THE Westminster Pulpit

VOLUME II

The Preaching of

G. CAMPBELL MORGAN

WIPF & STOCK · Eugene, Oregon

Wipf and Stock Publishers
199 W 8th Ave, Suite 3
Eugene, OR 97401

The Westminster Pulpit vol. II
The Preaching of G. Campbell Morgan
By Morgan, G. Campbell
Copyright©1954 by Morgan, G. Campbell
ISBN 13: 978-1-60899-311-6
Publication date 1/1/2012
Previously published by Fleming H. Revell, Co., 1954

THE
Westminster
Pulpit

VOLUME II

CONTENTS

CHAPTER		PAGE
I	THE FIGHT OF FAITH	11
II	MARAN ATHA	23
III	HUMANITY AND DEITY	37
IV	SANCTUARY	51
V	SIN	64
VI	THE NAME JESUS	77
VII	WORSHIP, BEAUTY, HOLINESS.	88
VIII	PROGRESSIVE REVELATION	101
IX	THE TRAINING OF OUR CHILDREN	111
X	SPARE THYSELF	125
XI	THE YOUNG RULER	138
XII	JESUS AND SINNERS	151
XIII	THE GREAT APOSTLE	164
XIV	CHRIST'S VISION OF JERUSALEM	177
XV	THE ALL-SUFFICIENT GRACE	191
XVI	FAMINE FOR THE WORD OF GOD	206
XVII	THE STUMBLING-BLOCK OF THE CROSS	217
XVIII	THE WORD BECAME FLESH	230
XIX	THE DEITY OF JESUS	243
XX	HARDENED	255
XXI	WITNESSES	269
XXII	SAINTS	282
XXIII	PREPARATION FOR SERVICE	295

CHAPTER		PAGE
XXIV	POWER FOR SERVICE	307
XXV	CHRIST'S KNOWLEDGE OF MEN	319
XXVI	CENTER AND CIRCUMFERENCE	332

THE ORIGIN OF THE WESTMINSTER PULPIT

WHEN DR. G. CAMPBELL MORGAN COMMENCED HIS UNIQUE ministry at Westminster Chapel in 1904 there was an immediate request for the publication of his sermons in order to extend the influence of his ministry.

On most of the Sundays in the year, Dr. Campbell Morgan would preach morning and evening sermons. As only one could be published weekly, the plan adopted was that each week Dr. Morgan would select the sermon most likely to be of world-wide interest and influence, and have it available in print at the close of each service on the following Sunday and for those attending the Friday evening Bible school.

In this way, the Westminster Pulpit sermons were given a wide circulation, and, in addition, through a subscribers' list, they found their way through the mail into all parts of the world. At the close of each year a large number of bound volumes were produced and published under the title of *The Westminster Pulpit*, which had a ready sale.

The value of these volumes is best understood if it is remembered that from the day when inquiries had to be answered, "out of print," requests have come from all parts of the globe for second-hand copies. And from those fortunate enough to obtain a single volume there has invariably come an inquiry regarding the cost of the remaining volumes of the set. The undersigned, who was largely responsible for the task of publishing *The Westminster Pulpit*, has in his library a complete series of this work, for which he has had many offers, without regard to price.

Dr. Campbell Morgan excelled in the art of expository preaching. It was his conviction that no minister would ever lack a congregation who adopted the expository rather than the topical method of preaching. In these volumes, which are being reissued after careful selection, the art of expository preaching is magnificently displayed in sermons covering a wide range of Biblical subjects.

I verily believe that those who obtain the first of the proposed ten volumes will not rest until they have secured the complete set; indeed, I strongly advise that the whole set be bespoken. I further believe that in launching and carrying out this project Fleming H. Revell Company will be making a valuable contribution to the greatest of all causes, the extension of the Kingdom of God.

ARTHUR E. MARSH

Westminster Chapel,
London, England

THE
Westminster
Pulpit

VOLUME II

CHAPTER I

THE FIGHT OF FAITH

Fight the good fight of the faith, lay hold on the life eternal.
I TIMOTHY 6:12.

WE ARE ACCUSTOMED TO SPEAK OF THE CHRISTIAN LIFE under different figures. Sometimes it is described as a pilgrimage in which, staff in hand and equipped for long and continuous marches, the pilgrim sets his face toward the country where he fain would be. Sometimes it is described as a voyage over seas in which today the blue of the sky is mirrored, and which tomorrow are swept by storm. Sometimes it is described as a race, to run in which the competitor must strip himself, lay aside every weight and set his face toward the goal, perpetually forgetting the things behind. In all these figures of the Christian life there is the suggestion of effort and of difficulty. I know there are those who speak of this Christian life as though it were easy, soft, weak. As a matter of fact, it is indeed, as the text suggests, a fight, fierce and terrible ofttimes, a constant warfare from beginning to end. It is a fight which requires all a man's grit and force if he hopes to win. It is in that way I desire to represent it to you, my brothers, to whom principally I speak this evening.

The words of the text constitute a part of the final

advice of the aged Paul to his young friend and fellow minister, Timothy.

The text is really a part of a threefold injunction which may be expressed by the three words which indicate it, "Flee," "Follow," "Fight." The first of these three words indicates what Timothy's attitude should be toward the evils which the apostle had been rebuking. The second affirms the true ambition of his ministry; the third indicates at once the strenuousness of his life, and by its connection with the latter part of the text, "lay hold on the life eternal," indicates the strength in which he will be able to fight his fight as he follows after righteousness and flees evil things.

I take the text away from its setting, and I do it no violence thereby, for while this is the word of the apostle to one who is called into the sacred and special work of the ministry, it has to do with life, and every man who is a Christian is in the ministry of Jesus Christ. Every man who has yielded himself to the King is called upon to fight the battles of the King in his own life and wherever he may be. Turning aside, then, from all its immediate and local application, I bring the text to you tonight as indicating this fact of the strenuousness of the Christian life.

What, then, is the fight to which men are called who follow Jesus Christ? Two forces are at work in the world. The force which gathers to the center and the force which drives from the center. First of all, the gathering force brings a man within his own personality into consistent life, and then brings man to man, heals the breaches and the wounds, and makes for a society which is pure, noble, self-sacrificing. The scattering force breaks a man up within his own personality, and drives men apart, severing man from man, brother from brother, the wide world over. The force of right and the force of evil are in array against each other. If I may express the warfare in another way I would say that there is a perpetual battle in the world between faith and fear. If, for a moment, you do not follow me in the antithesis, I pray you think that at the center of all evil as its inspiration is fear, at the center of all right as its inspiration is faith. If you take the Bible and trace your way through from beginning to end you will find these two principles are forever revealed as in opposition. You find men attempting to combine on the basis of fear, fear of each other, of some ultimate evil; and also men combining on the basis of faith in the unseen and eternal. Faith and fear are in perpetual opposition. All that which drives men to evil courses, and all that which divides man from man is based upon fear. All selfishness expressing itself in harm to other men grows out of the heart's fear. All self-sacrifice expressing itself in helpfulness to other men grows out of the heart's strong, firm courage and faith. In the world these two forces stand opposed. Every man is ranged on one side or the other. Every man's life is either a part of the force which scatters, or a part of the force which gathers. Every man's effort in every day of his life is a contribution toward the victory of evil at some point, or else it is a contribution toward the victory of good. I grant you that at the back of all expenditure of human effort by which we are surrounded, and of which we ourselves contribute a part, there is an infinite hunger and craving after God. The difference between faith and fear is the difference between attempting to satisfy this deep craving and hunger in the right and true way and in the wrong way. The wrong way is the way of evil. The right way is the way of good. These two forces are opposed even in a man's own life. A young man facing life sees before him some goal to which he desires to come; some ambition inspires him, prompts him, drives him. This in itself is not wrong. It is as it should be. God has made every young man capable of seeing lights in the eastern sky which lure him to endeavor. It is of human life, according to the plan of God, that young men should dream dreams and see visions, and build castles in the air, and aim at success. Every man who is a man has such visions and such desires. How are you going to gain your goal? By what way are you traveling toward your mountain height? How do you propose to translate your castle in the air into a solid piece of work squarely set on the earth? That is the question of importance. The suggestion that is made to the young man facing life is, on the one hand, a suggestion that he should take short cuts devoid of principle toward the goal he desires to reach. The other suggestion is that he shall find the one highway of stern duty and true principle and tramp it at all costs. The battle begins in his heart between the allurements and enticements of the short and easy method—as it appears to be—of evil; and the long, stern, and arduous method—as it appears to be—of good. In this great city at this hour the two forces are at work. The battle is set in array. Whoever may lead the hosts on the side of evil, the fact remains that through this city there are forces of evil waiting to lure men into ways of evil on the basis of fear, and other forces drawing men into the paths of righteousness on the basis of faith.

Whether it be in a profession or in business, here or there, the deepest thing in all your life story will be the contribution you make toward this great battle between evil and good, fear and faith. This battle is not one which is fought by preachers or teachers only. It is not a battle fought only by men who are openly vulgar, and are attempting definitely to demoralize human life—would God there were none such, but there are such! The battle is not one between the leaders merely. Every man in this house is in this great fight. You are fighting the battle in every hour and every moment of your life, as your life's force is being exerted on the side of good or of evil, according to whether the underlying inspiration is that of fear, which attempts to save self, or faith, which attempts to glorify God. That is why the apostle charges Timothy to "fight the good fight of the faith."

The leader of the forces of faith is Jesus Christ Himself. In the letter to the Hebrews the writer describes the heroes and heroines of faith through the ages. At last, passing from the eleventh chapter into the twelfth, you read these words which describe the One who is "The Author"—and now allow me to offer you a more literal and immediate translation of the Greek word—"the File-leader of faith." That is to say, the writer of this letter to the Hebrews puts Jesus Christ at the very forefront of the army that fights the good fight of the faith. Although in point of time and in appearance in human life He came long after the men already mentioned, Abraham, Moses, David, and the rest, yet Jesus Christ is the File-leader, the one moving first. The whole life story of Jesus, on the human side, is the life story of One who lived by faith. He saw the ultimate victory. He believed in the triumph of righteousness. He wrought with God along the mysterious way of human life and by victory gained over all temptation, and testimony borne in His own age, and at last by the infinite revelation and mystery of His passion, fought "the good fight of the faith." He it is who leads the armies of the faithful.

If a man is to fight this fight of the faith where is he to begin? He must begin with definite and personal submission to the great Leader of the army of the faithful. Every soldier in this fight must be enlisted of his own will and must yield his will to the will of the Commander. "He that is not with me is against me; and he that gathereth not with me scattereth." The personal application of that is that if a man would gather he must be with the Christ, and that if he is not with the Christ he is therefore scattering. You cannot "fight the good fight of the faith" until you have crowned the Christ. The first thing, then, in Christian warfare is enlistment under the leadership of the One who stands in front of us, the File-leader of faithful souls.

Then follows a statement of the all-inclusive equipment for the fight. The charge of the apostle here is not that a man shall fight to lay hold on eternal life, but that a man shall lay hold on life eternal in order to fight. I am afraid that has not always been the interpretation of this passage. We have very often read it as though the apostle meant that a man is to fight the good fight of the faith and presently to lay hold on eternal life. If that has been our interpretation it is because of a common mistake which postpones the possession of eternal life to the ages beyond. Eternal life is something for today.

What is eternal life? Some recent translators have, as I think, very beautifully expressed the thought in the words "age-abiding life," or the "life of the ages." Eternal life is not a condition to which a man comes after death. Eternal life is that mystic and wonderful life which is in all the ages, past, present, and to come. It is the infinite force at the back of everything. Now, says the apostle, in the midst of things present, in the midst of the battle against evil, in all the fierceness of the conflict, fight, laying hold on eternal life. The force in which man is to fight against fear and on the side of faith is that of the appropriation of this eternal life. Let me express this in a slightly different form. Eternal life is not merely a quantity. It is a quality. A man can live eternal life here in London just as well as in heaven. Unless he live it here how can he live it there? It is the life which defies change, the life which abides when all its varied expressions pass away. "Fight the good fight of the faith, lay hold on the life eternal." Take hold on this principle of life and in its power fight the fight of the faith.

How shall I find eternal life? The answers are as familiar to you as is the Book of God. You have heard them from childhood. Hear the words of Jesus, "This is life eternal, that they should know Thee the only true God, and Him whom Thou didst send, even Jesus Christ." Yes, but how am I to know the only true God and Him whom He has sent? Hear another of the statements of the New Testament, "He came unto his own, and they that were his own received him not. But as many as received him, to them gave he the right to become children of God, even to them which believe on his name: which were born"—there is the beginning of eternal life in the soul—"not of blood, nor of the will of the flesh, nor of the will of man, but of God." When a man sees Jesus Christ and obeys Him, yields to Him, in that moment he has taken hold on eternal life. He has put his own life in all its meaning into immediate connection with the life which abides, the life of the ages, and in that strength he is called on to go forth to this warfare.

What is to be the soldier's spirit? First of all, the man who fights after having crowned Christ fights in perfect confidence because he knows His leader and is convinced of the ultimate issue. In the letter to the Hebrews the writer says, "We see not yet all things subjected to him. But we behold . . . Jesus." The victory is not won. The final crowning of Christ Himself has not come. He is still waiting in the hidden mystery of the heaven until "his enemies be made the footstool of his feet"; but we have seen Him and to have seen Him is to be perfectly assured that He must win. It is impossible once to have looked into the face of the Son of God, to have seen Him in all the radiant beauty of His purity, the matchless majesty of His victory over sin, and believe that at last He can be defeated. If I am in the fight against evil in my own life and in the fight against evil in the world as a soldier of Jesus Christ, I fight in perfect confidence.

The man who fights under the direction of Jesus Christ fights not only in confidence but in cautiousness. The great word of one of the Old Testament writers is forever true in his experience, "Happy is the man that feareth alway." There is a foolhardiness which names itself courage, but is not courage. There is a species of pious blasphemy very much abroad in the world today about the power of the grace of God. I have heard men say that if they have once given themselves to Jesus Christ the grace of God is able to keep them in all sorts of places and conditions. It is not. The grace of God is able to keep a man in any place into which God brings him, however grave and perilous; but the grace of God is not sufficient to keep a man when a man deliberately puts himself into a place of peril outside the pathway of the Divine will for him. I have heard men say with regard to strong drink that the grace of God is sufficient to keep a man. So it is, if that man will obey the law of God and abstain absolutely and utterly from the thing that has marred him. If a man plays with fire he will be burned, notwithstanding his relationship to Jesus Christ. If a man attempts to try his courage by putting himself into a place of temptation he will fall, notwithstanding the fact that he has crowned Christ in his life by some act of submission in the past. The soldier who is to fight the good fight of faith is to "flee" from all evil. I pray you remember that there are moments in this great conflict of faith as against evil when you will demonstrate your courage more surely by using your spurs than by using your sword. There are places to which no man can go who is to fight this fight. The place of peculiar peril is to be avoided. The good soldier of Jesus Christ is the man who fears, and fears always. Not confidence merely, but caution also.

The good soldier of Jesus Christ is one, moreover, who understands that there must be conflict unto victory. That the victory is possible he believes. Then if it be possible, however stern, however strenuous, however terrible the conflict, he is to press right through until the end. You have heard the story of the Spartan son who returned home and said to his aged father, scarred by many a battle, "My sword is just a little too short for me." Said the old man, "Add a step to it." You tell me your sword is just a little too short for you to win. One step more, and one thrust harder. The last five minutes win the fight, not the hours that have preceded them. Some man here has been fighting his fight for weeks and months. You tell me you are just giving up. In God's name I charge you, fight through. It is the last five minutes that mean victory. There must be perseverance.

The soldier of Jesus Christ is not only a man having confidence and caution, and determined perseverance which issues in victory. He is a man who will endure hardness and so himself become hard, in that sense of the word hard. Hardness is a quality which comes only through enduring hardness. By hardness we mean not that hardness against which we are warned in the New Testament, the hardness of conscience and heart, but the toughness which enables a man to "stand . . . to withstand . . . and having done all, to stand." Hear one word as an aside. Some man says, "I lack that hardness. That is where I fail." I say to you, "Once more out upon the field, one more campaign, and you will be harder. Another victory and the fiber of your moral courage will be tougher." It is by fighting on until the victory is won by strong endeavor that man gains the hardness which makes him at last a valiant and victorious soldier of Jesus Christ. All these things are necessary if we are to "fight the good fight of the faith."

Where is the fight to be fought? In the first place, in secret. You will never be able to fight the good fight of the faith in London until you have fought it, and are fighting it, in your own heart and life. There are many ways of stating that truth. It is an old, a commonplace truth, yet one which I feel needs to be restated. There are so many men who desire to have something to do in the general moral uplifting of society who have never yet enlisted to fight against evil in their own hearts and lives. The first battle is the battle within, against wrong in the heart and life. Yet remember, as I have already said, this battle also, first and fundamental, can be fought only under the leadership of Christ. My trouble in dealing with young men is that so many of them misunderstand Christianity. They imagine that all they have to do is to make some confession of loyalty to Jesus Christ and that He will nurse them over all the way. Nothing of the kind. Crown Him. Follow Him. Fight under Him. The severest battles of a man's life are fought out in secret and in his own individual soul. Temptation to evil in its varied forms comes far more subtly to a man when he is alone than when he is with others. I begin my fight inside; in the secret recesses of my inner life, in the hall of the imagination, in the chamber of the affections, there the fight must first be fought. "He that is slow to anger is better than the mighty; and he that ruleth his spirit than he that taketh a city." I am not anxious to make any appeal to young men to fight the fight in the city. I am perfectly convinced you will be bound to do that if once you have fought in the fight in your own life. Your whole life, if that life be homed in the will of Christ winning His vistory, will be part of the force by which He lifts and purifies the city. The fiercest battles of the individual life, the longest, the most strenuous, are the battles fought in absolute loneliness. May I, with all reverence, illustrate what I am thinking from the life story of Jesus? Do not forget that in the will and economy and purpose of God He lived longer in private than in public. Think you there was no significance in that? Three years of public life, and, reckoning from twelve years of age, when He was a boy coming up to the Hebrew confirmation, eighteen years in quietness, hidden away. Where do you suppose, so far as the manhood of Jesus is concerned, the fiercest battles were fought, in the presence of the crowd or in Nazareth? I tell you, in Nazareth. There were battles to be fought in the presence of the crowd.

It is not particularly heroic to do right when you are in the midst of people who applaud you. It is easy for the men of this brotherhood to be pure on Sunday when they are in the brotherhood, and I am not at all sure that it is particularly difficult to be good in the midst of opposition. I tell you frankly, I have never quite understood the young fellow who does not love to put up a stiff fight for God when men are against him. It calls out the fiber that is in him. But, ah, me, my masters, when the comrades in the Christian war are not with me, when the soldiers who would oppose me and make me fight are away and I am alone, then the fiercest fight of my life is fought. There are curious notions abroad in the world as to ministers of the Word of God. Some people seem to imagine we are free from temptation on account of our calling. I tell you we are the special objects of the devil's attack. In the loneliness and seclusion of the study, with only books of religion about a man, oh, the temptation to sloth, to indolence, to pride, to fear, to traffic with the Word of God for some subtle motive. It is there, when I am alone, that the fight is fiercest. Unless a man wins there he will never win anywhere.

How shall I win there? By laying hold on eternal life. This Son of God who is the Leader of the hosts laid down His life in the light and the darkness of the cross—and let no man tell me there is no mystery in the cross. In that infinite hour of His agony He made it possible for me to lay hold on life, and if a man will lay hold on life by crowning Him, he can fight alone and win, he can fight with his comrades in arms and win, and he can fight against opposition and win. The first battle is ever in loneliness. That is the thought I desire more than any other to impress on you.

What is to be the final issue of this fight to which we are called? The triumph of right in our own lives and in the world. On that I am not going to dwell.

How are you fighting? Take the week that is gone. You have spent so much of thought, so much of energy. On which side has it all been exerted? Have you helped, by thinking and speaking and working, the victory of evil? Did you think and speak and work last week so that God Almighty got some help out of you toward the ultimate victory?

I call you in the name of the great Leader of faithful souls to fight the good fight of the faith, and I say to you tonight, you can fight that fight only as you lay hold on eternal life. I say to you finally, eternal life is yours here and now if you are His. It may come silently, gently, so much so that you hardly know the moment of its coming. When you take your life and hand it over to the great Captain of Salvation, you lay hold on eternal life, and in the power of that life you may begin your fight and win in secret and in public, in your own life and in every endeavor for the Kingdom of God.

CHAPTER II

MARAN ATHA!

If any man loveth not the Lord, let him be Anathema Maran atha.
                                          I CORINTHIANS 16:22.

THESE WORDS DO NOT CONSTITUTE A MALEDICTION. IF YOU ARE inclined to question the accuracy of that statement notice what the Apostle himself says about them. "The salutation of me Paul with mine own hand. If any man loveth not the Lord, let him be Anathema Maran atha. The grace of the Lord Jesus Christ be with you. My love be with you all in Christ Jesus. Amen." They are not a malediction, but part of a salutation.

Yet they are words of astounding severity and scorching heat, and are indeed words intended to make men stop and think, words gaining heat and force from the fact that they are surrounded by loving, tender, gracious words of salutation. They are a statement of a logical and inevitable sequence. If a man do not love this Lord Jesus "let him be anathema. Maran atha."

This is the close of a letter written to a Christian church, a church which had departed from the simplicity of Christ Jesus, a church which had lost its power of testimony in the midst of a great and wealthy city. This letter was written to correct the failure of such a church because its testimony was paralyzed, and it had ceased to be influential on account of its shortcoming and failure. The city of Corinth at this time was the home of learning and of wealth. It was full of a false wisdom or culture. Factions and rivalries existed throughout the city. The school men were quarreling amongst themselves concerning emphases and diversifications of ideas on nonessential things. Intellect was more highly esteemed than morality. Consequently there was abounding looseness of moral standard. Selfishness was dominant. There were a few wealthy people, living in luxury, while beneath them was a great mass of men and women in slavery. There was a popular denial of immortality. In one word, tragic and terrible, Corinth as a city was materialized, and the Church of Jesus Christ had been contaminated by all these things. Instead of fulfilling its mission as salt, and being pungent, antiseptic, it had lost its savor. Instead of being light, shining clearly, rebuking the darkness and guiding stumbling men back into the way of perfection, the light had become darkened. To correct the carnality which lay at the root of the spiritual failure in the church, this letter had been written. In imagination I see the apostle, suffering in all probability from such nearness of sight that he could hardly see what he wrote, taking from the hand of his amanuensis the pen, and writing, "The salutation of me Paul with mine own hand. If any man loveth not the Lord, let him be anathema. Maran atha. The favor of the Lord Jesus Christ be with you. My love be with you all in Christ Jesus. Amen."

So the great letter closes. That is the setting of my text. We must see it there if we would understand its meaning. The Apostle writing to a church of Jesus Christ, to men and women called saints, says in effect, "The claims of Christ are such that if they be once known and appreciated, and yet the heart does not answer in love, which is for ever more the inspiration of loyalty, then there is nothing for such a heart save that it shall be accursed, anathema." After the statement, to emphasize it, to defend it, to vindicate it, he writes, "Maran atha."

I have already several times recited those two words. Let me now say by way of explanation, before we proceed to a closer examination of them, that the Apostle in their use here defends the thing he has already said. That is their intention. He is not declaring that if men do not love Jesus Christ, when presently the Christ comes they will be accursed. They are already accursed. They are in the place of the curse. They are in the grip of the curse. Therefore, before we can understand the first part of our text we must understand the second part of it. Before we can fully appreciate what the Apostle meant when he wrote, "If any man loveth not the Lord, let him be anathema," we must inquire what he meant when he wrote, "Maran atha."

Therefore, I ask you, first, to consider with me the great fact: "Maran atha," and, second, the sequence: "If any man love not the Lord, let him be anathema."

There is great gain in the fact that our revision has written two words and not one, "Maran atha." There are certain things concerning these two words which are indisputable. There are other things which are doubtful, about which no final, dogmatic word can yet be said. There are two interpretations of their meaning. One affirms that they mean, "The Lord cometh." The other affirms that they mean, "The Lord has come." You will see that the difficulty arises concerning the tense of the verb. There is no difficulty concerning the substantive, the subject "Maran," the Lord; but whether the word "atha" means "cometh," or "has come," cannot be dogmatically affirmed. The central principle is not interfered with whichever interpretation be correct. I am not proposing for a single moment to argue as between the two. I will say, in passing, I am personally convinced that the words mean "The Lord has come," and that here the reference is not specifically and immediately to the second Advent but to the first, and yet to the second also. According to all the New Testament writers, the first involved the second. If you believe the words mean "The Lord cometh," then you also hold the fact of the first Advent. "The Lord cometh" for "the Lord has come." If you hold that the words mean "the Lord has come," then you also see that they mean the Lord is yet to come again, for He Who has come "shall appear a second time, apart from sin . . . unto salvation." The second Advent includes the first. The grace of the first demands the glory of the second. These words constituted a form of Christian salutation in the early days. Whether they meant "The Lord has come" or "the Lord cometh" matters nothing. The early Christians greeted each other in the market place or on the highway, saying, "Maran atha," and the reply would be "Maran atha." Whether the Advent referred to is past, or to come, the truth insisted on is that the true Lord is manifest—has been manifested or is to be manifested. The fact is not one of date, but of the manifestation in human history of the one supreme, lonely, imperial Lord of men, "Maran atha." The Lord has come, is coming: the Lord is coming, has come. The text summons us to the judgment seat of the one perfect Lord of men. When the Apostle with his own hand—stumblingly perchance, and in ·those large characters to which he referred in another letter—is writing his salutation, he sees his Lord. He has been following Him for years along the perilous and rough pathway. He saw Him first on the way to Damascus and he heard His voice. He has become familiar with Him. He knows Him for what He is. No other teacher divides his attention. No other lord makes demands upon his loyalty. He is the one Lord Jesus Christ, and Paul writes to these people in Corinth, "If any man loveth not the Lord, let him be anathema," and then, as though he had said, "He is the Lord, and He is revealed as such," he writes, "Maran atha." So finally he brings the saints of Corinth, and all Corinth, to confront the one Lord, and he says in the presence of that Lord, "Hear this, ye sons of men, if ye love Him not, ye are accursed." Logically, necessarily accursed. Not to love Him is to love the base, the mean, the ignoble. "If any man loveth not the Lord, let him be anathema. Maran atha." It is the great cry of a loyal soul bowing in adoration in the presence of the supernal royalty of the King.

The central fact suggested therefore is that of the Lordship of Christ.

This Lord Jesus Christ is Lord in a threefold sense. On His head are many diadems, but for us men, for the purposes of our salvation, I propose to speak of three only. He stands absolutely alone as Lord—first, as presenting a perfect pattern of human life; secondly, as paralyzing the paralysis which prevents men realizing the pattern; and, finally, as providing for men the power by which they may become what He reveals to them they ought to be. The territory covered by these three suggestions is small. I turn away from all the glorious diadems which rest upon His brow, and of which I might speak, because I want to speak of His Lordship as it presents itself to the needs of sinning men. I want us to see Him as the one Imperial and only Lord of the man who knows his sin and fain would escape it.

In the first place, I say He is royal in Lordship because He presents to men the perfect pattern of human life. I am not going to defend that statement. All I intend to do is to ask, What is this pattern He presents? What answer has Christ given to the old question of the psalmist, "What is man?" Christ's answer to that question is a threefold one. By His teaching He first of all declares that man is the offspring of God, that man is not of dust but of Deity, that in every man there is that which cannot be slain by the physical hand of his fellow man. "Be not afraid of them which kill the body, and after that have no more that they can do." According to His teaching, every man—the question of his bruising and battering and spoiling by sin is not now being discussed, in spite of these things—every man is a child of the eternities, offspring of the spiritual, in the deepest essence of his being related to God and eternity. That is Christ's first word about man. Then He has also revealed to us the fact that man is a being who can realize himself only within the realm of one simple and sublime law of conformity to the will of the One Who created him. By all His teaching He arrested the wandering will of man, and attempted to readjust it to the will of God. By all the deeds through which He manifested His thought and purpose for man, He sought to bring him back from the trackless desert of his own self-chosen wandering to the straight and narrow pathway of the good and perfect and acceptable will of God. So that Jesus said, and still says to men, "You can find your rest only in the will of God. You can find the answer to the deep questionings of your own life, you can find satisfaction for the perpetual sign of the deepest in you only as you find your way back again to God, and hand to Him your life, and choose His law as the law of your life.

Finally, Christ taught that man is created for service. He is an instrument for carrying the will of God beyond the circle of his own personality. That indeed is the teaching of the whole Bible. Man was not the final flower of Eden. He was its master. Man was not put into Eden for decorative purposes at the close of the great procedure. He was put in to dress it, to keep it, to govern it in co-operation with God. We have strange notions about the Garden of Eden. There are people who imagine it was an actual garden such as we see in this country of ours, beautifully laid out with flower beds and paths. Nothing of the kind. It was a rough bit of soil full of potentiality, blossoms in it, fruit in it, magnificence in it, glories in it, but not manifest. What were they waiting for? The touch of God's partner, man. God put man into the garden to dress it and keep it. Christ emphasized that in all His teaching: "The Son of man came not to be ministered unto, but to minister."

The great ideal of Jesus concerning man is that he is spiritual in essence, perfected within the law of God, and created for co-operation with God. He Who revealed that as the pattern of human life is the Master Teacher of the ages. I defy you to find me any such conception anywhere else. Other men have not dreamed of such things as these. Other teachers have said wonderfully luminous things concerning man, but they were all things of dust compared to these. He came to men, the Man of the home-made garment and little Nazareth, and in simple sentences and childlike speech He uttered great philosophies of human life, which have taken hold of the hearts of men; and we bow before Him as we say "Maran atha," the Lord, for none other has ever spoken of the possibility of human life as He spoke of it.

Had that been all He did, it would have been a great thing, but for me it would have been an awful tragedy. In the discovery of the spirituality of my being I should have found that I was orphaned, the offspring of God, and unable to find my Father. If I had found that my life could be conditioned only by the law of God I should have found that I was absolutely ruined, for I could not discover the law of God for me.

If I had been taught that I was created only for service I should simply have stood gazing out upon a lost dignity, for I had lost the secret of co-operation and fellowship with God, and the very garden of Eden would have answered me, not with flowers, but with the thorns of the wilderness. If this Man be Lord only by revelation of the pattern, He is Lord, I bow to Him, but bowing to Him I am undone.

He therefore presents Himself in a new aspect of His Lordship as the One Who touches with a strange and mysterious power the paralysis of man which prevents him realizing the purpose and ideal, until the paralysis itself is paralyzed, and man is set free. He comes to destroy the destroyer. The conception of man as material is forever more destroyed. From the lawlessness which had become another law working in my members and making it impossible for me to obey the law of God He sets me free. The self-life which had prevented my realization of God's purpose in serving God He crucifies. The process is not easy. But this is how He arrests me. He takes hold of me and reveals to me the pattern until I am ashamed, and just as I am hopeless, He touches me with some new power, and I feel that the forces which prevented my realization are relaxing their hold upon me, and if a man is saved by hope, I begin to hope. If a man is saved by faith, upon the basis of my hope I fling my trust out toward the Lord Who has revealed the pattern and has touched me with power. If a man be saved ultimately by love, I rise from hope through faith to love, and "if any man loveth not the Lord, let him be anathema."

Am I a spirit? He brings my spirit back into relation with the one eternal Spirit, and I live. Is it necessary for me to find the law of God. He presents Himself to me and says, "Follow Me. I am the Word, the incarnate revelation of the will of God, the thought of God rendered visible to thine eyes. Thou hast wandered away from the Father's home; follow Me; step by step, line upon line, precept upon precept I will lead thee in the way of His appointment." You can fling away the Ten Commandments then as an external law which you are attempting to obey: "I will write His law upon thy heart. I will come and dwell with thee. I am with thee all the days. I will lead thee step by step through all the pathway. I will be to thee the law of God which thou hast lost."

Finally, He communicates to me the energy of the Spirit, and out of the mystery of His Passion He gives me power. Out of the darkness of His death He gives me the light of life, and the life of light. So He confronts me not merely as pattern, but as power; not merely as revelation, but as energy. He brings to me in my loneliness and in my wandering all I need.

"Maran atha." The Lord, the only One Who has any right to such a title, the imperial, lonely, splendid, royal Lord, has come, is coming—which you like, both if you please. Between the "has come" and the "is coming," the Lord is here. In the words of the Apostle, in the presence of His royal Lord Jesus the Revealer of the ideal, the Destroyer of the paralysis, the One Who communicates power, in the presence of this Lord who has in His government everything that sinning man needs. "If any man loveth not the Lord, let him be anathema."

I return to the statement which constitutes the first part of my text. "If any man loveth not the Lord, let him be anathema." This is wholly in view of the Lordship of Jesus. I can imagine that someone here is at once startled and alarmed by the peculiar term of the Apostle, "If any man loveth not." Some soul trembling upon the very brink of yielding to the Lordship of Jesus may say, 'I do not love Him.' Why did the Apostle use that word? He did use that word, and as a matter of fact, if you would rightly understand this passage, as Mr. Rotherham, in his Emphasized Bible, has beautifully and as I think accurately rendered it, you must read, "If any man *dearly* loveth not the Lord." It is the thought of supreme affection for the Lord Who lays His claim upon man and demands his allegiance. Yet I recognize the difficulty. Why does the Apostle use this word? Do not forget he is writing to saints, to such as have heard the Word and have yielded obedience thereto, and have already come into some measure of light, and he mentions the ultimate stage in relation to Jesus. What are the matters which precede love? I take you back for a moment to his letter to the Romans. In the course of that letter concerning salvation Paul wrote these words, "Belief cometh by hearing, and hearing by the word of Christ." That is how you would state the Gospel to the man who has not yet obeyed it. Take that verse and state it in the other order. "The Word of Christ," that is, the whole Evangel. What then? Hearing it. What then? Faith in it. In the Corinthian letter, writing to saints, he takes all these things for granted, as though he had said, 'You have heard the word of Christ. You have believed the word of Christ. If any man do not love Him, then let that man be accursed.' That is to say, in the thinking of the Apostle, if the Word be presented and if the Word be heard and be obeyed —and of set purpose I substitute the thought of obedience for that of faith, for the only faith that saves is the faith of obedience—then necessarily, always, absolutely without exception, the experience of the obedient soul is the experience of love. This word of the Apostle indicates the final stage in the relation. I do not mean that it is postponed. There is some soul who has come into this house tonight. You hear the Word of Christ, the Word of His Lordship. You hear it, you believe it obediently, submit yourself to it in all honesty, then at once you will begin to love Him. Love comes in the pathway of obedience. You do not love Him, you tell me. Then where have you failed in this order? Have you never heard the Word of Christ? That can hardly be true of anyone here. You have heard it now. The Word heard, what will you do with it? Will you believe it? I do not mean theologically. I do not mean intellectually merely. I do not mean, Do you assent to the fact of His Lordship? I mean that first, for there can be no submission on the part of any honest man to any but absolute royalty. I cannot be loyal to inferiority, so help me God. My King must be royal. He must appeal to all that lies within me and demand my loyalty by what He is in royalty. Have you seen the Royalty? Do you know that this Christ is the one Lord of men? Will you obey? If you say No, you pass away, it may be in reverent recognition of His imperial majesty but without one pulse of love. Do you say Yes? Then you will begin to love Him tonight. I do not say, "Perhaps," or "Peradventure," or "It is reasonable to suppose." I affirm it dogmatically. No man can see the light and obey it without feeling the love.

Hear me again for a moment. How will that love first manifest itself? Not in your consciousness always as love for Him, but far more commonly in your love for someone else, and your desire to bring that one to Him. The first movement of the love of God in the soul of man, woman, or little child, is a love impulse which drives that one out to bring in someone else. Do you not at once see what that proves? Father, tonight you obey, and immediately you think of your boy, and your heart says "I would fain bring him to Christ." You love your boy, and if you love him you would hardly lead him to any but the One you loved supremely. You demonstrate your love for Christ by the love which drives you to bring someone else to Him.

When obeying, you begin to be anxious about father, mother, wife, husband, child; it demonstrates the fact that although you have hardly dared say it, yet in your heart there has come love for the Christ.

Thus the Apostle is stating the logical sequence. If a man is separated from the Lordship of Christ of his own will and choice, then he has no true vision of his own highest possibilities, he has no understanding of life's truest laws. There is within that man no force making for perfection and permanence. That man is already in the grip of destructive forces. If you turn your back upon Christ when He has shown you the spirituality of your being, what have you done by that action? You have consented to the materialistic conception of your own life which proceeds to corruption. If you turn your back upon Christ when He reveals Himself to you as the revelation of the will of God, then you turn your face toward lawlessness which lies at the root of all evil and calamity; you are already in the grip of disintegration and break-up. If you turn your back upon Christ when He calls you into service and co-operation with God, then your life henceforth must circle around your own selfish desire and motive and lust. The self-centred man has created for himself the grave in which he must lay his own individuality. So that if any man love not the Lord, it needs no Apostle to curse him, but it does need that the Apostle with the pen of inspiration should write that he is already accursed. "If any man loveth not the Lord, let him be anathema."

As the old year passes away from us and we come again to the turn of the highway and to another mile post, this message is alive and as real in London, in Westminster Chapel, as when the Apostle wrote it upon parchment for the Corinthian Church centuries ago. Here and now and everywhere, "If any man loveth not the Lord, let him be anathema." He is in the grip of destructive forces; and all the subtlety of his brain, the cleverness of his intellect, and ingenuity of his mind cannot deliver him from dire and irremediable ruin. "If any man loveth not the Lord, let him be anathema." Hear it, ye sons of the new age. My brothers, sisters, living in the midst of our boasted civilization and progress, "Maran atha." There is but one Lord. There is but one Master of men. There is but one Revealer of the true ideal. There is but one Redeemer of failure. He is here in spiritual power and presence, in our very midst tonight. Do you love Him? Are you loyal to Him? Have you crowned Him? If from the heart even tremblingly there comes the answer Yes, then the last part of this verse is reversed. 'If any man love the Lord, let him be blessed' and blessed is he! Already in him there burns the light that shineth more and more unto the perfect day. Already in him operate the forces which at last will bind the universe about the feet of God in perfect and eternal harmony. Already in him thrills the love that cometh forth from God and returneth back to Him in the cycle of the centuries. Blessed art thou, brother, sister, mine, in the midst of the burden-bearing and strife and toil, testing and tempting, if thou hast crowned this Christ, all hell cannot destroy thee. All the forces of evil in the universe cannot accomplish thy undoing.

If your answer is No, already the touch of eternal death is upon you. Already the break-up that ends in the eternal and infinite disorder is within your soul. "Maran atha." I bring you this final word. Back again to the Lord, the one and only Lord of men. "The Word is nigh thee, in thy mouth, and in thy heart: that is the word of faith, which we preach." You are familiar with it. Will you obey it? If never before, now answer it obediently.

Oh that all alone, forgetting your past history, and present difficulty, and neighbor and friend whom you have brought with you to the sanctuary, oh that now you would look into the face of the one Lord Jesus Christ and say to Him simply as a child, with all the courage and conviction of your manhood, "I will trust in Thee and follow Thee, Thou Lord and Master of men." Then He will enwrap you with His love, and lead you in His light, and bring you into His life.

CHAPTER III

HUMANITY AND DEITY

Being then the offspring of God.
ACTS 17:29.

THE TEXT OCCURS IN THE COURSE OF THE ADDRESS WHICH Paul delivered on Mars Hill. I am quite conscious that Paul has been somewhat criticized for the method he adopted at Athens. It has been said that he attempted to adapt himself to local conditions and surroundings and signally failed. Moreover, it has been affirmed that when presently he wrote to the Corinthian Christians, and said, "I determined not to know anything among you save Jesus Christ, and Him crucified," he was in his own mind reflecting upon the mistake he had made when, coming to Athens, he had attempted to speak to the Athenian listeners in a language which they would be most likely to understand. I have made reference to this view of Paul's attitude simply to say that I hold it to be utterly unwarrantable and false. He always manifested his great sense of the need of adapting the manner of his message to the men who listened, while he was careful never to change its essential note or lower its highest claim by one single hair's breadth. I submit to you that when he wrote to the Corinthians, "I determined not to know anything among you save Jesus Christ, and Him crucified," he neither intended to put his message to them into comparison with his method at Athens, nor did he mean that the only message he had to deliver to men anywhere was the message of the cross. His reason for so writing was that they were still living a carnal life, and he could not pass away from the first principles of Christianity because they had not made response to the claims of that earliest declaration. The cross was not Paul's ultimate and final message. "It is Christ Jesus that died, yea rather, that was raised from the dead." All the spaciousness of his message was created by the fact that while he never forgot the fundamental truth of Christianity, that of the cross, he left the first principles and passed on to the perfection of teaching as he attempted to lead men to see how in resurrection life they had possession of all that was necessary for the realization of the purpose of God within them.

If Paul's method at Athens is not to be criticized, it must be examined and understood. I ask you to notice that in the words of the text, "Being then the offspring of God," the Apostle was reaffirming the truth of which these people were already in possession intellectually. He was protesting against their attempting to make to themselves likenesses of God. His whole spirit had been stirred within him as he found them to be not—as the Authorized Version incorrectly rendered it—"too superstitious," but "very religious." He discovered all through Athens evidences of the religious character of the people. That was the great thing which moved his heart. Their deep, underlying interest in religion was manifest in their temples, their altars, their idols. So much was this so that they had even erected an altar to "the unknown god." Recognizing the underlying religious capacity of the Athenians, Paul protested against the way in which they were attempting to satisfy it. He tells them God "is not far from each one of us; for in Him we live, and move, and have our being." This "unknown god" to whom you have erected an altar I declare unto you. You have said that I am "a setter forth of strange gods." I am the setter forth of the God to Whom you have already erected your altar. "He is not far from each one of us . . . as even certain of your own poets have said. For we are also His offspring."

Of set purpose, quietly and deliberately he reaffirmed this truth, and proceeded to make the application which was necessary at the moment. "Being then the offspring of God, we ought not to think that the Godhead is like unto gold, or silver, or stone," that is, we ought not to imagine that we can make something like Him of something which is less than ourselves. When you make likenesses of God in gold or silver or stone, you degrade the God Whom you yet know to be the One of Whom you are the offspring. So much for the setting of the text.

I bring you this message today, although its application is a different one. Being then the offspring of God, ye ought not to degrade yourselves by being satisfied with anything less than that which Christ laid down as the supreme and final injunction of His ethic, "Ye therefore shall be perfect, as your heavenly Father is perfect." Being then the offspring of God, the one true passion of every human life ought to be to become like Him, and so to be true to the underlying fact and force of personal life.

It is a great truth, though I am inclined to say, improperly used by some people. False deductions have been made from it, and still are being made, and because improperly used by some, it is feared by others. I believe that as we see this truth individually, we shall be prepared to listen to the call of Christ to come to Him for life; as we understand this truth collectively we shall be busy in the enterprise of making known the great Evangel to the men at home and in the far distant places of the earth. I do not hesitate to say that it is this conviction which is the driving inspiration of all my life and ministry and work.

Man is the offspring of God. What is this word "offspring"? It occurs about twenty times in the New Testament and is translated in seven ways. It is translated "race" seven times. It is translated "offspring," as in our text, three times; "kinds," three times; "kind," twice; "countrymen," twice; "stock," twice, and "kindred," once. You will at once see that running through all these words there is one thought, or one particular quantity, and it is to that I desire to draw your attention. I think perhaps we come nearer to the true sense of the Greek word here translated "offspring" by using the Latin word which has come into the common speech of today, *genus*. A genus includes all the species which, differing in proportion and color, are yet of the same life essence, and there you have the thought in the word translated "offspring."

I shall do no violence to the text if I change the word and say the poets declared and Paul reaffirmed that man is kin of God, that by first creation he is intimately related to God. Man is not in any essential power of his personality the creation of the devil. Man is in every essential power of his personality the creation of God. Every man is a thought of God, created, wrought out into visibility. Every man is made, according to the teaching of Scripture, in the likeness of God, in the image of God, and every man has entered into the power of his own life by the inbreathing of the breath of God. The life I live now—I am not speaking of my Christian life, that inner mystic life which gave me a new vision and a new understanding, and a new capacity for realizing myself— I am speaking of my first life—call it natural if you will—is God created. It is life which is kin to the life of God, so that when I am told that all humanity is of God, I am told that which is perfectly true according to the teaching of Scripture. Yet, let us follow this. Where does it lead us?

There are three lines I shall attempt to follow. First, the evidences of Deity in humanity. Second, the failure of the Divine in the human, and, finally, the restoration of man to God. To omit any one of these is to omit something of Christian truth and doctrine. To begin by the declaration of man's restoration to that which he has never lost is illogical and foolish. To begin by declaring that man has failed to realize the possibility of his own being, and to deny the possibility is again illogical. On the other hand, to begin by declaring that man is essentially kin of God, and to deny the fact of wrong and sin and evil, is to contradict the common experience of every man who has lived an ordinary life in the midst of the things of this world. The three things are necessary if we would understand what Christ has to say to this and every age concerning man.

First, then, the evidences of Deity in humanity. When Wordsworth sang

> Trailing clouds of glory do we come
> From God who is our home

he sang as one of the seers. A study of humanity in the light of God's self-revelation results in an almost overwhelming mass of evidence for the kinship of man to God. The ultimate conviction of such consideration is that all the essentials of humanity are kin to Deity. Only the accidentals are unlike God. Do not read into my word accidental anything less than ought to be in it. An accident may be a tragedy, a catastrophe. Only the accidentals are unlike God. Take some few of the evidences.

You will find in every human being a passion for life.

Have you ever asked yourself what the passion for life really means? How is it that everywhere, in all circumstances, in all ages, all men manifest a hunger for life; that the deep cries of humanity which are recorded for us in the simple terms of Holy Scripture are the cries of humanity everywhere; that when the young ruler looked into the face of Jesus and said, "Good Master, what shall I do that I may inherit age-abiding life?" he was simply speaking out of the depth of his humanity? He was saying what every man says sooner or later. Wherever you find a human being you find a being in revolt against death asking for life. What is this passion for life? It is born of the consciousness of the infinite. It is born of the fact that in the soul of man there is a profound consciousness from which he never escapes, of the fact of age-abiding life. His mind encompasses infinitely more than he can understand. He tells you he cannot grasp the thought of the infinite either as to time or space; but the man who knows a thing is unknowable has grasped that thing. In the moment when I know that I stand at the center of infinite reaches and stretches and forces, there is born within me a passion to hold, to possess, to grasp. It is that which puts man into the attitude of revolt against death.

Wherever you go you will find men characterized by a passion for dominion. The campaigns of humanity demonstrate the truth of it. Man is forevermore attempting to win his territory and reign over it. Wherever you find me a man determined to hold the scepter I show you one of whom the psalmist sang long ago. "Thou hast made him but little lower than God"—for dominion. The passion for dominion which is in the human heart is demonstration of man's relation to God.

Again, wherever you find man, you find a thirst for knowledge. If you have any children in your home and will listen to them you will learn wonderful lessons. You will find in those days when they are first beginning to talk that the words which most often pass their lips are "Why?" "How?" "What?" In asking these questions the child proves its capacity for knowing, and if you will follow that child through all its years, to youth and manhood and even old age, you will find it asking the same questions. Man is asking to know. He begins as a little child: "Why do flowers grow, mother?" and when he is an old man he has not answered that question unless he has listened to Christ as He says to him, "Consider the lilies of the field. They toil not, neither do they spin, yet your Father garbs them with a glory which Solomon never knew." That is the answer. Christ summarizes all truth about knowledge when he says, "This is life eternal, that they should know Thee, the only true God, and Him Whom Thou didst send, even Jesus Christ." Wherever you see a man seeking knowledge—he may be seeking it wrongfully, but the fact that he seeks it demonstrates him the offspring of God.

Again, take man's eagerness to create. All the inventions of the centuries demonstrate man's eagerness to make a new thing. The artist will tell you that art is a passion for creation. The passion for the new is always evidence of man's desire to create. It may be journalism, it may be theology. Man, foolishly, or otherwise, is after the making of something new. The passion for creation is demonstration of man's kinship to God.

Take yet another illustration. The appreciation of beauty which you will find everywhere in the world is demonstration of the same thing, whether in art, sculpture, poetry, or music. Of course, I take it for granted that no one will say to me, "What has beauty to do with God?" If you do ask that question, I remind you of the words of the ancient prophet who, in an ecstasy of worship cried out, "How great is

His goodness, and how great is His beauty." The admiration of beauty is everywhere. It is demonstration of the fact that humanity is offspring of God.

Take another illustration on a higher level. Man's admiration for goodness. You say, "Is that universal?" Absolutely universal. Remember, I said "admiration"! I do not mean that all men are good. Far from it. I do mean that you cannot find me a man in all the circle of your acquaintanceship who in the deepest of him does not admire goodness. He may affect not to admire it, but in the deepest of him he knows that it is high and noble. It is there—the conviction of the goodness of goodness, the beauty of holiness.

Once again, man's capacity for love is an evidence of his relationship to Deity.

None of these things has come into human life as the result of the influence of sin, evil, and the devil. All these are found in humanity as a whole. In some measure they are found in every man. In some men some one essential is more prominent than the others. These facts are demonstrations of the truth which the poets sang and which Paul reaffirmed, that man is the offspring of God.

If I sent you away with that as the only message I should be false not only to the Bible, but to all your experience. Think for a moment of the failure of the Divine in the human. When Heber sang

> Where all the prospect pleases
> And only man is vile,

he uttered the most tragic and awful truth. He sang a thing we would fain blot out of our hymnbooks, but we dare not. It is true. It is when I see man in his magnificence as offspring of God that I really understand his ruin. It is the sense of man's true kinship to God which reveals his awful failure as nothing else can do. Inter-human comparison may satisfy me, but this dignity of which I have been speaking demonstrates the degradation which I find all about me. If man is not kin of God in specific and special manner by creation, what is he? If he be merely of the dust and only of the dust, only so much related to God as the flowers are related to God, I quit my preaching. If that is all the truth about man, then man is doing very well. If indeed man is the outcome of the dust by the force of the one life common in the flower and man and God, then let me find an honest occupation; because man is climbing up, let me leave him to his climb. Why should I interfere? If that be true, there may still be room for the ethical cult, but the vocation of preaching the Evangel is a past vocation, and has been a ghastly mistake and an awful failure. But when I see in every human face the stamp of the image of God, and when I know that man is more kin of God than any other form of creation, then I begin to see man's degradation, and in every one of the illustrations I have taken to prove man's relation to Deity I have evidence of man's failure in that respect. Man's passion for life is confronted with the necessity for death, and he cannot by any means escape. Man's desire for dominion is defeated by a sense of slavery. The thirst for knowledge is intensified by the feverishness of agnosticism. Agnosticism never has been and never can be an intellectual resting place. No man who is an intellectual can rest there. He may have to declare his agnosticism, but it will make him more than ever restless. If he be indeed intellectual his thirst for knowledge is forever answered by a point beyond which he cannot go, until the Word of God has spoken the mystic secret in his ear.

Man's eagerness to create is ever unsatisfied in that nothing is ever new. The love of the beautiful is ever conscious of an unattained beauty, and here is the principal point, the admiration of goodness is the agony of inability to realize. Is it true that men everywhere see how good goodness is? It is equally true as Paul wrote—and he voiced not merely a theological creed but the actual experience of life—"The good which I would I do not; but the evil which I would not, that I practice." If it is true that when a man takes strong drink he is engaged in a quest for God—and I believe it is true—is he finding God that way? The man stooping over the stagnant pool is seeking water, but is he finding water? Is it not unutterable folly for that man to attempt to satisfy his thirst with the water of the stagnant pool when the living streams are gushing from the rock just at hand. All these are demonstrations of a degradation which needs some power to lift it. In every human life there is this paralysis. There is the vision of goodness but no virtue that can translate the vision into history. The capacity for love is ever suffering for lack of the final center. The sum total is failure. All fail in greater or less degree in every man. Flaming exceptions are all partial. Every demonstration of man's kinship to God is evidence of his degradation, his failure.

What message has the Christ of the New Testament to this double fact in human life? I make my answer first by saying that Christ recognizes the double fact. It was His recognition of the double fact which created the passion of His heart. When He saw the multitudes as sheep without a shepherd He saw them in their ruin, and at the back of the ruin He saw the Divine intention. Let no man imagine that he has recently discovered the fact of man's relationship to God. Christ proclaimed it long ago. He saw not merely the great capacity, He saw also its paralysis, and His heart was moved with compassion in the presence of it. The whole meaning of Christ's mission in the world is that He addressed

Himself to the two facts, the fact of man's kinship to God, and the fact of man's degradation. When Isaac Watts sang,

> In Him the sons of Adam boast
> More blessings than their father lost,

he sang a solo with all the infinite harmonies of the Evangel sounding behind and through it. Jesus confronts man in his kinship and ruin and makes possible the realization of the kinship of God by the negation of the forces of wrong which have brought man to the place of degradation. How does He do it?

First, consider this fact. The things I have said of man are true of Christ in part, but only in part. The things I said first of man are all true of Him. The things I said of man secondly are not true of Him. Remember that first of all He realized all that which man feels himself capable of by creation, and yet never can realize in actual experience. Men feel the passion for life. Jesus possessed it so that He could say, "No one taketh it away from Me, but I lay it down of Myself. I have power to lay it down, and I have power to take it again." They are words He actually uttered. If I cannot understand all the depth of their meaning, I can understand the first simplicity of them, and in that simplicity I find that Christ declares that no man can take His life from Him. In the laying down of it He will do it voluntarily and take it again. Did He take it again? On your answer to that question depends your relation to the Christian fact. If you say, No, then He did not rise. "Then is our preaching vain, your faith also is vain . . . we are of all men most pitiable." If you say Yes, He did take it again, then His taking of it again demonstrates the fact that He laid it down and that no man could have taken it from Him had it not been His will to lay it down.

Man seeks dominion: He exercises dominion. Standing once upon the mountain heights, Christ said to a group of fishermen, "All authority hath been given unto Me in heaven and on earth. Go ye therefore, and make disciples of all nations." They started, and all the triumphs of Christianity have been won in the name and power of Christ. He rose from the dead and grasped the scepter of universal empire.

We speak of knowledge and the desire to know. Our knowledge is limited. Jesus said, "This is the age-abiding life, to know God." He also said, "Father, I have known Thee." He possessed the ultimate secrets. I speak of the desire to create: He said, "I make all things new." We speak of man's admiration for beauty and his inability to overtake it: He declared—and the centuries demonstrate the truth of it—"I am the bright and morning star." Other men admire goodness and cannot realize it. He stands challenging the ages by His words, "Which of you convinceth Me of sin?" "I do always the things that are pleasing to Him." Other men have capacity for love. He stands in the center, the flaming, eternal vision, and says, "I . . . abide in His love." So that all man is in kinship to God by first nature, this Man is. All that man is in degradation, this Man is not. Identified with the essential human nature of the sinner, He is separated by infinite distances from all the sin of the sinner and all the limitation of knowledge resulting from the sin of the sinner. The lonely Man! But I am not saved by that fact. The contemplation of the great ideal never communicates dynamic to a paralyzed man. I may gaze upon the beauty but I am not thereby transformed into it. I may see the perfection of His life, and all it does for me is to bow me to the dust in shame Have you seen it? Then do you not know it in your own experience? I say to you tonight, in the name of God, that the man who tells me that he has seen Christ, and hopes within his own life by some effort of his own to reach Him, has never seen Him.

To see the vision, to see the spotless, matchless purity, to see human life in Christ is to know how weak I am, how low I am in the scale, how far off I am from Him, it is to know the power of the poison that paralyzes me, and to cry out in agony of soul, "If that Man has done none other for me than to reveal to me the beauty of human life He leaves me upon the highway bruised and helpless."

Thank God, I have an Evangel! The Evangel tells me that this Man perfect in realization in His life entered into all the limitations resulting from sin, was numbered with the transgressors in birth and baptism, and all the circumstances of poverty and pain, and yet I am not so saved, for by sympathy no man can save his brother. I follow Him reverently until I see Him in the hour of a great cross—a cross that grows upon my vision in its height and depth, and in the wide sweep of its outstretched arms, the cross upon which I once saw the Galilean carpenter, but upon which I now see God manifest in flesh. There in the mystery of that cross I know that He has entered into the very place of the ultimate issue of my sin. When you are told that we of the Evangelical faith declare that one man by dying saved the race, say it is not true. We make no such affirmation. We do affirm that the one lonely Personality in all the ages Who was man and God, God and man, God-man, God manifest, by dying provided plenteous redemption for the whole race. There in the cross, in which there is wrought out into visibility the eternal verities which I never could have known otherwise, I see how I, kin of God, yet ruined, may lift my face again toward the light, for by the sacred, hallowed, overwhelming mystery of the cross I have life.

Every man is capable of Deity. When Christ calls He

calls to the deepest in man. No man can realize the possibility of his first creation who has once sinned a sin that leads him into distance and paralysis, save as he is born again, born anew of the Spirit, and as he abandons himself to the grace of God.

CHAPTER IV

SANCTUARY

A glorious throne, set on high from the beginning, is the place of our sanctuary.
JEREMIAH 17:12.

JEREMIAH'S PROPHECIES WERE UTTERED WHEN THE RELIgious and moral conditions of the ancient people of God had become idolatrous and profligate. They are full of the sorrow of his heart, and yet thrill with vehement denunciation of sin. Notwithstanding these facts, it is quite evident as one reads this book that in common with all the messengers of God Jeremiah lived and spoke with strength born of a perpetual consciousness that however chaotic the circumstances of the hour may appear, the foundation is secure. In our text we have a radiant revelation of the prophet's conception of the character of that foundation. At the center of all he saw an established throne. As I have indicated, he shared this conviction with all the great messengers of God, whose words have been recorded for us in the Scriptures of truth. There was a day when they said to David, "Flee as a bird to your mountain, for, lo, the wicked bend the bow, they make ready their arrow upon the string, that they may shoot in darkness at the upright in heart. If the foundations be destroyed, what can the righteous do?" He replied, "How say ye to my soul, Flee as a bird to your mountain? . . . The Lord is in His holy temple, the Lord, His throne is in heaven; his eyes behold, His eyelids try the children of men."

There was a day when Isaiah was passing from the first phase of his ministry into a larger and more trying one, a day when the throne of his people became vacant, and he said, "In the year that King Uzziah died I saw the Lord sitting upon a throne, high and lifted up, and His train filled the temple." So here Jeremiah is facing a ministry full of difficulty; his heart is failing, his flesh is trembling, he is afraid; yet the word of God, as he says, burns within his bones and he is driven forth. He goes in spite of fear and trembling, with a courage and heroism that almost startle us as we read the story. Why was he courageous in spite of fear? The answer is to be found in his declaration, "A glorious throne, on high from the beginning, is the place of our sanctuary."

The conception of my text is that right relation to the throne of God is the place of sanctuary. Notice carefully that he does not say that the sanctuary is a throne, but that the throne is a sanctuary. If Jeremiah had declared the sanctuary to be a throne it would have been true; but it would have opened before our minds an entirely different aspect of truth. It then would have said to us that the sanctuary, using the word in the Hebrew sense, the place of worship and approach, was also the place of government. That is true, but that is not the message of the text. That is not the vision which made Jeremiah and all the messengers of God strong to face opposition and declare the truth. It was the conviction that the throne of God is a sanctuary, that if a man would find sanctuary he must find the throne; if a man would find the place of refuge, of quietness, of peace in the midst of trouble and turmoil and distress, he is not to seek it by the way of asking for a solution, but by putting his life into right relationship with the established throne of the abiding government of God.

Since the days of Jeremiah all the externals have changed. Human ideals, the habits and manners of men, and the customs of the age are all different; but the essential stream of human life flows on, and the laws of its progress are also unchanged.

We take this text out of the midst of the prophecies, turning from the man who uttered it, and all the strange and appalling circumstances in the midst of which he found himself, and we take the words and declare them to be a statement of truth for us. "A glorious throne, on high from the beginning, is the place of our sanctuary." I shall ask you to notice, first, the meaning of sanctuary, and second, to consider the final declaration of the text, that the place of our sanctuary is the throne.

The idea of sanctuary is a very old one. Indeed, it is as old as human history. Wherever you read human history you will find this idea obtaining. In the architecture of ancient Egypt there are found what are called sanctuary temples. They were temples which consisted of one simple chamber, so simple that a person finding his way into it was hidden, and yet no enemy could be hidden from him therein. They were the sanctuaries into which men in hours of great stress and danger came for safety. In the history of the ancient people of God you read of how men came and took hold upon the horns of the altar, which means they sought and claimed sanctuary. Not only in the ancient history and the history of the Bible, but in the history of our own country we find the same story. In olden times every church and churchyard offered what was called sanctuary. We are close to an illustrious instance of what I am now referring to. Dean Stanley says of Westminster Abbey, "The precincts of Westminster Abbey were a vast cave of Adullam for all the distressed and discontented in the metropolis who desired, in the phrase of the time, 'to take Westminster.' " That is to say, men in debt and danger, and discontented—I am quoting the words concerning Adullam—found their way in the olden days into the church or churchyard, and there were considered safe, and their confidence was respected.

What, then, does the idea suggest? There is a twofold note in this thought of sanctuary. Man's consciousness of his own danger and his desire for escape therefrom; his consciousness of unrest and his longing for a place of rest; his consciousness of peril and his desire after protection. The cry of man after sanctuary in all ages has been the cry of man in the midst of stress and strain and danger, of peril and conflict, and unrest; his cry for protection, for some place in which to hide himself, for some sphere in which the forces which have been buffeting, beating and bruising him will be unable to reach him. The idea of sanctuary is the idea of a place of quietness, of peace, of privacy, of protection. The deep meaning of the word is indicated in the fact that in all the instances I have quoted, and many others which I might have named, the thought of sanctuary is intimately related to religion—false or true matters nothing for the moment—whether the ancient religion of Egypt, or the revealed religion of Israel, or the religion of our own Christian times, the fact remains the same. When a man sought sanctuary he sought the things of religion. In that seeking is evidenced the fact that man associated with sanctuary the idea, first, of purity or holiness; second, of privacy, or perfect silence; and, finally, therefore, as a corollary to these two, the idea of protection, of being guarded from the things which were against him.

The idea of purity, of separation by holiness, sanctuary, in all these illustrations, was in the thinking of the men who sought it, a place in which there was no lie, no deceit. The holy of holies in the sanctuary of the Hebrews was a perfect cube, suggestive of regularity, of exactness, of integrity. Sanctuary, therefore, was a place which had no complicity with the evil things which made sanctuary a necessity to man. Man, in the midst of evil—whether in the sense of wilful sin, or in the sense of the limitations and calamities which follow thereupon—evil, hampering, hindering, bruising, battering him, wants sanctuary, a place where evil is not. He is seeking some place of purity that he there may find refuge from the forces of impurity which have disturbed his life and harmed him.

Sanctuary suggests not only purity, and perhaps this is the subconsciousness of desire—it suggests privacy, a place guarded by the forces of its own holiness from intrusion which is either inquisitive or revolutionary. It is a place of silence, a place of quiet—witness the great shrines of all religions, false and true. At the heart of every one is a place which few are permitted to enter, of which the chief characteristic is peace because there is privacy. In following me you will understand that I am not defending any form of religion. I am illustrating a truth. At the heart of many a religion in the place of silence, quietness, there is enthroned as deity that which is degrading. I simply ask you to notice the desire of the heart of man first of all for a religion untouched by evil, because evil has harmed him, and, second, for a place of quietness.

Men will take sanctuary in the most actual way even yet. You cannot walk through Westminster Abbey or St. Paul's Cathedral without seeing some poor, bruised, battered soul getting quiet. I never see such in the great cathedrals but I experience a twofold emotion—prayer for them, that they may find the secret place of hiding, and the desire that all our churches might always be open for such to pass inside, and sit and seek that quietness and find rest.

Then as a necessary corollary to this desire after purity and privacy, and now perhaps I have reached the first sentiment of the man who seeks it, seeking sanctuary is seeking protection, seeking to be guarded against the things which have troubled and harmed. Overcome in the conflict, bruised and broken in the battle, the spirit of man flings itself toward some religion of purity, privacy and protection, and in so doing at least indicates the fact that by submission to its law of holiness and peace he will be protected from the forces which have been against him.

Such are some of the suggestions of the great word sanctuary. Today the strenuousness of life is more terrible than it ever was. In the age in which we live perchance there are fewer cataclysms, catastrophes, than in olden days; but if the hours red and horrible with tragedy are fewer than they were, the sum total of unrest is greater than it ever was. The strain and stress of life have invaded places which were characterized by immunity therefrom. We still sing,

> Thou hast Thy young men at the war,
> Thy little ones at home,

but even our homes today are invaded, and the little ones are touched by the competitive fever of the age in which we live. Never perhaps have men more keenly felt the need of sanctuary.

Never has the subconsciousness of common humanity more cried out after some place of rest, some relationship which will make the heart firm and steady, some attitude of life which will correct all the feverishness arising from the complexity and strain of life. Where shall we find our sanctuary? This is background that I may bring you to the text.

"A glorious throne, on high from the beginning, is the place of our sanctuary." A glorious throne. That is the sum total of the revelation of Scripture to men. There are many things included in that of which I am not going to speak. I am not going to attempt to dissect, or analyze, or find out all the component parts of the great truth. From Genesis to Revelation the one truth the Bible declares is that the throne of God is man's resting-place, the throne of God is the place where man will find the answer to his desire for quietness, to his passion for peace, to his search after sanctuary.

In a rapid survey go over the Bible with me. In the early Bible history the throne is unnamed, but it is always there. In the early movements chronicled for us I find men in relation to the throne, submissive, at peace; in rebellion against the throne, disturbed. The throne of God is everywhere. I come at last to the point where the chosen people make their great mistake, and I hear God's explanation of it, "They have rejected me, that I should not be King over them." I come further on until I find this selfsame chosen people in the midst of circumstances full of terror, Ahab and Jehoshaphat are the reigning kings. In the first book of Kings, for the first time in the Bible, the phrase, "the throne of God," appears. When the thrones of men which had been set up in folly were proven disloyal to the principles for which they stood, and suffering and darkness had settled over the people, the messenger of God reminded them of the one throne of God. The devotional and prophetic books are full of references to the throne of God. In the Gospel story Jesus speaks of the throne of God, and the burden of His message is always that of the Kingdom of God. In the Acts I see Him, the Son of man, having passed to the throne as the final place of His power. When I come to the Revelation, that last book of the canon, declaring the final movements that usher in the eternal state, the throne is mentioned more than in any other part of the Bible. It is the book of the throne of God and the government of God. It is the book of the Kingdom of God. Its one message to men is, if you would find sanctuary, find the throne; if you would find peace, kiss the scepter; if you would be safe, get into right relationship with the one abiding and eternal throne. "A glorious throne . . . is the place of our sanctuary."

Mark the suggestiveness of the idea. What is a throne? It is the symbol of authority. It is the basis of law. It is the place from which the laws which govern are uttered. It is more, it is the symbol of administration, and not merely the symbol of law. It speaks of rewards and punishments. It speaks of the fact that the laws which are for the governance of all submitted to it are enforced by its majesty. It is the throne of arbitration and the settlement of disputes. This is sanctuary. The Bible idea of sanctuary is not that men shall find peace by escape to the pity of God, but to the judgment of God. The Bible idea of sanctuary is not that man shall find peace because God as a Father takes him and lulls him to sleep while in his heart man is still in rebellion. The Bible idea of sanctuary is that man shall find peace when he returns to the will and government of God in submission. This is not to contradict the meaning and message of Jesus. Jesus came not to persuade God to have pity on men who to the end of their career would remain in rebellion; but to establish the law and make it honorable, to preach the Kingdom and, blessed be His name, to make it possible for any bruised and broken man, returning toward the throne, to be healed and made strong. The ultimate in the purpose of Jesus was to bring men to sanctuary by bringing them to the throne. "Seek ye first His Kingdom, and His righteousness; and all these things shall be added unto you."

Not only did Jeremiah speak of the throne, he used a phrase which runs all through Hebrew figurative speech. "A glorious throne, *on high*." Even in the Revised Version we have the rendering "set on high," the word "set" being introduced, as is shown by the italics, in order to indicate a thought. I venture to think that here, as so often, there is more grandeur, more rugged splendor if we translate literally, "A glorious throne, on high from the beginning, is the place of our sanctuary." Mark that Hebrew figure of height. It is but a figure, but it is a suggestive one. The figure of height runs through all Hebrew imagery, and is always indicative of safety. In Psalm 46, one of the great psalms which has become the common property of trusting souls, we read "The Lord of Hosts is with us; the God of Jacob is our refuge." You have noticed the marginal reading of the word "refuge," "high tower." Again in Proverbs it is written "The name of the Lord is a strong tower: the righteous runneth into it and is safe"—set on high. It is a peculiar Hebrew figure of safety. How is this safety produced? By setting man on high above the things which are against him.

Go back to the threefold fact of sanctuary. Man coming to the throne of God comes to a throne on high and is lifted above the evil, therefore, into a place of purity. He is lifted above disturbance, therefore, into a place of privacy. He is lifted above enmity, and therefore, into a place of protection. This is sanctuary. It is this thought of height symbolizing safety that emerges in the wonderful words of Jesus with which we are very familiar, "Now is the judgment of this world: now shall the prince of this world be cast out. And I, if I be lifted up from the earth, will draw all men unto Myself. But this He said, signifying by what manner of death He should die." He did not mean merely, "If I be lifted up a few yards from the ground on the rough Roman gibbet."

He meant, "If by that pathway of suffering and sorrow, I am lifted high above evil, high above distraction and enmity, I will draw men to Myself." As He was lifted to the place of the throne by way of the cross He was lifted to a throne on high from the beginning, and as men find their way to Him on the throne through the mystery of His cross, they find their way to purity which is above evil, to privacy which is above disturbance, to protection which is above enmity.

Yet there is another phrase, for the prophet has not said the final thing. "A glorious throne, on high from the beginning, is the place of our sanctuary," "From the beginning." Again you are familiar with the phrase. It is one of those commonplaces of Scripture running from the first book to the last, from the first chapter to the final one, the simple phrase "the beginning." Take the highways of the phrase, "*In the beginning* God created." Come on into the sweet song of Solomon concerning wisdom, sung while the seeds of the decay of earthly kingship were already scattered, the song in which he sings, "The Lord possessed me *in the beginning* of His way, before His works of old. I was set up from everlasting, from the beginning, or ever the earth was. When there were no depths, I was brought forth." In Isaiah's prophecy in the midst of the failure of earthly kingship, speaking of the one King, he declares that He sees "the end from *the beginning*." It is used by John in introducing the Gospel which reveals the inner life of Christ, "*In the beginning* was the Word." The Master Himself when correcting the casuistry of men who were asking Him questions about social order and quoting something Moses had said, swept behind Moses and said, "From *the beginning*," so indicating the permanence of the moral order. It is used by John again in the epistle, which has as its key words, life, light, love, showing from what source these things have sprung, "That which was from *the beginning.*" Found again at the commencement and close of the Revelation of Jesus Christ which He sent and signified to His servant John, "The beginning." Some of you remember the words of Dr. Parker about that wonderful phrase. No words of mine can as beautifully and forcefully convey their profound significance. He said, "The beginning, the remotest date that has yet been suggested. Science has its slow rising and slow falling centuries. Yet 'the beginning' —the dateless date—includes them all, and drowns them in a deeper sea. On that ocean millenniums are but tufts of foam."

"A glorious throne, on high from the beginning, is the place of our sanctuary." That is to say, the government of God is based upon the reasons of things and finds its expression not in the rules of a passing hour, but in the principles of eternity. So that if God shall order my life for the next half-hour the reason of His ordering lies back in the ages that I cannot measure. That is Calvinism at its deepest and best and truest. That is the great fact which we still believe, that every flower that blooms on the sod under the Divine government has its roots of life and thought and suggestion far back in the ages we do not know.

Jeremiah had to preach to rebellious people, footmen to weary him, horsemen to tire him, in a land of peace, and amid the swellings of Jordan. How can he do this work in the midst of the opposition? How can he continue? "A glorious throne, on high from the beginning, is the place of our sanctuary." If this tiny, short life of mine is conditioned by the law of the throne on high from eternity, there is no room for panic in my heart. There is no room for fear and trembling. Let me but learn that law, let me but find the place of true relationship to that fact, and I have found sanctuary.

The fixed point in the universe is the unchangeable throne of God. The laws which emanate from it, the supreme will that enforces those laws, the infinite and unchanging wisdom which arbitrates amid all the conflicts, the certain wisdom and eternal youth which preside over the strife and battle, these, when my life is in harmony, create the only perfect sanctuary for human life. Our loyalty to the throne is the law of our liberty.

In the present life on every hand are mysteries that baffle and perplex. Oh, the perplexities and the problems about us. Let me not speak in generalities. Let me speak to one man or woman here. Buffeted man, tempest-tossed soul, the circumstances of the hour are circumstances of chaos. You cannot see how there is to be deliverance. It may be in matters material, mental, or spiritual. Here you are, an atom of humanity, and the surging sea of the multitude does but add to your unrest. You are seeking sanctuary, a place of peace, of privacy, of purity. Oh, to be high lifted above the things which seem to break and scar. Listen, this is the Gospel of hope, "A glorious throne, on high from the beginning, is the place of our sanctuary." Oh, the inexpressible comfort of knowing that unseen by the vision that is physical, but surely apprehended by faith, "the throne of God is for ever and ever: the scepter of His Kingdom is a right scepter." And, oh, my soul, the deeper comfort when individual life is immediately related to that throne by submission to its authority. Then indeed is man able to sing:

> Father, I know that all my life
> Is portioned out for me,
> The changes that are sure to come
> I do not fear to see;
> I ask Thee for a present mind
> Intent on pleasing Thee.

How may I find that throne? It is not far to seek, for the King Himself, in grace and tenderness and compassion, is at hand, and without material sign you may find the King, and finding Him thou shalt find the abiding throne, the glorious throne lifted high from the beginning. If thy life and mine may be surrendered to Him, we shall have found sanctuary.

CHAPTER V

SIN

Sin is lawlessness.
I JOHN 3:4.

Lust when it hath conceived beareth sin.
JAMES 1:15.

IN THESE TWO BRIEF PASSAGES WE HAVE INCLUSIVE STATEments of the nature and the genesis of sin. I am proposing to consider this subject in the most personal and immediate way, desiring to discuss the question of sin in the individual life, as to what it really is, and as to how it comes about.

What is sin? "Sin is lawlessness." How does a man sin? "Lust when it hath conceived beareth sin." We exclude from our consideration, first, the question of sin among the unenlightened peoples; and, second, the question of racial inheritance. Concerning those who have never heard the Evangel there is but one thing to be said, that the Judge of all the earth will do right. Concerning the subject of racial inheritance, or, if you will, the subject of heredity, I am not proposing to speak, save to say that while it is perfectly true that very many of us may have inherited tendencies from our fathers, it is equally true that we all have another inheritance, mightier than the inheritance of evil. The mightier inheritance is our inheritance in God, both by creation and redemption. We are living in the midst of the sanctions of the

Christian ideal. Wherever the ideal came from, the common consent of enlightened humanity agrees that it is right. There is no man in this house but that in the deepest of him consents to the standard of life revealed in the ethical teaching of Jesus. The standard of right and wrong for us is necessarily the Christian standard. We are all living in the light of that conception of life which has come to us through Christ, and we are all, in the deepest of us, consenting to the beauty of that conception.

Moreover, we are all conscious, however much we may debate it philosophically, of our power of choice. The man who, today, or yesterday, or the day before, committed sin, knows full well he need not have done so. I grant that there may have been unnatural predisposition to sin; I grant that the surroundings may have been very difficult; yet if a man be perfectly honest he will confess that he never yet committed an act of sin but by the choice of his own will. If the act of sin was not by the choice of his own will, then it was not sin. If you can conceive of circumstances in which a man is compelled by physical force to the doing of a thing which his conscience does not approve, circumstances in which a man has no choice left, under such circumstances he does not sin. Sin is always in the realm of the will. I am not discussing evil. Evil is a larger subject. Evil is all that is hurtful and harmful, whether as to cause or effect, whether material, mental, or moral. I am discussing sin.

Let us first, then, consider John's definition, "Sin is lawlessness." In order to understand this, we must take time to look at these two words, "sin" and "lawlessness," and see what they really mean.

"Sin." The word translated "sin" here is one of doubtful origin. From the philological standpoint, there is doubt as to its derivation. We are in no doubt, however, when we trace its use, as to what men meant by it. The very simplest definition of the word possible is "missing of the mark." It was made use of by Greek writers in at least three ways, always with the same underlying thought and intention.

The word was used in the physical realm. A man casts his spear and misses his mark.

It is used in the mental realm. A man sits down to write a poem and fails. That is a missing of the mark.

It is used in the spiritual realm, of failure to realize, coming short of the high ideal.

Turn to the other word, "lawlessness." Philologically, it means "without law." Greek writers, however, never use the word to indicate the condition of being without law, but always with reference to the breaking of law.

Now, take these two words and look at them as they constitute the one definition of my text, "Sin is lawlessness." May I change the words and indicate the meaning? "Missing of the mark is due to the breaking of law." While the word "sin" alone might indicate a condition for which the one sharing in it might not be responsible, this whole definition declares the condition to be the result of choice and action. Thus the element of guilt enters into the thought and fact of sin. The mark is missed because the law is not observed. The prize desired is not gained—and this is for the young men here—because the rules of the games are not observed. It is not merely that a man is disqualified and flung out by a judicial decision of someone outside; but that there is only one way in which to reach the prize, and that is by the observance of certain rules. If a man break the rules he misses the mark of the prize of his high calling. That is sin. Sin is first a decision and choice of the will. It is, finally, the ultimate disaster of failure, resulting from that choice of the will. It was when I knew, and disobeyed, that I sinned. It was when I came to the parting of the ways, and had the right, the power to elect, to choose, to decide, and I did so in the way of disobedience, that I sinned.

A young fellow in a business house told me an almost grotesque thing. He had become a teetotaller, and had kept his pledge for some time, when one night in a mad frolic, and exhibition of wickedness, the other men in the house absolutely forced him to swallow brandy. He did not break his pledge. He did not sin. They sinned, but he did not. I know the illustration is rough, almost grotesque, but it gets to the heart of what I want you to see. How often that has been true in your life is another matter. You talk to me of the seductions of a certain hour and place. Why were you in that hour and place? I should need to cross-examine you very carefully before I would be willing to agree that there was no guilt in your sin. You speak to me of the fact that you have in your blood, in your life, tendencies to evil, things that drive you. Have you put proper guard upon those tendencies? Have you used the common sanity of the athlete in your fight against them? I am not speaking yet on the highest ground, but on the lowest. Is it not true of the vast majority of men who are sinning today that they "have not yet resisted unto blood, striving against sin"? Until a man has resisted unto blood in his striving against sin, he has no right to say he could not help his sin. If sin is never sin in the sense of guilt until a man violates law, directly a man does violate law it is sin. When you state excuses for your choice of wrong, state also in common honesty the resources which were at your disposal, which you neglected. There are many excuses. There are men in this house tonight who live in the midst of circumstances very difficult for them, men who come to see me and talk with me, and write to me—I thank God for every such chance of helping men. All the environment in which you have to spend six out of your seven days is difficult. I grant it. I know it. Over against the difficult environment and the difficulty of the tendencies which you say you have inherited put the resources which are at your disposal if you will but avail yourself of them: the resources which are at your disposal in God, of which you may avail yourself if you fulfil His one condition of crowning Christ, the resources which are at your disposal in the comradeship of the saints, the resources which are at your disposal in prayer, prayer on the highway, in the midst of the environment, when the forces of evil are massed against you, prayer, which is but a sigh, a sob, the uplifting of the heart, but which touches the very hand and heart of God and brings deliverance to men. When next you tell me you are bound to sin, be careful that, first of all, you have considered not only the difficulties by which you were surrounded and the perils in your way, and the things which were against you; but be careful that you have also taken into account all the resources which were at your disposal.

In turning to James I want to read a few more words than the actual words of my text. "Each man is tempted, when he is drawn away by his own lust, and enticed. Then the lust when it hath conceived beareth sin: and the sin, when it is full-grown, bringeth forth death." This is a remarkable passage. In it three things are clearly revealed concerning sin. First, the basis of it, lust. Second, the method of it, a man is drawn away, enticed by his lust. Third, the issue of it, lust, being drawn away, conceives and bears sin. When I see the external act of sin, I ask what lies behind it. An enticement and a drawing away. And behind that what?

"Lust." It is absolutely necessary first of all that we should understand that deepest word in my text. What is lust? We have come to use this word almost exclusively in one sense. What does this word mean as it appears upon the page of the New Testament? Let me give you one or two illustrations where it occurs, which will prove that it does not necessarily, or indeed radically, mean what we have come to associate with the word in our speech today. When Jesus was approaching the end, coming near to the Cross, He sat at the table of Passover with His disciples, and said to them, "With desire I have desired to eat this passover with you." To translate that in another way would be to read, "With lust I have lusted to eat this passover with you." It is the same word exactly, the suggestive Greek word *epithumia*. Peter in his letter, speaking of the great redemptive work of Jesus, says, "which things angels lust to look into," "desire" as we have it translated. It is the same as the word in my text.

Once again, Paul writing in that wonderful letter, so radiant in its revelation of Christian experience, to his children at Philippi, said to them, "having the lust to depart, and be with Christ." I am sure you see at once what I am trying to bring you to understand about this word "lust." Desire is not sin, and there is no sin that men commit but at the back of it there is desire which is not sin. If only you can get far enough back into the mystery of your sin you will find desire which is not wrong in itself. Go back to an illustration which I am perfectly sure I have used more than once in this pulpit. I take it again as being the most graphic I know. Paul in writing to the Ephesian Christians said to them, "Be not drunken with wine . . . but be filled with the Spirit." That seems a strange bringing together of opposites. Behind both is the common lust, the same desire. Why does a man drink wine? Because the taking of it opens a window, lifts him, exhilarates him. I dare not say enthuses him, for the difference between enthusiasm and excitement is radical. The word "excitement" simply means things in rapid movement without order. Enthusiasm means God-filled. But the man is after vision, light, excitement, lilt, and lift. What does a man obtain when he is filled with the Spirit of God? Vision, lift, enthusiasm, the thing that puts him high above all the troubles of life and enables him to keep beneath his triumphant feet the very things which perplex and harass and make difficult the way of man. The desire for the vision, for the lift, for the sense of fulness of life—it is that which drives a man to drink. If I should tell a man that when he appeals to drink for the satisfaction of that desire he is on his way to find God, I should lie. He has then, in answer to the cry of his soul after God, turned his back upon God. Desiring to find life, he has deliberately turned his face to death. Seeking the sun rising, he has knowingly begun to follow the will o' the wisp which leads him on to the swamps from which there is no return, save by some miracle of the redeeming grace of God. It is perfectly true that lust, desire, is in every life, and in every advance of evil to man; every suggestion of evil is made to something which at its root is right. Lust is not sin, but sin comes out of it.

Mark the method. "Each man is tempted, when he is drawn away by his own lust, and enticed." I think with rare discrimination James here makes use of two words and they are both remarkable.

"Drawn away." It is a hunting figure, a figure of a man who is engaged in trapping animals, and the word means seduced from safety into snares. The next word "enticed" is a fishing figure, and includes the thought of a bait held out. The thought of the word enticed is "seduced by a fancied advantage." Mark the process in your own soul while I try to describe it to you as in mine, for, ah me, I know it, and you know it. There is desire in my life. Here is a suggestion that I shall satisfy that desire by being drawn away from the straight line which I see in front of me. I am enticed by the bait that offers me immediate realization of the thing I am after. I turn away, mark the word, turn away from the law which is in my conscience of right and wrong, I turn away to satisfy the lust. Lust is right, but the suggestion is that instead of answering the desire of my nature within the realm of God's holy law, I shall attempt to answer it outside. I am enticed. I am drawn away. The desire is right; the peril is that I am asked to satisfy proper desire by breaking law. Preaching some time ago on the subject of temptation, I illustrated this fact in the temptation of our blessed Lord. Every appeal of the devil was an appeal made to something which was perfectly right, but the suggestion of the devil was that there should be satisfaction of the proper desire by turning aside from law, being enticed, drawn away. You have not yet reached sin. Lust is not sin. Temptation is not sin. Desire is not wrong. The fact that you are drawn toward lawlessness is not sin. The fact that you are enticed by suggested advantage toward breaking law is not sin. You are yet upon the highway of rectitude. Christ desired, but He never sinned. Christ was tempted, but He never sinned. You may have come as far as this many a day and yet have not sinned. You will perpetually have to come as far as this. You will be conscious of desire for all kinds of things for which you have been made of God. Allurements will come and enticements and suggestion that you should step outside the proper line of rectitude which you know full well and satisfy your craving by some illicit process. That is temptation, but it is not sin.

When does sin begin? James is careful to tell us. "Then the lust, when it hath conceived." We may translate this word "conceived" here in order to help us, by a number of words —to clasp, to seize, to arrest, to capture. Here is a desire in my life. It is not sin. Here is temptation luring me from the line of rectitude. That is not sin. The will within me decides that I shall turn from the line of rectitude and take this suggestion and lay hold upon it, seize it, capture it. What then? The act is committed. That is sin. When I seize the bait the hidden hook seizes me. The hook is not sin. The hook is the penalty, the first pang of hell. The sin is in the deliberate choice of the will and the determined act by which I turn aside to answer, not my desire, but the allurement to the fulfilment of desire in an improper way. When you turn toward evil courses, when you go out upon the highway or into the hidden and secret and shameful place, you are not seeking God, you are turning from Him. In your heart and conscience you know the thing which is right and the thing which is wrong. There is desire within you for vision, light and life in its fulness. Oh for the thrill and throb of a great life. Who does not desire it? Every man does who is physically, mentally and spiritually sound. He desires it. It is the cry of his life after God. But when you turn to the ways of lust and licentiousness you are not answering that cry, you are answering the seduction which suggests that you turn by short and illicit methods to satisfy desire. Sin is the answer to the suggestion that I break law to satisfy desire.

A man wins when he says, "Desire is perfectly right. It is right that I should desire vision and life at its fullest, but I must find these things along the line of law." If you listen to the voice and turn aside, know this, and know it forever—be not deceived, I pray you; "God is not mocked"—you sin, and you are not seeking God. Listen to me, you are trying to dodge God and get your prize without God, and you cannot do it. Lust, desire is enticed, is drawn away, and if man with the will shall seize upon the bait, then he sins.

Remember, this is not only a revelation of the genesis of

sin. It is also a revelation of the nature of sin. It is not a thing to be pitied. It is a thing to be smitten, to be punished. Its punishment lies in the line of its own activity. If a man will turn away he turns to death, for mark the last word of James, "The sin, when it is full-grown, bringeth forth death." The man who is indeed alive, desires fulness of life, vision, sense of God, and turns to find fulfilment for these things in the evil and pernicious ways of ungodliness, is not after God, he is attempting to get round God and win something which his nature wants without God, and he never succeeds. This is sin, not merely against himself, not merely against the community, but against the cosmic order. Sin as the wilful choice of wrong is not a part of God's cosmic process. It is rebellion. It is treason. It is chaos. Let every man who feels allurement to satisfy desire apart from the way of God know this, that when he turns in answer to it to the house of evil, to the method of wrong, he is not after God, but lifting the fist of rebellion in the face of God. There can be but one issue for all such high treason, and that is the nemesis and the ruin of alienation from God and the consequent cutting off of the possibility of all that man most seeks after.

So I come to our common use of the word "lust." There is a poetic accuracy in it. What is lust? Desire. Yes, but get a little lower down. What is lust? The Greek word suggests hard breathing, passionate desire, earnest desire. If man attempts to satisfy desire without God, what is the answer? Desire which never can be satisfied. There are appalling illustrations of the truth of that which cannot be used here and now. God help me to say this thing solemnly to you. Take hold upon any proper and natural capacity of your life, I care not what it be, and attempt to satisfy it outside the lines of God's law, and you do but intensify the desire and never satisfy it. That is perdition. The craving for the thing which never comes. The God-created desire without the God-provided bread. That is the issue of sin. There are men in this house tonight who know something of it. There are men here, I dare venture to affirm, who are conscious of the fact that the more they attempt to satisfy the craving of some inner desire without God, the greater the craving becomes. Take an illustration which is commonplace. Christ's supreme illustration of evil is mammon. I pray you watch the man who attempts to satisfy his craving for possession without God. The craving for possession is perfectly right. God made man to hold a scepter and wield power. Jesus did not tell men they were not to answer the craving for possession. He did utter words sadly and awfully forgotten by the Christian Church and the world at large, "Lay not up for yourselves treasures upon earth." He did not say, "Lay not up treasures," but "Lay not up . . . treasures upon earth." Then also He said, "Lay up for yourselves treasures in heaven." The desire to possess is perfectly correct, it is part of the proof of your relationship to Deity. Here is a man who turns his back upon God, or, if he still names His Name, breaks His law of love. Did you ever find a man come to the moment when he said, "I am satisfied with my getting"? Is there not always an insatiable passion for more gold? A grasping devilishness that blights everything that is human in the man and makes him cruel and hard and cynical, grinding all others to the dust that he may make his gold. You need not envy the man who, without God, has piled his millions. There is a greater hunger in him after possession than ever, and the more he possesses, the more he hungers. Lust, which is desire at its deepest, attempting to be answered outside the line of God's law, becomes in itself a very consuming fire, the "worm that dieth not" and the "fire that is not quenched." That is the issue of sin.

I warn you with all love and earnestness, with all the passion of a strong conviction, and with all loyalty to my ordination vows to preach the Cross of Christ, I warn you do not be deceived by any philosophy which declares to you that sin is one of God's processes. It is man's poison and God's enemy. It is the one thing which has brought in its wake bitterness, anguish and sorrow. If you answer the desire of your inner life outside the line of God's will, which you know full well, then the lust which was proper becomes a fire which cannot be quenched.

Who here has never sinned? I am not asking whether you are a sinner by nature or not. I am not discussing that subject now. I pray you remember that in the mystery of Incarnation and Atonement there are forces provided greater than the forces which you inherited by nature. Actually and personally, who has never fallen? I mean into actual sin, as men count sin, sin of the flesh, or of the mind? Of course the mere moralist of the hour will reckon that the sin of the flesh is an evil thing. We are on other and higher ground. We recognize also the sin of the mind, the desire for safety, for ease, for all the things which are merely self-centred.

It is for the man who has sinned that Jesus came. The Evangel of the New Testament is for the sinner.

Where does the Gospel begin? It begins where sin ends. Mark the process. Lust, enticement, yielding, sin, death. Not death postponed. Not physical death. But death here and now. Dead in trespasses and sins. Jesus Christ brings men as His first gift, life from the dead, a new vision, a new sense of strength. The man who has become the slave of the evil thing, to which he has turned himself, may know his chain broken, the fire quenched, the passion stilled as the Master stilled the storm upon Galilee, and all the incompetence of the broken will made strong again. There is but one condition, and it is that man should turn from his sins to Christ and trust Him wholly and absolutely. Though you have answered lust outside law until lust has begun to be your judgment and your pain, even here tonight, He will quench the fire and break the bands and set you free.

Do not, I beseech you, give these last words away in generalities. I am getting weary of generalities. I mean you, my brother, hidden away. Thank God, you are hidden away. No eye is resting upon you save the eye of the Master. You are hidden away in this crowd, in the grip of sin. Its power can be broken tonight and forever as you turn to the Christ of God and trust Him with all your soul and mind and body and estate. May God help all such as feel the force of sin to turn to that mighty Saviour.

CHAPTER VI

THE NAME JESUS

Thou shalt call His name Jesus; for it is He that shall save His people from their sins.
                                    MATTHEW 1:21.

EVEN TODAY THE NAMING OF A NEW-BORN CHILD IS AN EVENT full of interest. The principles of choice are varied in these complex and somewhat superficial days. Children are given names because the names have been borne by their fathers before them. Sometimes names are still given to children as expressing a hope on the part of the parents, but as a rule they are simply given on the basis of preference.

The Hebrews meant far more by their names than we do. That will be discovered as the Old Testament history is read. They were often wrong in their naming of the children. The very first name, Cain, was a wrong name. Eve called her first-born Cain—Acquired. She was doomed to disappointment. She had hoped that the promised seed had already come. And the second name was also a mistake. She called her next boy Abel—Vanity. There was far more to satisfy the mother's heart in the coming years in Abel, even though he suffered death, than in Cain.

Sometimes the names were tragic names. Hosea, that prophet of the wounded spirit and the broken heart, as children were born into his home named them, and in their naming is seen the terrible conditions of the chosen people. He called the first Jezreel, judgment threatened! He called the second Lo-ruham mah, mercy not obtained! He called the third Lo-ammi, not My people!

When Mary's Child was born, Joseph named Him Jesus. And this was by special instruction conveyed to him by the angel. That angel was the messenger of heaven's thought, and of God's will. The Babe was registered Jesus in heaven. And that name, given by Joseph in obedience to the instruction of the angel who had received his command in heaven's own high court, was a name which expressed heaven's confidence in the Child now born. Earth's salvation will come as earth shares heaven's faith in Jesus; and the giving of the name at the first was expressive of this confidence of God in the newborn Child.

This story of the giving of the name is one of supreme interest. Do not be angry with me for bringing to you a text you have known from childhood, but let us come back to this name, which every child here who has begun to read at all, can spell, and try to understand some of the things signified by the giving of this name. A few moments first, then, with the name given; and, second, a consideration of the reason for giving this name to this Child.

I would have you, first of all, remember the humanness of this name. It was a very common Hebrew name. Doubtless many a boy living in Judea in the days when the Babe was born was called Jesus. And doubtless it had been for long years, for centuries, a popular name in Jewish families; for of course you remember that Jesus is but the Greek form of the Hebrew name "Joshua." There were many boys called Joshua, and in the Greek dialect obtaining at the moment, many boys doubtless bore this name of Jesus. There is nothing startling in the name. When the neighbors heard that

Mary had called the new-born Boy Jesus, they did not stop to ask what she meant. Many another Jesus was running about in Nazareth and Judea, and all through the countryside it was one of the most common names, almost as common as John is today.

Thus God took hold of a name perfectly familiar, which set the new-born Child among the children of men, rather than separated Him from them. He took hold of a name that men were using everywhere, "Thou shalt call His name Jesus," the name that the boy next door has, the name that men have been calling their boys by for centuries. "Thou shalt call His name Jesus."

But how came it that this name was so familiar? What were the associations of the name in the Old Testament history? It was a name associated with two men pre-eminently—the one who first received it, a leader; and, then, another who made it conspicuous, a priest.

The first man who bore the name was the great soldier who succeeded to the leadership of the people after the passing of Moses, the man to whom there was committed the stern, hard, fierce fight that was necessary to establish the people in the land. This man was born in Egypt, in slavery, lived there about forty years, and then followed Moses as he led the people out of Egypt; then spent the next forty years in the wilderness, passing through all its experiences. Finally, he led the people with the sword and terrific conflict into possession of the land. That is the man who first received this name. So far as the Bible is concerned, and in all probability so far as Jewish history is concerned, the name had never been known before. It was made for him by Moses. His name was originally Hosea or Hoshea: but Moses changed it and called him Joshua.

The next man who bore the name conspicuously was a

priest in the days of restoration under Haggai and Zechariah.

Now this Child is born, and heaven, taking a name familiar in the homes of Judea, a name conspicuous in Hebrew history because of its connection with the soldier leader and the restoring priest, commands, "Thou shalt call His name Jesus; for it is He that shall save His people from their sins."

Let us examine the matter more closely. We have seen that the name was common among Hebrew boys. We have seen that the name was thus popular because of the historic association. Now, what does the name mean?

In the story to which I have already made reference, in Numbers 13, it is told how men were sent to spy out the land: princes of the tribes. Among them was the prince of the tribe of Ephraim, Hoshea, which name means salvation, or deliverance. In the course of that story in Numbers we are told, as I think parenthetically, that Moses changed his name from Hoshea to Joshua, and the reason for it will be found presently when the spies returned. You know the story well, how the majority report was against going up to Canaan; but the minority report—and it is a very interesting thing to notice in human history how minority reports are almost always right—the minority report was, We can possess the land. Joshua was the spokesman, and what did he say? He declared that Jehovah was able to bring His people into possession in spite of all the difficulties. I think it was because of that word, and because of that fact and of that confidence that Moses with insight and foresight, seeing what this man meant to the nation, changed his name. It was a good name before: Hoshea: salvation. Yes, but this man was not depending on his own right arm. He had no dream in his heart that he could bring salvation to his people. He declared that it must be the work of Jehovah; and, consequently, Moses weaving the two names together, Jehovah and Hoshea, called him Joshua, for Joshua is the combination of the two words, Jehovah and Yawshah, which is Hoshea, and which as we have said means salvation. The name Joshua signifies Jehovah saves, or Jehovah will save, or Jehovah's salvation. Jehovah and salvation are thus woven into one name. It was high honor conferred on the new leader to bear such a name as that, and a wonderful revelation of the insight of the man who gave it to him. The original name, Hoshea, salvation, is a fine one, but this man knew that he could not lead the people in, even though his report be a true one; but he also knew that God could, and Moses said, Your name is changed, and into it is brought the name of the God Who can save. So the name was made. And Joshua led them in, but he never gave them rest.

The high priest of a later day, who had the name, came very near fulfilment of some of its significance as he bore the iniquity of the people, the filthy garments signifying this fact. Presently he was crowned. It was all prophetic and symbolic, but he failed, as the subsequent history of the people proves. The centuries have gone, and the high and noble thinking of the name has never been realized in actual life. There is a hush in the outer court of the inn, and a little Child has come into the world, and the world is quite careless, but heaven is not. Stars are shining, angels are singing, wise men are feeling the touch of the upper spaces, and are journeying toward the manger. Who is it? "Thou shalt call His name Joshua; for it is He that shall save His people from their sins."

God took hold of a common name of the boys playing about, and called His Son by that name. God took hold of the great historic name of the past, the name of the great leader and the name of the priest of the past, and gave it to His Son new born. Yes, but what is the deepest thing? Call Him Jehovah, Yawshah; Joshua, Jesus. Call Him by His own

Father's name, Jehovah, and so indicate the truth about His nature. Call Him by the supreme passion of His Father's heart, salvation, and so indicate the meaning of His work in the world.

We pass it on from age to age in printed page, and from mouth to mouth in spoken word: Jesus! But in that name is wrapped up essential truth concerning Him. Jehovah, Yawshah. Call Him that. He is my Son. He is My Servant Who shares My nature. He comes to do My work. Now I understand Him when in the coming years I hear Him say, "I and My Father are One." Call Him Jesus, and I understand Him when I hear Him say, upon another occasion, "My Father worketh even until now, and I work." Call Him salvation, and link your two names together into the infinite music; whether it be Hebrew, Greek, or Anglo-Saxon, matters nothing. You cannot rob it of its music. Carry it into all languages and dialects, and in sweet tones it breaks upon the listening ear of humanity.

> Jesus, the name high over all,
> In hell, or earth, or sky,
> Angels and men before it fall
> And devils fear and fly.

That is the tone of His triumphant march to victory. But there is another tone.

> Jesus, name of sweetness,
> Jesus, sound of love;
> Cheering exiles onward
> To their home above.
>
> Jesus, oh, the magic
> Of the soft love sound,
> How it thrills and trembles
> To creation's bound.

This name has appealed to every generation, and to all classes of men because it is a great name. It is the name of the boy who plays in the street. It touches you. It is Jehovah, Yawshah. Call Him that, said the Father to the angel, and the Boy's name was registered in heaven, God's name linked with the great word that declares His mission in the world.

Second, the reason for giving this name. "Thou shalt call His name Jesus; for it is He that shall save His people from their sins." You notice that slight variation in translation, certainly a great gain. The real thought is that of a contrast. "Thou shalt call His name Jesus; for it is *He* that shall save His people." I repeat, the form of the sentence really suggests a contrast. A contrast with what? With all the aspiration of the past, which had never become achievement. With all the strong and strenuous attempt that had ended in defeat.

Take the man who first bore the great name. Joshua is one of the greatest men upon the pages of the Old Testament in many ways. And yet in all full realization, he failed; and the writer of the letter to the Hebrews tells us, "For if Joshua had given them rest, he would not have spoken afterward of another day." So the great leader of the past failed. He led them in, he led them with great sternness and severity, and magnificent triumph against Jericho, and Ai, and on, but he certainly never gave them rest. And all the history of the coming years was the history of perpetual restlessness. Joshua never led them into rest. Well, call *His* name Joshua, for it is He that shall save His people from their sins.

And Joshua, the high priest in the days of the prophets Haggai and Zechariah, not much is said of him, but there he appears, the representative of religion, urging the people under Zerubabel to their building, helping the office of the prophet with his priestly intercession. There he is seen in symbolic language, clothed with the filthy garments, representing defiled Israel. But he could not take away sin, and the filthy garments remained upon Israel, and Israel failed to fulfil the great function for which she had been created a nation, that of speaking the message of God; and Joshua the priest failed, as did Joshua the leader.

Very well, then, call *His* name Joshua, for He *shall* save His people from their sins. And so, brethren, that emphasis of contrast leads us to see that this name indicated, or the declaration associated with the name indicated, not merely a mission, but a method. The angel did not say to Joseph, "Thou shalt call His name Joshua," for He shall lead the people in. He did not say to Joseph, "Thou shalt call His name Joshua," for He shall bear away the filthy garments, and enable the people to bear their testimony. He might have said these things, but what He said was deeper. "He shall save His people from their sins." My brethren, this is a revelation of the assured success. Joshua failed to lead the people into rest, why? Because of the people's sin, with which he could not deal. Joshua the priest failed to realize in Israel God's purpose, that which should be his message to the nations, why? Because of his people's sin, which he could not carry. So that instead of dealing merely with the surface of things, or speaking of issues, the angel's message goes down to the depths and says, "Thou shalt call His name Joshua," for He will lead His people into rest, and to the fulfilment of their vocation by saving them from the sins which prevent rest, and which give the adversary power.

Call this new-born Child Jesus, "for He shall save His people" from these things and from the consequent ruin. If His people are saved from sins, they will find rest; if His people are saved from sins, they will fulfil their vocation, and be and do all that God means they shall be and do.

THE NAME JESUS

"Thou shalt call His name Jesus; for it is He that shall save His people from their sins." I pray you remember that the phrase, "His people," is significant at this point. It marks limits, and indicates limitlessness. What are the limits it marks? *His* people. No, brethren, I will begin with the other word. How does it indicate limitlessness? It does not say, He shall save the people of His own nation. It does not say, as has often been pointed out, He shall save God's people, but His own people. "His people." He is coming to make a position, to create a people to be a Kingdom, and to set up the Kingdom; and the people who are His He will save from their sins. There is your limit, but there is your limitlessness. How may a man become one of His people? Simply by believing on Him and crowning Him. It is a statement that overlaps the boundary line of Judaism. It is a statement that includes the wise men who come from afar to Him, as well as shepherds singing on Bethlehem's plains. This is the story of the first naming of the Child.

But as you take the story you will find this Child grows up, and He stands amongst multitudes of men, and He comes out of the border line of Judea, and touches Tyre and Sidon, and Phœnicia. He goes to Samaritans finally, and at the last commissions His disciples to go everywhere. Standing amongst men, He says, "Come unto Me, all ye that labor and are heavy laden, and I will give you rest." "Him that cometh to Me I will in no wise cast out." It is a universal invitation that He utters. Will you come? Are you coming? I am addressing in imagination the whole nation, and from here and there they come, they crowd. Who are those that come? His people. What will He do? Save them from their sins. Unless you make yourself His by birth, He cannot save you from your sins. Unless you yield to Him, you cannot be His. It is the call of Christ which constitutes human opportunity.

That opportunity taken, and men yielding to it, what then? Then they become His, and He saves such from their sins. So that He brings men into rest, who come to Him, and that Joshua could never do. So that He enables a man to fulfil the Divine vocation who comes to Him, and that the high priest, Joshua, could not do. But our Jesus does it by saving us from our sins.

Brothers, when this name was given to Joseph by the angel it was, so far as man was concerned, a prophecy. So far as God was concerned it was an affirmation of faith, of absolute assurance and certainty. Thou, Joseph, shalt call His name Jehovah—Salvation, for He shall save His people from their sins. So spake heaven; and as men heard it, it was a prophecy, it was an indication, it was a hope. There is a sense in which it is true that He did not receive that name finally until He went back into heaven, and Paul tells us all the gracious story when he writes, "Who, being in the form of God, counted it not a prize to be on an equality with God, but emptied Himself, taking the form of a servant, being made in the likeness of men; and being found in fashion as a man, He humbled Himself, becoming obedient even unto death, yea, the death of the Cross. Wherefore, also God highly exalted Him, and gave unto Him the name which is above every name." What name? "That in the name of *Jesus* every knee should bow."

The angel uttered it, heaven's confidence, a prophecy of hope to men; and the Babe bore it, and carried it through the simplicity of childhood, one Boy among the many who bore it in those Judean villages; and the Boy passed out into youth, and bore the same name, Joshua, Jesus, in purity, and in resistance to all evil. And He bore it on through the years of public ministry, and He bore it on the Cross, and never so universally as there. Who is this upon the Cross? The Babe

Whose name is Jesus. But Who is He? Joshua, Jehovah, Salvation.

Can He do it? Can He take sins away, and bring rest? Can He take sins away, and enable me to fulfil my vocation? I do not know. He is dead. They have buried Him. I do not know. I am one of the disciples, I am afraid. I do not know. I hoped, but I am not sure. What is this the women say? He is risen? He has appeared first to them, and then to the eleven, and then to Peter all alone, and then to others, and to five hundred at once. He gathered them about Him on Olivet, the risen One, and He went up, bearing with Him the same sweet human name that boys bore at their play in Judea, bearing up the name the leader of the past bore, who failed to bring into rest, bore it up triumphant into heaven itself; and He received it there anew, no longer a prophecy for men, but an evangel!

And there at the center of God's universe at this moment of human time is the Man Who bore the name, glorified, our Joshua, Hallelujah! He is able to lead us into rest. He is our High Priest, clothed no longer with the filthy garments, for He bore them away on the Cross; but with the miter on His head, and many diadems upon His brow, Jesus, the enthroned One. May God help us to hear the evangel of the name, and to know assuredly that what the name prophesied He has perfectly accomplished.

CHAPTER VII

WORSHIP, BEAUTY, HOLINESS

O worship the Lord in the beauty of holiness.
PSALM 96:9.

THE WORD THAT ATTRACTS OUR ATTENTION IN THIS TEXT IS the word "beauty." "O worship the Lord in the *beauty* of holiness." Whether in application this word is of supreme importance may be another question. The very fact of its attractiveness compels us to consider its setting. In that consideration we shall discover its suggestiveness and importance.

The particular word translated "beauty" here is used only five times in the Scriptures: once in Proverbs 14:28, where it is translated in the Authorized Version "honour," and in the Revised Version "glory"; again in I Chronicles 16:29; in the psalm which was sung when the ark was brought from the house of Obed-edom to its resting-place in the tent or tabernacle; again in II Chronicles, in the story of Jehoshaphat's arrangement of the singers who were to precede the army, who were charged in their singing to "praise the beauty of holiness"; again in Psalm 29, and in the text.

It is a somewhat rare word therefore. Our English word "beauty" does most perfectly express the real meaning of the word, of which it is a translation. It suggests honor, or glory, or beauty, not as a decoration, but as an intrinsic value, an inherent quality. The Revised Version suggests in its marginal reading in each case that we should read, "Worship the Lord in holy array." But this does not for a single moment interfere with the essential thought of the passage, for it cannot refer merely to material clothing, but to that outshining of inner character which is the true array of the soul in its approach to God in worship, that outshining of inner character which makes even sackcloth beautiful, and homespun a thing of ineffable glory. We do not forget that when our Lord was transfigured, that transfiguration was not the shining upon Him of a light from heaven, nor even, as I venture to believe, the outshining of His Deity, but rather the shining through of the essential glory and perfection of His human nature. Eye-witnesses tell us that His very raiment became white and glistening, and yet as we read the story we know that it was the appearance of the glory of a raiment due to the essential glory of His own character there manifested to them for their sakes rather than for His.

And so with our word "beauty" here the thought is that of an inherent quality, not a decoration, not something put on as from without, but something manifest to the eye, and appealing to the emotion and the mind, as being in itself glorious and beautiful, and yet belonging essentially to the fact with which we are brought into contact. The text is a cry, calling upon men to worship, and declaring what is the true condition of worship, and so incidentally revealing the true nature of worship. Only once does this particular word occur apart from the same kind of setting—in the book of Proverbs. Everywhere else it is associated with worship, holiness. "O worship the Lord in the beauty of holiness."

These words lie in the midst of language in which the psalmist is appealing to men to praise God, calling them to recognize His greatness, calling them to recognize His glory, calling them to think of His power and His majesty, and urging them to answer the things their eyes see, and their hearts feel, by offering praise to Him.

In this call so poetic and full of beauty there is a revelation of the deep meaning of worship, of its abiding condition, and glory. "O worship the Lord in the beauty of holiness." The supreme thing is worship. But how is worship to be rendered? "In the beauty of holiness." Wherever you find beauty, it is the outcome of holiness. Wherever you find beauty as the outcome of holiness that beauty in itself is incense, is worship. To attempt to worship in any other way is to fail. To live the life of holiness is to live the life of beauty, and that is to worship.

What is worship? The essential and simple meaning of the word, and therefore the fundamental thought is that of prostration, of bowing down. Worship suggests that attitude which recognizes the throne, which recognizes superiority; that attitude of the life which takes the low place of absolute reverence in the presence of that which takes hold upon the life and compels it. It is a word full of force, which constrains us, and compels us to the attitude of reverence.

The word "worship" runs through the Bible, and the thought of worship is to be found from beginning to end. The thought of worship is on the part of man, the recognition of Divine sufficiency, the recognition of his absolute dependence upon the Divine sufficiency, the confession that all he needs in his own life he finds in the life of God. And the spoken answer to that conviction of the abandonment and surrender of the whole of man to God is worship. I worship in the presence of God as I recognize that in Him I find everything that my life demands, as I find that in myself I am incomplete everywhere, save as I am brought into relationship with Him. A sense of my need and His resource, a sense that all my life finds only its highest and its best, and fulfils itself in relation to Him, produces the act and the attitude of worship. The attitude of worship is the attitude of a subject bent before the King. The attitude of worship is the attitude of a child yielding all its love to its Father. The attitude of worship is the attitude of the sheep that follows the leading of the Shepherd, and is content in all that pasturage which He appoints. It is the attitude of saying Yes to everything that God says.

The height of worship is realized in expression in the use of two words which have never been translated, which remain upon the page of Holy Scripture, and in the common language of the Church, as they were in the language where they originated: "Hallelujah," and "Amen." When I have learned to say those two words with all my mind, and heart, and soul, and being, I have at once found the highest place of worship, and the fullest realization of my own life. "Let all the people praise the Lord, Let all the people say, Amen." And when I pass on presently to the end of the Divine Library, I hear in heaven, "a great multitude . . . saying, Hallelujah. . . . And a second time they say, Hallelujah"; and the great responsive answer is Amen. Amen to His will, and Hallelujah the offering of praise. I know it is but a simple symbol. I know it is but the saying of an old thing, but I address my own heart as much as any of you, my brethren, and I say, Oh, soul of mine, hast thou learned to say Amen to Him, and that upon the basis of a deep and profound conviction of all His absolute perfection in government, and method and providence? Canst thou say, not as the boisterous shout of an unenlightened soul, but as the quiet expression of a heart resting in the perfection of God, Hallelujah and Amen? Then that is worship, that is life.

I am not going to stay to speak at all upon secondary worship, save to refer to it and recognize it. The outward acts are sacred. The songs of praise that tell of the goodness and the grace and the sufficiency of God, the prayer that pours out its burden because it is confident in God's resource to meet all human need, the quiet attention to the Word of God as we meditate upon it: these are the outward acts of worship, and behind the praise and the prayer, and the meditation upon His Word is this great consciousness that all I need is in Him, and that in proportion as my whole life is abandoned to Him, in that proportion my need will be met, and so my life itself, restful in God, powerful because of my relationship to Him, will be a song, a psalm, an anthem; or if I may go back and borrow the words, God's own poetry, God's own poem, the music that glorifies Him.

So, brethren, the outward acts are the least important parts of our worship. If I have not been worshiping God for the last six days, I cannot worship Him this morning. If there has been no song through my life to God, I am not prepared to sing His praise, and the reason why so often

> Hosannas languish on our tongues

is because "our devotion dies." This is a pause in worship, and expresses a perpetual attitude. The worship of the sanctuary is wholly meaningless and valueless save as it is preceded by and prepared for by the worship of the life.

We may now press on to ask the meaning of the psalmist when he says, "O worship the Lord in the beauty of holiness." Let us fix our attention in the most simple way upon the word "beauty," in our common use of it.

When Charles Kingsley lay dying, he said, among other things, "How beautiful God is!" We are almost startled by the word. We do not often think of it in that connection. We speak of His majesty. We speak of His might. We speak of His mercy. We speak of His holiness. We speak of His love.

And yet, brethren, there is nothing of God which He has made more patent to men than the fact of His beauty. Every ultimate thought of God is beautiful. Every manifestation of God is full of beauty. I recently came across some old verses of Tupper's. They are quaint, and somewhat curious. He says:

For beauty hideth everywhere, that Reason's child may seek her,
And having found the gem of price, may set it in God's crown.
Beauty nestleth in the rosebud, or walketh the firmament with planets;
She is heard in the beetle's evening hymn, and shouteth in the matins of the sun;
The cheek of the peach is glowing with her smile, her splendor blazeth in the lightning;
She is the dryad of the woods, the naiad of the streams.
Her golden hair hath tapestried the silkworm's silent chamber,
And to her measured harmonies the wild waves beat in time;
With tinkling feet at eventide she danceth in the meadows,
Or, like a Titan, lieth stretched athwart the ridgy Alps;
She is rising in her veil of mist a Venus from the waters,—
Men gaze upon the loveliness,—and, lo, it is beautiful exceedingly:
She, with the might of a Briarens, is dragging down the clouds upon the mountains,—
Men look upon the grandeur,—and, lo, it is excellent in glory.
There is beauty in the rolling clouds, and placid shingle beach,
In feathery snows, and whistling winds, and dun electric skies;
There is beauty in the rounded woods, dank with heavy foliage,
In laughing fields, and dented hills, the valley and its lake;
There is beauty in the gullies, beauty on the cliffs, beauty in sun and shade,
In rocks and rivers, seas and plains,—the earth is drowned in beauty.
Beauty coileth with the water snake, and is cradled in the shrewmouse's nest,
She flitteth out with evening bats, and the soft mole hid her in his tunnel;

The limpet is encamped upon the shore, and beauty not a
    stranger to his tent;
The silvery dace, and golden carp, thread the rushes with her;
She saileth into clouds with an eagle, she fluttereth into tulips
    with a hummingbird;
The pasturing kine are of her company, and she prowleth with
    the leopard in his jungle.

Go back to the first lines of it with me for a moment—

For beauty hideth everywhere, that Reason's child may seek her,
And having found the gem of price, may set it in God's crown.

That is the key to it. Tupper saw beauty in all these things. We are so blind, and seldom see beauty, but he saw God's handiwork, evidences of God's presence and God's power, and God's law operating in the blossom of a perfect beauty.

My brethren, these are commonplaces to us. Yet how often do we see them? I am not here to remind you of these things. I am here to take you back to the thought of the beauty of God, blossoming in the daisy on the sod, blazing in the starry heavens, to bring you back to my text, "O worship the Lord in the beauty of holiness," to remind you of the fact that every ultimate thought of God is beautiful, and that ugliness and deformity are never of God. All the beauty of flowers in form and color and perfume are of God. All the beauty of the seasons as they pass: spring and summer and autumn and winter, all that is beautiful in man physically, mentally, spiritually, and all that is beautiful in the interrelation between man and man, is of God.

To put this same truth for one moment from another standpoint, everything which is of God is beautiful. The marring of a flower which makes it ugly is not of God. That in a man which is repulsive is not of God. God is a God of might. God is a God of glory. God is a God of love. But He is also the God of beauty. It is well for us to think of it for a moment and remember it.

I remember staying, some years ago, while conducting some special services, with a friend in Devonshire. There came by the morning mail to him some roses wrought in silk by deft fingers here in London. And he put some of these roses wrought in silk by me, and said, "They are very beautiful." And holding them up in my folly and short-sightedness, I said, "They are perfect." He replied, "Are they, really?" And he brought his microscope, and put the rose beneath it, and the very silk itself became coarse as sackcloth. Then he brought from his greenhouse a spray of God's roses, and put them under the microscope, and the more closely I looked, the more perfect they were. The beauty of God as manifest in the tiniest cell of the flower as in its completion is manifest in the blossoming of the flower, as in the rhythmic order of the heavens about me. Brethren, God is very beautiful, and everything which is of God is essentially beautiful.

Therefore, do not let us be afraid of our text when we come to the subject of holiness. "Worship the Lord in the beauty of holiness." In God's works beauty is the expression of holiness.

> The Beauty is His handiwork,
>   The Light glows from His face,
> The perfume is His sweetness,
>   All Earth's beauty is His grace.

If God's ultimate thought is realized only along the line of His law, then the law is that which creates the beauty; and everywhere beauty is marred by the breaking of law. Holiness, then, is rectitude of character, the condition of beauty.

What is "the beauty of holiness"? The realization of a Divine thought by abiding in the Divine law. That is the one and only condition of worship.

Let me illustrate again. The flowers that blossom on the sod are worshiping God. But how are they worshiping? They are worshiping by their beauty. And what is their beauty? The beauty is the result of the operation of the law of God; and in answer to the laws of their life, not by effort, not by garments other than the garments of essential glory wrought out from their inner life, they worship. They worship in beauty because they worship in holiness. They worship within the realm of law. "The trees of the Lord," said one of the ancient writers, "are full," and I often regret the addition in translation which imagines that the Hebrew method of expression is so imperfect that we must add to it to complete it. Our translators have written, "The trees of the Lord are full of sap." They thought it was poetic. I think it was prosaic. I think they had been looking at a tree, and they thought there was nothing but sap. The Hebrew word is "full." Change the word "sap" to "beauty," and that would still be incomplete. There are things which are subtracted from by adding to. "The trees of the Lord are full," full of sap, full of beauty, full of health, full of poetry.

But let me introduce the word "beauty" here. "The trees of the Lord are full of beauty," and are they not? Oh, it is good to get away and stand among the trees. "The trees of the Lord are full." "The voice of the Lord breaketh the cedars." What did the psalmist mean? He says, "The God of glory thundereth . . . the Lord breaketh in pieces the cedars of Lebanon." The Word of God, the enunciation of law is upon them, and they have heard, and have answered, and in the uprising of their life, they have blossomed into fulness of form and beauty. Did you ever see an ugly tree? I have, but it was a tree some fool of a man had tried to cut into the shape of a bird. But a tree is full of beauty. What is its beauty? It is the beauty of law. You spoil the law of the tree, and you will rob it of its beauty, and you will rob God of His worship.

You may climb higher. The cloud rises in the sky, and you with your incipient infidelity grumble because the sun is shut out from your patch of earth. Presently the cloud is giving itself away, flinging itself out upon the earth; and gradually it exhausts itself, and ceases to be. Every rain shower is the worshiping of a cloud, its fulfilment of the purpose of its being. It is its answer to the movement of God in the economy of life. And as the cloud pours itself out it worships, it worships in the beauty of holiness. The tides that come and go worship, and worship in beauty, worship in majesty, the deep diapason of their voice roaring around us, until we are deafened, but it is all an anthem of worship. But what is their beauty? The answer to law, the fulfilling of the purpose of God.

So we climb by these illustrations to man. When does a man worship. A man worships when he is what God meant him to be. I may sing every song in the hymnbook, and never worship. I may recite every creed that was ever prepared, and never worship. I may inflict all manner of scourging upon this body of mine, and never worship. I may kneel in long lonely vigils of the night, and never worship; and the song, and the sacrifice, and the prayer are nothing unless I am, in this one lonely individual life of mine, what God Almighty meant me to be. When I am that my whole life worships.

How can I be that? Only as I discover His law, only as I walk in His ways; and here is the difference between the flower and man. The supreme dignity, the tremendous and overwhelming majesty of your life and mine is that of our power to choose, to elect, to decide, to will. Consequently the worship of the soul that can choose and decide and elect and will is profounder, mightier, greater than any other worship could be. It is not in the antiphonal song of choirs, or in the chanting of music to which we listen, or even in our own singing; it is in taking hold of our individual life, and the putting of it into such relationship with God that it becomes what He means it should be.

I do not worship God by going to China as a missionary if God wants me to stay at home and do the work of a carpenter. I do not worship God by aspiring to some mighty and heroic thing for Him if the capacity He has given me is for doing the quiet thing, and the simple thing, and the hidden thing, and the unknown thing. It would be very foolish for the hummingbird, instead of entering the tulip, to try to beat back the air and combat with the eagle. It worships by staying where God puts it. It would be very wicked for the eagle to cultivate a mock modesty, and say that it preferred to remain among the tulips when it ought to be soaring sunwards.

So that if I have spoken to you about the fact that God has foreordained works, that we should walk in them, I now remind you that if you worship when you find God's appointment, and when you walk in the way God has appointed, you realize your own life. Worship consists in the finding of my own life, and the yielding of it wholly to God for the fulfilment of His purpose. That is worship! You say, Would you tell us to find our life? Did not Jesus say we must lose it? Yes, "He that findeth his life shall lose it," but He did not finish there: "He that loseth his life for My sake shall find it," not another life, not a new life, not a new order of life, not an angel's life, for instance, but his own life. The Cross is necessary, restraint is necessary, sacrifice is necessary, self-denial is necessary; but these things are all preliminary, and when Paul describes the Christian life at its fullest, he does not say, I am crucified. That is the wicket gate, that is the pathway that leads out, that is the beginning. "I have been crucified with Christ: yet I live; and yet no longer I, but Christ liveth in me: and that life which I now live in the flesh I live in faith, the faith which is in the Son of God."

Or again, he says, speaking of Christ Himself, "It is Christ that died," but that is not the last thing, nor the final thing, "yea rather, that was raised from the dead." And so if the Cross be absolutely necessary, and it is—your cross, my cross, my individual dying to the ambitions of selfish desire, all that is necessary; but beyond it, life. What life? My life. The new birth is but the passing into the possibility of the first birth. The new creation is but the finding of the meaning of, and the fulfilment of the purposes of the first creation. "O worship the Lord in the beauty of holiness." Discover His law, answer His law, walk in the way of His appointing. Let Him Who made you lead out all the facts of your life to the fulfilment of His purpose, and then your whole life is worship.

Then, brethren, you will see that worship does not begin when you come here. This is a very valuable part of worship, but it is secondary worship, symbolic worship. This is the day in which we cease the worship that perfectly glorifies Him in order that in song and praise and prayer we may remind ourselves of the perpetual and unending truth that life lived within His will, and according to His law, the life of holiness is the beauty that glorifies God. This service is but a pause in which in word and attitude we give expression to life's inner song. And if there be no such inner song, there is no worship here. Worship is the perpetual poetry of Divine power and Divine love expressed in human life.

Angels worship not merely when veiling their faces

they sing of His holiness, but when ceasing their singing at His bidding, they fly to catch the live coal from the altar, and touch the lips of a penitent soul who sighs. It is true "they also serve who only stand and wait." But it is equally true that they also worship who serve, and serve perpetually. And it is in the service of a life, not specific acts done as apart from the life, not because I teach in the Sabbath school, or preach here, that I worship. I may preach here today, and never worship. But because my life is found in His law, is answering His call, responsive to His provision and arrangement, so almost, without knowing it, my life has become a song, a praise, an anthem. So I worship! I join the angels, and all Nature, in worship when I become what God intends I should be. And in that blossoming of His ideal we sing the song of His greatness and His love.

> Our midnight is Thy smile withdrawn;
> Our noontide is Thy gracious dawn;
> Our rainbow arch, Thy mercy's sign;
> All save the clouds of sin are Thine.
> Grant us Thy Truth to make us free,
> And kindling hearts that burn for Thee,
> Till all Thy living altars claim
> One holy Light, one heavenly flame.

And so I pray that when the service is over, and the Sabbath day has passed, we may go back to know that in the shop, in the office, in the home and market place, in all the toil of the commonplaces, we can worship the Lord in the beauty of holiness. Where there is holiness there is beauty. Where there is beauty there is worship. However ornate the worship may be in external things, if it lacks the beauty of holiness, it never reaches the inner sanctuary, and never glorifies God.

CHAPTER VIII

PROGRESSIVE REVELATION

I have yet many things to say unto you, but ye cannot bear them now.
JOHN 16:12.

THESE WERE SOME OF THE FINAL WORDS OF JESUS TO HIS disciples, spoken amid the messages of which we speak as His Paschal discourses. They were uttered in the hearing of that inner circle of souls who had gathered about Him, loyal to Him, having tabernacled with Him, had listened to His teaching and had become familiar so far as was possible with His Person. To these men He says, "I have yet many things to say unto you, but ye cannot bear them now."

This has always been so. God has ever had more to say to man than man has been able to bear. And God has ever patiently waited for man's ability to bear before speaking to him other of the things that he ought to know.

You will remember that Isaiah was criticized by men who mocked at his method, and said that he was a man of "strange lips" and "another tongue," that he was a man who spoke to them "line upon line, precept upon precept; here a little, there a little." We have come to include these words in our prayers of thankfulness for God's patience with us, saying that He deals with us thus—"precept upon precept; line upon line . . . here a little, there a little." We are perfectly right. But the lips that first uttered those words were the lips of men who laughed at the method. They criticized God's servant, saying "Whom will he teach knowledge?" That was his method. It was made necessary by their blindness and sin, and even though the prophet did not declare it at the moment, we, looking back, see the infinite grace and patience of God manifest therein.

And the method obtained even after our Master had passed back into heaven. You will remember that Paul in his great Corinthian letter says, I cannot feed you with meat because you are not able to bear it; you are yet carnal. The carnal mind cannot discern the deep things of God. He said, I am determined to know nothing among you save Jesus Christ, and Him crucified. Why not? Because they were carnal, and not able to bear anything else. We have made that the watchword of the preacher. It is, however, a misinterpretation of the meaning of the Apostle. Upon another occasion he says, "It is Christ Jesus that died, yea rather, that was raised from the dead." The Christian preacher has never preached the whole Christian message until he has preached the resurrection and the ascension, and the infinite issues of positive life that come from the narrow and straitened gateway of the Master's death. To these Corinthian Christians the Apostle said, I cannot go further on in my instruction, I am bound to keep you in the region of first principles, because you are not able to bear it.

Thus having seen that the method obtained in the old prophetic age, and in the apostolic age, I come back to my text, and I find Jesus standing amid His disciples. After the three years of instruction He was about to leave them, and looking into their faces, He says, "I have yet many things to say unto you, but ye cannot bear them now."

Shall we listen to that word of Jesus, first as a statement

of the Divine method of revelation, second, as a basis of faith, a secret of peace for all our hearts; and, third, as a trumpet call to the life of receptivity.

In order that we may appreciate the value of that final thought, let us dwell upon the first. In this text we have an illustration, as I have already indicated, of the perpetual method of God in revealing Himself to men.

In reading the Divine library we discover that every dispensation has grown out of a preceding one, the preceding having prepared for it; and every distinct and successive dispensation has prepared the way for another, which was coming after. The line of development is to be discovered in man's appreciation and appropriation of something new revealed. In proportion as man has learned the lesson of a particular period, God has been prepared to pass on to something else. There are many ways of tracing that line of development in the Old Testament Scriptures. Take the broadest, and therefore in some senses the least satisfactory, and yet for the moment the most easy. Taking the history of man as a sinner, leaving out from our present thought everything that goes before it, we find that God has been teaching humanity lessons one at a time, never the second until the first was learned.

We find God dealing first with individual man, and teaching him the lesson of his responsibility to God. Then, dealing with man as to his social interrelationship, the meaning of the family, and of society; and gradually the emergence of the national ideal. Then the meaning of community of worship, and gradually, through long and tedious processes the great monotheistic lesson, the fact of the one God.

Then after a lapse of centuries we have the incarnation, the coming of the one God into human life, rendered necessary by man's sin and failure; and from that incarnation until now, still the same line of development—progressive revelation. I believe that the catholic consciousness of Christ—I use the word in its simplest and truest sense, including within its gracious and spacious and radiant sweep all the children of God of every denomination—at the moment is the greatest and the grandest that the world has ever had, as the result of a progressive unfolding of all the essential truth concerning God which came to men by the way of the coming of Christ. Not all at once did the light come, but it has been increasing little by little, line upon line, precept upon precept.

Progress has always depended upon realization of the truth. God has never led humanity forward into any new truth concerning Himself, save as they have realized and obeyed the measure of truth already manifested. This law of Divine revelation still stands.

It is God's method with the individual. If I speak experimentally, it is in order to illustrate the truth. What is His method with me? "Line upon line." Yes, but when did I come to the second line? Never until I had learned the first. By learning the first I do not mean committing it to memory, or accepting it theoretically, but obeying it, and being transformed into its intention; for truth is always a sanctifying force. Truth is not a commodity that a man has any right to place upon his shoulder and label. Truth possessed by a man is valueless. Truth possessing a man is valuable, and it is when any particular truth concerning Jesus Christ has come to me not merely as an illumination, but has become part of me by sanctification of my life, that I am ready for some other lesson.

Brethren, here is the meaning of the arrest of development in Christian character which is so often manifest in our own lives. How is it that some of us have lost our first love for the Word of God, have lost our appreciation of things

Divine, are looking back with a sigh of regret to days long gone when the light was clear? In every case because somewhere we disobeyed the truth, we refused to submit ourselves to the light that came to us. There can be no advancement or development until there has been obedience to the particular thing God said to us. Where? I do not know! You know! One year ago, ten years ago! Some of you may have to tramp your way back for twenty years to find the point where development was arrested, and it was because you refused to obey light at that point. God cannot advance in the unfolding of essential truth because as yet you have not been prepared for the greater truth by obedience in the first thing He said to you.

I have said that the catholic consciousness of Jesus Christ is far finer today than it has ever been, but is it not a sad thing that it is nevertheless so imperfect as to create divisions within the catholic Church. Oh, these divisions! How can they be healed? There are men this morning in the Christian Church, absolutely sincere in their loyalty to Jesus Christ, and yet we are absolutely opposed in certain views concerning Jesus Christ and Christianity. Why? You cannot answer that individual question by individual examination. You must take the larger and wider outlook. You must become conscious of the Church, the whole catholic Church of Jesus Christ before that question can be answered. And when you have become conscious of it, then the answer is to be found in this conclusion, that the Church itself has not been true to the things which have been certainly revealed to her somewhere. And all divergence of opinion means, somewhere, disloyalty to truth.

Our responsibility consists in finding out whether or not we are true to the thing about which we are absolutely certain, and convinced. If we get down to the simplicity of our

Christian life, to the fundamental things about which we are all agreed—and thank God there are such things—are we true to these things? Have we obeyed them? So long as the Church holds truth as an intellectual quantity it becomes its curse, its bone of contention, its reason of division, the rock upon which it goes to pieces. But when the whole Church of Jesus Christ in its individual membership will answer the demand of truth, and walk in the light of the revelation, then there will be the coming together of those that have been divided, not by any organic attempt at reunion, but upon the basis of God's unfolding of His new meaning.

We are quarreling about some things He has never revealed. Men are differing, even to bitterness, about the future of the wicked. God has said no final thing in Scripture about the future of the wicked. He has said quite enough to lay upon the heart of every preacher the awful responsibility of what it may mean for a human soul to cut itself off from God. But no man has any right to anathematize me, or anyone else who does not hold his view upon the future of the wicked. These things are not fully revealed.

For centuries the Church has been divided about Arminianism and Calvinism. God has not said the last thing about the great problem, and why should we quarrel about it? We have disobeyed light and wasted time trying to discover other light, while still disobedient to the thing He has spoken. This is the perpetual method of God. The law of revelation still stands, that He can never reveal new truth to those who have disobeyed the truth received. I find in my text a basis of faith, and therefore a secret of peace.

In spite of what I have said concerning the necessity for obedience to truth, before we attempt any further intellectual apprehension of its meaning, is it not a fact that there is nothing the heart of man rebels against so much as the sense of mystery? The rebellion against mystery is that by which man has beaten his way into new discoveries which on the other side have been new revelations from God. And yet we have to admit that the mystery is still there, in every department of life. There is no pathway that I traverse long before I come face to face with mystery. But mystery is another word for human limitation. Finally, there is no mystery. At the heart of mystery is intelligence. "God is Light, and in Him is no darkness at all." That is the great and essential word that denies mystery. Mystery to me, surely yes! Mystery in every flower that blossoms, and every day that comes. More mystery I think within my own personality than anywhere outside it. Mystery, yes, but not to God. At the heart of the mystery is the Light. Behind the clouds through which gleams of glory break occasionally upon our waiting vision is the Light itself. As God is essential Light, so Jesus Christ, God incarnate, is Light. He said upon one occasion, "I am the Light of the world." He brought into human life all that human life needs of illumination, of instruction, and of intelligence. So to Him in the things that I desire to know there is no mystery. "I have yet many things to say," and the things that are mysteries to me He holds in trust for me, and He holds them in order that I may know them; the essential light is to come in gleam after gleam until it burns to the eternal brightness upon my life. He holds in trust, but He reveals them to me line by line, and precept by precept as I am able to bear.

To my own heart this morning that is a foundation for faith. The thing which today is a mystery to me, tomorrow will be a revelation. The very veil that prevents my seeing through to the heart will resolve itself into the method of revelation presently.

> Soft they shine,
> Through that pure shrine,
> As beneath the veil of Thy flesh divine,
> Beams forth the light,
> That were else too bright,
> For the feebleness of a sinner's sight.

He veils in love, but my heart says in the presence of the veiled mystery, He knows, He holds in trust the things He holds for the moment! Consequently I wait in my limitation by faith in Him.

Take Him away from me, remove Him from before my eyes, tell me that He also is a struggler amid the mists, attempting to find out; tell me moreover that He is a half-informed personality in human history, then I have no focusing for essential light. I am more afraid of light than darkness, I will hark back to the mist to escape the blinding glare of the Throne of the infinite Knowledge.

But Love, standing before me in this Man Who is also God, says to me, I know these things, troubled heart. There are things you do not know, and I have them to say to you, but you cannot bear them yet. The reason of My withholding is not capricious. It is not that you are to be perpetually shut out from final knowledge concerning all your problems. It is because your eyes are not ready for the light. The mind is not trained to grasp, is not prepared for the apocalypse. I have the things to say, but you are not yet able to bear them.

If that be the basis of faith, it is also the secret of peace. His very chastisements are grievous, but afterward I learn that the very processes of His discipline are leading me into larger capacity for revelation. My friend, Margaret Bottome, of the United States, founder and president of the King's Daughters, was telling me some time ago of how upon one occasion a friend of hers came into possession of a chrysalis of one of the most gorgeous butterflies. She took care of it toward the day of emancipation when it should find its color and beauty. She watched patiently the struggle of the life within, and thinking it a pity that there should be such a struggle, she took her scissors to help it out. Oh the disaster of it! That butterfly never found its wings, nor lived its life. God might help me out of some present pain, some present anguish. He might make it easier for me, but He would cripple my wings. And through the process of mystery and even of pain and withholding He is not withholding, for He is preparing me to see.

And so, finally, and, as I think, naturally, the text becomes a trumpet call to the life of receptivity. His will is to reveal to us the deep things of God, but He waits for the fulfilment of condition on our part. What is my responsibility? Quick response to the demand of the truth that He has revealed. As I make that response the truth makes me free, sanctifies me, and I am prepared for another line, another precept, a little advancement. The trouble with us all is that we are so fearfully content not to know. I am never so anxious about the soul who rebels in the presence of mystery if that soul will remit the story of rebellion to Jesus Christ as I am about the man who is content to sing the hymns he sang ten years ago, as though they were the finality of Christian experience. One or two things at the beginning, and the revelation did not proceed. Why not? Why was it that we did not get further? We make up for lack of growth in development by singing:—

> Where is the blessedness I had,
> When first I found the Lord?

If we were true to Jesus Christ the blessedness of this morning would eclipse in its glory any blessedness that preceded it. The trouble is that we are content not to know the deep things of God, to live upon the surface of things. I have heard people say that they will be quite content if they get just inside heaven. Just to get inside is pure selfishness. Oh that there might come upon us the passion to know the deep things of God, to look into the mist with eyes intense in their longing, until we see it disappear, and the light break. Oh, to ponder the things He has said until we hear their clamant call, and obey. He will lead us on into deeper things, and higher things, and better things.

Surely if we hear Him say, "I have many things to say unto you, but ye cannot hear them now," we ought to reply, "Oh, Master, prepare us to receive them. Bring us back to the point where we were disobedient." You know where you lost the line of your development. Something He told you to do, and you have not done it, though the years have rolled away. Something He told you to cease doing, and you are still doing it. Some call of truth disobeyed. Back to it, my brother, this morning, back to the point of your disobedience, and there obey.

CHAPTER IX

THE TRAINING OF OUR CHILDREN

Train up a child in the way he should go, and even when he is old he will not depart from it.
PROVERBS 22:6.

ONE IS INCLINED TO COMMENCE THIS MORNING BY ASKING in the presence of this text a somewhat startling question. The question would be whether Christian people generally today believe the Bible to be true. A great many who would quite readily answer the inquiry in the affirmative would nevertheless halt, and attempt to qualify, and so begin to indulge in their own peculiar method of criticism in the presence of this particular text.

"In the beginning God created"—yes! "And God so loved the world that He gave His only begotten Son"—certainly true! "Whatsoever a man soweth, that shall he also reap"—there can be no question about that! "Train up a child in the way he should go, and even when he is old he will not depart from it"—well, that is open to question; we are not quite sure about it. This text is not so often preached from, nor so often quoted today, as in olden days; and that is because people are not quite sure whether it is true.

New methods and new ideals concerning children have made men question the absolute accuracy of this Old Testament word, the word of the preacher of long ago. Indeed, you will find sometimes that if this truth be insisted upon with anything like vehement emphasis there will be an equally vehement protest. Whether in conversation among friends, or in general discussion, or even in preaching, you insist upon it today that if a child be trained aright, it must end right, people begin to question, and I have heard personally a most angry protest against the statement of this truth on the part of Christian people whose own children have gone wrong. Ah, there you touch the secret reason why this text is not believed as it was believed, or is questioned more today than it was in the past.

Well, my brethren, this morning at any rate I intend to treat it as an inspired statement, as a declaration of truth, as something which the preacher was inspired of the Spirit of God to write because it is essential truth, and to which there are no exceptions.

Believing this I shall ask you to consider in the simplest way first the condition, "Train up a child according to his way"; and, second, the promise, or perhaps it would be more accurate to speak of it as the sequence, the necessary result, the inevitable issue, "and even when he is old he will not depart from it." In dealing with the condition, the word that arrests us necessarily is the first word of the verse, "train." "Train up a child." I want to say two or three of the simplest things about this question of the training of children. I speak with more doubt about it than I should have done seventeen years ago, but I speak out of personal conviction, and in all tenderness and love to my brothers and sisters who have the charge of children in their own homes, and especially in the hearing of those of you who have charge of children in the Sabbath school, or Day school. To all such as are privileged to touch child life, and to be in any way responsible for it, I desire to speak.

And the first is that training involves an ideal. There can be no training save to some goal. A result must be desired, and training simply means working toward that result. There can be nothing capricious or haphazard about true training. Unless there be some goal toward which we are moving, some ideal that we desire to realize, some great purpose ahead, there can be no training, and we shall never train the children of our own home as they ought to be trained, neither shall we train the children of our Sunday schools except we have some underlying conception of an ultimate for them. Training means going in a direction toward an ultimate. It means a great deal more than that, but that is the first thing.

And we are living in an age, brethren, when I am afraid in the Christian Church—and I have no message in this respect to the men and women who are outside the Christian fact; my first word to all such is, You must be born again; I have no ethic for the man who has not been born again, because he is absolutely unable to obey; he is dead in trespasses and sins—but within the Christian fact, within the circle of such as accept Christ as King and Saviour, and share His common life, I am afraid today that the ideals that we have for our children are often very low; and it is because our ideal for the child is a low ideal, that our training is a false training, and so much of the ruin and disaster that appals us constantly in the case of Christian people results from this fact.

Too often our ideal for our boys is that they shall be educated, gain a position for themselves, and, alas, to use the phrase that so constantly is upon the lips, even of Christian people, "get on in the world." Too often for our girls we have the ideal that they shall be also educated, and refined, and accomplished, and presently, again to use a phrase which if I could I would cancel absolutely from the thinking of

Christian parents, "get settled." Well, brethren, these as ideals are anti-Christian and pagan. I am not undervaluing education. It is the duty of every man to give to every child he has the best education that he possibly can. I am not undervaluing position. Let every lad be ambitious to be the best carpenter, the best doctor, the best lawyer, in the whole district. Let our girls in very deed and very truth be educated and cultured and refined, but if these are the ultimate, then what are we removed from pagans? This is not the ideal with which we must start in the training of the child. What then is that ideal? I might put it in many ways. Let me take one of a hundred. That the child shall realize Jesus Christ's estimate of greatness. By realize it I do not mean theoretically merely, but practically. What is Jesus Christ's estimate of greatness? That a man is great in proportion as his character is what it ought to be. In the great Manifesto of the King, that wonderful enunciation of the ethic of the Kingdom of God, never a single blessing is pronounced upon having, never a blessing pronounced upon doing. All the blessings are upon being. And the true ideal toward which we are to move, and for which we are to train our children, must be the realization of the character upon which Jesus Christ has set the sevenfold chaplet of His benediction. That the boy may be a Godly man, that the girl may be one of the King's daughters all glorious within, that first. Everything after, but that first. To neglect that as the ultimate, to lose sight of that as the goal is to ruin our children by love which is false love, is to harm them by the very method in which we attempt to serve. Simply to take your boy, my Christian brother, and desire that he shall be a successful merchant and business man and make money, I am not sure that it would not be kinder for you to shut your front door upon him, and let him fight his way through slum and up. To take your daughter, Christian father and mother, and simply desire that she shall shine in human society, with never a thought in your mind of how she appears in the palaces of the King, is cruel and dastardly, and not kind. Training means moving toward an ultimate, and the first thing in the training of the child is that we should see to it that the ultimate upon which our eyes are set is the true ultimate.

And now a second thing. The training of a child involves personal discipline. And as God is my witness I preach to my own heart this morning. What I want my child to be, I must be. I should like to bring that a little closer home to my heart and yours by stating it thus. What I want my child to be, that I am. Some man says, Not that; I want my boy to be better than that, truer, higher, nobler, purer! No, sir, you do not, or if you do, you desire a thing that can never be, by your influence at least. For remember this, you will make your boy what you are, and not what you tell him to be. How constantly Emerson's thought comes back to the mind when one thinks or talks of character. He says in thought, not in actual word, I cannot hear what you say for listening to what you are. That is what your boys are saying about you this morning. You say to your boy, Be good, and you are not good! He will be what you are, and not what you say. You say to your boy as he starts out on his life, Be pure, and in your own heart there is impurity. Your boy will answer what you are, and not what you say. And this is not merely the thought of a preacher, it is the science of life. If you are going to train anyone to anything, you must yourself be that, or able to be that toward which you are attempting to train. There was a gymnastic display here last night. I was sorry I could not be present; but I am quite sure they are not going to appoint me the trainer for next year. And if you saw me on parallel bars, you would know why. I cannot train the lads to gymnastic excellence. Would that I could, but I cannot do it. It is too late. There are things I think I could help a boy to do, but not that. Why not? Because I am not an athlete. Now lift your thinking back. You cannot expect your boy to be a Christian athlete if you are weak and anemic in your Christianity. If you neglect prayer, and if the family altar is a thing you can lightly lay aside, your boy will never erect it in his home presently. I can make my child only what I am myself. Dear teachers, remember it. God bless you and help you this morning. Do not forget that, as you gather your class around you Sunday by Sunday, you influence them only by what you are in yourself. It is true of the preaching. God help me to remember it. I cannot influence any congregation by what I say, unless behind it there is the mystic force of a life true to the preaching. Thank God for the children in our homes, not merely for the privilege of training them, but for the fact that they train us. And how they train us! There is something in my own make-up which is perhaps mischievously independent, and if a man tells me I should not do this or that, I always feel like saying, Mind your own business. But if a man says, How will this thing that you do influence your boy? I am alert and listening.

And I must answer that conviction of personal necessity for discipline. If I am to train my child I must see the goal toward which I desire the child to press, but I must go that way too. I cannot persuade the children of my home to set their faces toward the King's city and Kingdom if I am a rebel.

Then, brethren, again, training involves a recognition of certain facts about the child, and that thought is enough to take our whole morning. I am going to deal with it only briefly, and yet attempt to say two or three things which seem to me to be important in this connection. I think there are two things we need to remember when we look into the face of every little child, and they are: first, "Foolishness is bound up in the heart of a child"; second, that child has upon it the mystic sign of the Master's Cross. There is no child for which He did not live, for which He did not die. And as I look into the faces of the children about my feet, in my own home, in this church on Sunday, in our Sabbath school, I must remember if I would help them and serve them these two things. First of all, account for it as you will, I care very little about the philosophy, but I care a great deal about the fact, that there is enough of iniquity in the heart of every child to work the ruin of a race if you let it work itself out. But I remember this also, that there is not a child born that is not born to the inheritance of the Christ of God, and that is far mightier than the forces which are against them. So I have these two things to remember in the training of every child, that there is in the child, first of all, the capacity for evil, but beneath it, deeper than it, truer than it, is the capacity for good, and at the disposal of the child for the realization of the good as against the evil is all the grace of God.

These things being remembered—and, my brethren, you see how much one would care to say about these things, but I pass them—these things being remembered, now I come to the main message of my text. "Train up a child according to his way." And here is where the home is important, and where neither Sabbath school, nor Day school, can ever take its place. I suppose it is necessary in these days that we should teach children in crowds. Would to God we could escape from it. But at least we can in the home, and it is of the home I am principally thinking this morning. Every child is a lonely personality, a special individuality. You know the phrase that is often made use of concerning remarkable men. I have heard it said, and I doubt not you have too, that God made Oliver

Cromwell, or John Wesley, or Abraham Lincoln, as the case may be, and He broke the mold. That is one of those curious sayings which have in them so much of truth and of falsehood. It is perfectly true that God made Abraham Lincoln and broke the mold, but what do you mean when you say that? Do you mean to infer that was the lonely and exceptional method, that occasionally God makes one man and breaks the mold so that there may be no other like him? I tell you, that is God's regular method. God made you, and broke the mold. He made every child in my home and broke the mold, and there are no two alike. Those blessed with children in the home know how true it is. They contradict each other, and disagree, and conflict in that sense is not always evil. You cannot find me two children in your own home alike. Listen, train up your family of two, or three, or four, or five, on exactly the same lines, and you may hit the goal in the case of one, and miss it in all the rest. No, you must specialize. Every child you have demands special consideration, and lonely attention. "Train up a child according to his way." You must discover what the child is if you would train the child. I think we have suffered in every way, socially, may I say, politically, and most certainly religiously, by the habit of imagining that we can deal with children in crowds, and treat them all the same way. It cannot be done. For the teaching of certain things that they must know it is necessary. But not when you are going to train a child, educate a child—not instruct a child. There is all the difference in the world between instructing and educating. To instruct is to build in. To educate is to draw out. But when you are going to train a child, to educate a child, you must find out what the child is. Let me give you one or two illustrations.

Here is a child of sanguine temperament, always hoping, never to be suppressed. Now the one business of the trainer is to put the hand upon that child, and see to it that the child is humbled. No, I did not say "snubbed." And don't you misread the English language so far as to imagine that humbling means that. The child must be kept humble, or else the child will break its own heart, when presently some morning which dawned brightly becomes a day gray and ashen. The child must be treated with such judicial care as shall save it from following the gleam that is not light at all, but which leads to darkness.

Here is a child despondent. You have tried to treat them both alike, and when it has been necessary not to encourage the sanguine child overmuch, you have nearly broken the heart of the despondent child with your lack of appreciation. That despondent child needs to be praised for every good deed done. There should be for such words of helpfulness.

Here is a child skeptical, forever asking questions, an agnostic from birth, a child who will ask you more theological questions in the course of one day than you will be able to answer in a lifetime. What are you to do? Are you to tell the child that asking of questions is an evil thing? Certainly not. You must reason, and answer the questions, and take time to do it.

Here is another child, brother of the other, or sister, it may be, who is credulous, and believes all things without inquiry. Your business with that child is to ask it questions, to show it that there is a necessity for testing the spirits, and being perfectly sure of things.

Here is another child born, as scientific men are very fond of telling us, with a religious temperament. Guard that child carefully. Be afraid lest the temperament should lead to fanaticism.

Here is a child born with an irreligious temperament, with no leanings toward spiritual things. Then that child must be led into the light, the interest must be awakened, and that by showing the child that all the things of dust, which it most loves, are allied to Deity.

The illustrations are imperfect. I trust the philosophy is clear. You cannot take half a dozen boys and girls and treat them all in the same way. You must take them child by child. "Train up a child according to his way," and the business of parents supremely is that of attempting to discover what God has put within every child, in order that it may be led out to fulfilment.

I think therefore that the training must be twofold. First of all, it must be positive. The children must be taught that they belong to Christ, and led to the point of recognizing this fact and yielding themselves thereto. In the second place, the children must be taught that sin is their enemy, and therefore God's enemy, and it is therefore to be fought perpetually. It is the old-fashioned method of the Sunday school that we need to get back to, and not away from. Did I say "method"? Perhaps you will let me change the word. It is the old-fashioned *passion* of the Sunday-school teacher we need to get back to. I have read with great interest during the last days a book entitled *Bible Teaching by Modern Methods*, containing papers and reports of discussions at the Round Table Conference recently held in connection with our Sunday School Union. If you have time for nothing else, borrow the book—not mine, because I want it—and read the first and last lectures, Dr. Davison's lecture, in which he again emphasizes what indeed is the true aim of Sunday-school work; and Dr. Adeney's lecture, in which he emphasizes the fact that our teachers must be trained, and the work must devolve upon the ministry. Our first business is to bring the child into a recognition of its actual relationship to Christ, and a personal yielding thereto. Let it be done easily and naturally. Do not be anxious, if indeed your home is a Christian home, that your child should pass through any volcanic experience; but as soon as possible the little one should be able to say, Yes, I love Him and I will be His. It is as simple as the kiss of morning upon the brow of the hill, as the distilling of the moisture in the dew, or it ought to be. Thank God for men who, having wandered far away, have come back by volcanic methods, but thank God for the little ones who have been led to the point of yielding and finding their Lord before any other lord has had dominion over them. Training should be toward that. Every child is called of God to specific work in the world, and the specific work ought to be discovered by those who train them; and when the capacity is found, then let a child be trained toward it.

Now one or two words concerning the text's declaration of sequence. "Train up a child according to his way, and even when he is old he will not depart from it." I desire in this connection, first of all, to observe that only upon the fulfilment of the conditions enunciated have we any right to expect a fulfilment of the promise made. I have no business to expect that my child will fulfil the true purpose and intention of its own life if I neglect the training of the early days. I want to say also in this connection that this whole text answers objections. For instance, you may say to me in the presence of the text, and of my insistence upon this training, Then the untrained must go wrong. If I fail to train my child, the child must go wrong. No, not necessarily. I say that with reserve, and yet I am compelled to say it. You may neglect your child in your own home, and some Godly Sunday-school teacher may do the work you have neglected. Then you say to me again, Then the wrongly trained must go wrong. Not necessarily. It is not always so. There are children wrongly trained at home, who yet at last have found life and its great fulfilment. But what I want to say to you is this, that the man or the woman who finds the child, and really trains it up to the high ultimate, will possess the child in the ages to come, for we still believe that the things of time are finally the things of the eternities, and that the relationships of time can be the relationships of eternity only as they are fulfilled in the power of the eternal things. I want to put that, if I may, more superlatively, although I shall not enlarge upon it. I hear people sometimes who have been very careless about their children, very careless about their training, very careless about their Godliness, who thought of all the things except these things, when their children are taken from the world, speak of their hope that their little ones will meet them when they also cross the border line. Well, I do not know. Yes, perchance, but remember, your child if you fed it and clothed it, and educated it, and neglected its relation to God, will be more eager to meet the Sunday-school teacher who led it to God than you. Spiritual relationships, after all, are the final relationships. No, you and I have no right to infer negative conclusions from the text, although we should take solemn warning from the fact that we cannot infer conclusions. The promise is a positive one, and we stand by it. It does not say if we do not train our children our children must lose their way. But it does say, "Train up a child according to his way, and even when he is old he will not depart from it." That is, he will fulfil his life, he will fulfil God's thought for him, and purpose for him, and intention for him, the intention that lies within him as a prophecy and a potentiality. The promise is the declaration of a sequence. It is not a capricious word spoken to men, but the unveiling of a law which operates, and from which there is no escape.

And I make an appeal. With such an ideal, and such a training, and such a promise, the only fear we need have about our children is fear for ourselves. You tell me in answer to all this, Ah, but there have been such failures. Well, why? And who am I that I should judge? You know how constantly it is being said that the children of ministers so often turn out ill. Why? Well, I do not know, but I will make you these suggestions. Children turn out ill from Christian homes sometimes because of the laxity which imagines that a child's happiness consists in self-pleasing, imagines that for the child to be perfectly happy it must have its own will. There is all the difference between letting a child have its own will and its own way. To train a child in its own way crosses the ill sometimes. But never do it with passion. Passion burns to destruction. Reason fires to construction, and we must always make this careful differentiation. You mean well by your child. Are you too gentle, too tender? Have you an anemic conception of love?

Or, on the other hand, it may be and I give you this as a personal conviction, it is more often due to, the sternness which forgets the needs of young life. How often I have seen it. You talk to me of a Puritan home and upbringing, and you know the sternness of the moral policeman regime, and the moment the boy crosses the threshold, with a sigh of abandonment he is into every excess of evil. Said a man to me some years ago, "How is it I have lost my children?" And I said to him, "I do not see you have lost your children, they are sitting round your board, most of them, and you do not seem to have lost them. They respect you, and look up to you." "Oh, yes," he said, "but there is not a boy round my board who trusts me." And I said to him, more for the instruction of my own heart than to imagine that I could help him. "What do you mean?" "Why," he replied, "there is not one of them makes a confidant of me." And I looked the man in the face and said, "Did you ever play marbles with them when they were little?" And he said at once, "Oh, certainly not." And I said, "That is why you lost them." My brethren, this thing is a burden on my heart. I am not talking pleasantries. We do not lose our children when they are seventeen. We lose them when they are seven. I am not talking to mothers. I never do! And that is not a flippant remark. I would like to hand all the bairns over to mothers for their theology. It is the fathers of the Christian Church who have failed with their children. You are a good man, and a hard man, and your children know it, and they respect you, but they do not trust you, and you lose them. There may be a laxity that is too gentle, a love that is anemic. There may be too much iron in your blood, too much sternness.

How shall I find the happy medium? Be very much and very constantly in comradeship with Jesus Christ. That is the last thing I have to say. If I am going to be so severe as to be true, and so tender as to hold, I must know Him, the Man Who could look right into the soul of a Pharisee and scorch it with His look, and into the eye of a little child and make the child want to come and play with Him. Oh, I must be much with Christ if I am to be with children. In God's name, if you do not know Christ, keep your hands off the bairns. You cannot train the boy to be a carpenter unless you are a Christian man and in fellowship with Him constantly. The parents' responsibility cannot be relegated to Sunday-school teacher, or Day-school teacher. To do that will injure me and place my child in great danger. I have tried to talk to you. God knows how much I have talked to myself, and all I can do in the presence of the old affirmation of ancient scripture which is fresh in its application today is to pray that my Father will keep me so near to Himself that I may know how to be a father to my children.

CHAPTER X

"SPARE THYSELF!"

From that time began Jesus to show unto His disciples, how that He must go unto Jerusalem, and suffer many things of the elders and chief priests and scribes, and be killed, and the third day be raised up. And Peter took Him, and began to rebuke Him, saying, Be it far from Thee, Lord: this shall never be unto Thee. But He turned, and said unto Peter, Get thee behind Me, Satan: thou art a stumbling-block unto Me: for thou mindest not the things of God, but the things of men. Then said Jesus unto His disciples, if any man would come after Me, let him deny himself, and take up his cross, and follow Me.

MATTHEW 16:21-24.

THIS CHAPTER CONTAINS A MOST STARTLING CONTRAST between the two conversations of Jesus with Peter. The first is full of light and revelation and gladness. The second is full of darkness and misery and sadness. The first part of the King's mission, so far as the disciples were concerned, was accomplished. The second part was about to begin. He had first of all to teach them that He was the Christ, and at last one of their number had looked into His face and made the great confession. He now had to teach them that the Christ must suffer in order to accomplish the deepest purpose of His mission.

They had thought of the Christ, the Messiah, as of a King who would correct all that was wrong in the externality of things. They had to learn that the method of Christ was not that of beginning at the circumference, but at the center; not of dealing first with the issues of the sins, but with the sin itself, and that in order to this the process must be one of suffering. He began immediately upon the confession of Peter to tell them that He must suffer and be killed, and be raised again the third day.

I think it is of great importance that we should pay special attention to this statement of Jesus concerning His coming passion. The Son of man must "suffer . . . and be killed . . . and the third day be raised up." Had He simply said He must "suffer . . . and be killed," I might have been inclined to imagine that He spoke as one who merely foresaw the natural issue of what He had been teaching and doing. But He said more than that. He said, first of all, the Son of man "must go unto Jerusalem." He said, finally, the Son of man must rise again. If the foretelling of what His enemies would do to Him was merely the statement of what He knew of them, why must He go to Jerusalem? Why not escape them? That is what Peter asked Him to do. The "must go unto Jerusalem" has in it something deeper and profounder than Jesus' foresight of what His enemies desired to do to Him, for He might have escaped them. The "must go unto Jerusalem" was the result of His loyalty to the will of God, and the impossibility of His deviating from it by a hair's breadth.

Yet it may be said that the "must go unto Jerusalem" leaning back upon the will of God, followed by the must "suffer and be killed," merely meant, I must be true to the will of God, and I now see what the issue will be, these men will kill Me. But when He looks through the blinding mists of the coming passion to the blazing glory of resurrection morning, declaring—"the third day be raised up"—I know He is more than a man submitting Himself to fate. He is a Conqueror moving through battle to victory, through the crisis inevitable, not merely by the will of sinning man, but in the economy of God, to the great and final issue of resurrection and triumph.

The very first recorded word of the Master was, "I must be about My Father's business." He never changed and never deviated. Through teaching and through work, through rebuke and through tenderness, in long journeys and lonely vigils, was always the keynote, "I must be about My Father's business," and as He approached the end, it was the same "must" still. "I must be about My Father's business," and that takes Me to Jerusalem, and that takes Me to suffering, and that takes Me to death, and that takes Me to resurrection.

This morning our attention is to be centered supremely upon Peter, and the effect this new declaration had upon him. Peter taking Him aside, said, "Be it far from Thee, Lord." One wonders whether those words carry to our hearts the real meaning of the thing he said. It was, as a matter of fact, an ejaculation. It has been variously translated. Dr. Young translates it thus—Spare Thyself. I personally think that gets nearer to the heart of Peter's meaning than any other. In the Emphasized Bible, Mr. Rotherham has translated it thus—Mercy on Thee, Lord! It has been translated, God pity Thee, Master! My own feeling is that the introduction of the word God there spoils the real thought and intention. I go back to the word as Young gives it to us, Spare Thyself, Lord! One is almost startled by the vehemence of the Master's reply, "Get thee behind Me, Satan: thou art a stumblingblock unto Me," an offense, something in the way, hindering My progress. I must go to Jerusalem and suffer, and be killed and rise again; thou art in the way, a stumbling-block to My going to Jerusalem, to My suffering, to My dying and My rising. "Get thee behind Me, Satan!"

May I now attempt to fix your attention on these two men, Jesus and Peter. We will allow all the other things in this wonderful chapter to stand on one side, in order to see these two. They stand facing each other, representatives of two opposing ideals, one representing humanity according to God's intention, the other representing humanity in the heart and essence of its failure. Both speak in the presence of the eternities, with hearts strangely moved within them. Both speak the deepest thing that is in them. All the surface things are out of sight.

Peter was absolutely honest and poured out in the word he spoke to his Lord his own thought and conception of life and the way it should be lived. Jesus, in His first declaration, and then in His answer to Peter, as clearly revealed His thought and His conception of life, and what it ought to be.

This is a permanent antagonism. So this morning, as I try to take you back to that scene at Cæsarea Philippi, I want you, if you will, gradually to forget the rocky fastnesses amid which these things happened, and the different robing of these men of the past, and the different circumstances in the midst of which they lived, and God help you, and God help me, to bring ourselves to the test of this revelation. I am standing this morning with Peter or with Christ. Which? I shall make no confession, but I pray God to find out for me and to show me ere this service be over. May He do so also for you.

First, what is this that Peter said, and what is this that Peter meant? The language of Peter was the language of angry and short-sighted affection. I am very anxious to insist upon it that it was affection. If you are going to put into absolute contrast realizations rather than ideals of life, you must contrast Judas with Jesus. Peter had come far upon the way. He had seen the Lord, and Jesus had said to Him, "Blessed art thou, Simon Bar-Jonah: for flesh and blood hath not revealed it unto thee." I want you to see how the highest and the best in humanity, other than Christ, is leagues away from Him. It is Peter who stands in contrast with Christ, the one disciple who had made the confession, the one who had seen the most clearly, and spoken most accurately the truth concerning his Master. It is in this man I find the contrast. His language was that of affection. Lord, pity Thyself. Have mercy upon Thyself. Spare Thyself. And there is infinite pathos in the second part of what he said. Sometimes you may gather a whole tragedy into a word. As Peter said "this," he saw his beloved Master in the hands of the brutal men who had been plotting to take His life. He saw in imagination, keen, awful, accurate imagination, that sacred form battered and bruised, and mauled by the hands of brutal and lawless men. "*This* shall never be unto Thee." I am inclined to think there were tears in the man's voice, that in that moment his love—and how he did love his Lord—was driving him. This going to Jerusalem to suffer and be killed, this be far from Thee. Peter would not see his Master suffer. That is love, but love intermixed with other things, is paralyzed, blinded, and makes mistakes. Doubt very much, I beseech you, any philosophy which declares to you that love is all, unless that philosophy also declares that God's love contains within it not merely pity and mercy, but holiness and rightness and justness. This word was a word of love, but love mistaken, love not understanding perfectly.

If I have said there were tears in the voice of Peter as he said "this," let me add to that at once: it was indeed the language of anger. The word means to chide. He took Him aside and began to chide Him, to rebuke Him. This does not contradict the other. Love can be angry. Love can speak in tones of bitterness, sometimes when it ought so to do, sometimes when it ought not so to do. Here is a man rebuking His Lord. Pity Thyself. *This* be far from Thee. This was the language, not of love only, not merely of angry love; it was also the language of short-sighted love. Is it not remarkable that all through the story of those last days, Christ never spoke to His disciples about the Cross without also speaking of the resurrection. Yet how evident it is that the men who listened never heard, or never understood. When Peter said to Him, Pity Thyself, this be far from Thee, what did he mean? The third-day resurrection? No, the suffering and the Cross. Why did he thus ignore the resurrection? Because he did not perfectly understand, or because he did not take time to think and understand, and because in his own heart's thinking nothing could be considered sufficient to balance suffering and death. It was so all the way through. These men never seem to have heard about the resurrection. It was short-sighted affection. Affection blinded in blood. It was affection which could not see far enough. I am almost loth to take an illustration here, for the subject is high and sacred, yet I think I will. Here is a little child suffering from some form of disease which can be healed and cured by a painful operation. The mother says, Yes; but a friend says, Oh, no. It is a shame the child should suffer. They both love the child, but which loves the child the most? The mother who sees through the pain to the redemption and freedom, and to the lack of pain that lies beyond. Peter loved his Lord. He was angry with his Lord. He was short-sighted. He did not see through to the end of the suffering.

This language of Peter, which was the language of angry, short-sighted affection, expresses the common philosophy of fallen human nature. First of all, the language of Peter indicates man's misconception of the first duty of man. What did Peter mean when he said, Spare Thyself? He meant, Master, your first duty is to yourself. Please forgive me putting Peter's word into so up-to-date a form as that. You have often heard that. You have often said that. A man's first duty is to himself. How constantly we hear it. You hear it inside the Church, among the saints. When you get outside the Church they express the same philosophy in a more brutal way. Each for himself, and the devil take the hindmost. That is a great mistake. The devil generally gets the foremost in that race. That is the philosophy. Master, your first duty is to yourself. Jesus knew that was a lie born in hell. He knew that His first duty was to God. "I must be about My Father's business." That is the first duty.

In the next place, Peter's language, this common expression of the false philosophy of humanity, was a misconception of the value of sacrifice. Peter meant to say to Him, Master, this will be failure, the direst and most disastrous failure. Nothing can be gained by dying. How often you will hear that said. People say, You will kill yourself, and what then? Resurrection and heaven, according to Christ! Defeat, direst failure, and death, according to Peter! Master, I have just confessed Thee Christ, and Thou hast approved my great confession. Master, Thou hast spoken about building a great ecclesia, a Church, and about keys. How are you going to do this if you die? Sacrifice means failure. To hand Yourself over to Your foes, and let them maul, and brutally ill-treat, and murder You, is to fail. I need not argue the other side. Nineteen centuries have proved that by that defeat He won.

> He death by dying slew,
> He hell in hell laid low.

Peter meant that sacrifice was a mistake.

Once again, this common philosophy of fallen man is a misconception of the value of men. I do not think I do any violence to what Peter meant when I say that in his heart he was thinking something like this— It is the kind of sentiment we applaud. It is the kind of sentiment that still obtains.—I think in Peter's word to Christ this inner thought finds expression, These men are not worth Thy suffering. These men have wronged Thee, they have persecuted Thee, and if they but can, they will lay their hands upon Thee, and put Thee to death. Spare Thyself. I think in the heart of Peter there was some underlying conception that his Master had some purpose of love in being determined to go to Jerusalem, and he said to Him, They are not worth it. Men are not worth suffering for in this way. How much Thou hast suffered, how much of misinterpretation and misunderstanding Thou hast suffered in these days of ministry. Give it up. Pity Thyself. Deliver Thyself from all this. Men are not worth it. Jesus Christ's answer is, that however black the deed of His murder, however dastardly the sin that finds expression in His dying, the men who put Him to death are worth dying for. "I must." It is the "must" of God's will, and the "must" of God's love, and the "must" of God's determination to make it possible that the men who put Him to death should find their way into life.

Now turn to the other side. How will Christ deal with this philosophy and this suggestion? My heart and mind are every day more and more amazed at the Master's method and His wisdom. He first named the origin of the philosophy. "Get thee behind Me, Satan." James Garfield said that what the age supremely needed was men who would dare to look into the face of the devil and call him devil. There was a time when I was somehow hurt, or anxious, that Christ should call Peter, Satan, but I have come to see that His naming of Satan here was out of the compassion of His heart. Peter, I know that voice. I know that philosophy. I have heard that suggestion, not once or twice, but through all the years, and supremely once, in the lonely vigil with which My ministry commenced. In the awful loneliness of the wilderness I heard the voice which said, Pity Thyself, and take the kingdoms of the world by giving me one moment's homage. "Get thee behind Me, Satan." So the real enemy who had been speaking to the King, through Peter, was unmasked.

In the next place, our Lord revealed the true character of the suggestion. "Thou art a stumbling-block," an obstacle to progress, something which will not help, but will hinder. Peter, desirous of helping, was hindering.

Finally, the Master analyzed the motive. "Thou mindest not the things of God, but the things of men." Will you put these things into contrast as they stand revealed here for a moment? The things of men, as I see them at Cæsarea Philippi, are not vulgar things, not things against which men conduct missions, and institute the signing of pledges. What are the things of men which Peter was minding? Ease, fame, wealth and pomp. These were the things in Peter's view. A king with keys upon his girdle, and his high officers of state. A king more occupied with his own dignity than with the welfare of his people. A king seeking his own ease, his own safety, his own comfort. The things of men, false ideals of human greatness and human royalty. What are the things of God? Peace based upon purity. Rest only after the conflict which destroys the things which create restlessness. Joy lifting itself into song because the fountains of sorrow have been dried up. Glory and honor, not won by the way of compromise, but by the way of fidelity to the eternal principles of right. These are the things of God. If a man is minding the things of men and seeking ease, and earthly pomp, and glory, living a self-centered life, he is against Christ. If he is minding the things of God, the Kingdom of God which cannot be established save as the forces and evil things which have been against it are dealt with and destroyed, he must go to the Cross. By all of which I desire to say that when Jesus said "I must," it was not merely that He yielded Himself unintelligently to the will of God, but that He knew full well that the will of God which marked his pathway through Jerusalem, and suffering, and the Cross to Resurrection, was the good and perfect and acceptable will. We tell each other, and rightly so, that we are to submit ourselves wholly and absolutely to the will of God without questioning. Yea, verily, but why? Because His will must always be will impulsed by love, and by light, and therefore will be of the highest and noblest and best. It is not mere blind submission to mechanical force, this yielding to the will of God. It is reason linked with faith handing the life over to what must be the highest and noblest and best. So it was with Christ. He minded the things of God. We all know the figure of the Potter and the clay. Have we not often done violence to the great figure by looking more at the clay and the principle than at the Person? If you tell me this is the principle of life, that I am the clay and God is the Potter, and you tell me nothing about God, but only that I am to submit myself wholly, absolutely to Him without regard to what He is in Himself, I cannot obey. But I watch the Potter at work on the clay. I know the Potter. I know the thought in the mind of the Potter is a thought of love, a thought of beauty and of purity, and I yield, not to the mechanism of a superior force, but to the love that can make no mistake. Peter had not seen this. He had not yet learned it. Presently he will, and I shall see him rejoicing that he is considered worthy to suffer. For the moment he has not seen this, but Christ has. "I must," because I mind the things of God, not merely the purpose and program of God, but the heart and character of God.

As at the beginning, so at the close let me say to you that these two conceptions of life divide us as a congregation into separate camps. I would God that it might be that we are all in Christ's camp; but I am going to find no verdict, to pass no sentence. Hear me: you are living and I am living, answering one of two master principles, either, Spare thyself, or Do the will of God. The first is devilish. "Get thee behind Me, Satan." When Christ has put His measurement upon a thing, I have no appeal, and desire to make no appeal. The other is Christian in the deep, true, profound sense of the word. I must obey the will of God and that always means suffering in a world where sin is. In the presence of sin and in the presence of wrong, those who put the "must" of the Divine will at the center of their lives and answer it must come after Him, must know something of fellowship with His suffering. You can know nothing of fellowship with His suffering until you have put the will of God as the master passion of your life. You may suffer, but your suffering is not in fellowship with Him while you are persisting in sin. No man living in answer to lust and desire, suffer as he will, is in fellowship with Christ. Let us beware of specious blasphemy. When a man has yielded himself to Christ, when the will of God has become the master passion of a man's life, then if His will means passing down to Jerusalem, and suffering, and death, so be it. I want to make a distinction carefully here. Jesus did not deliberately choose suffering. He did not deliberately choose sacrifice. He chose the will of God, and because suffering and sacrifice lay in that will He chose them; but He did not imagine that He had to seek for the most unpleasant thing and do it. How many Christian people have that idea. How many people have the idea that they must do the thing that is most objectionable in order that they may be in the will of God. That is not Christ's idea. There are some people who carry that to the last extreme, and I hear of hair shirts and tortures for the flesh. Jesus Christ never scourged Himself. Jesus Christ never inflicted pain upon His own physical being. Jesus Christ never deliberately chose mental anguish. He chose the will of God, and when the will of God led Him through infinite and intolerable suffering, then He went. That is the master passion of life.

It is perfectly true that no man has any right to commit suicide. It is perfectly true that no man has any right to use the strength which is God's strength outside God's will; but no other man has any right to come in and interfere between the servant's loyalty and his Master's command. A man must be very careful that it is God's will when he is in the way of suffering. A man must search himself in the midst of suffering as well as in the midst of joy, as to whether it is God's will.

We need supremely today a Church of Jesus Christ, reformed to the pattern of Jesus Christ. I admit that I have said it is not right to choose suffering simply because it is suffering. A man must choose only the will of God; then if it lead through suffering or joy, he must rejoice alike in joy or pain if it be God's sweet will. Yet surely this voice of Peter is heard on every hand today in the Church. Oh that the Church could be brought to the high level of abandoning her comfortable ease and vulgarity, and come after her Lord with the "must" of God driving, then the world would see that the wounded Bridegroom has a wounded Bride, that the suffering King has a suffering army, that the Head wounded and heaped with abuse has in sympathy with Himself the souls that follow Him to do the will of God, even through suffering.

What then? On every cross there shines the light of Easter day. If you will not have the cross, you will never reach the Easter day. If you shun this rugged road of the will of God, you will never come into the far-reaching magnificence of the King's own great new country.

Someone here is suffering in the will of God. My last word to you is this: We come to the green hill. I have not brought you to the green hill as men who need salvation, but as a company of the children of God. You are in the midst of suffering. You might have missed it if you had been disloyal to truth and to your Lord. You might, young man, have had promotion in the world, but you were true, and you are poorer, and you will be all your life. Already upon that life of yours, limited perhaps, and bruised and broken in the will of God, the light of Easter day is shining, and flowers—not the flowers of earth, the grass that today is and tomorrow is cast into the oven—but the flowers of immortality that bloom from the blood of the Cross are in your pathway and upon your brow. So when we get to the Cross we are at the center of the universe, and all its measurements are the measurements of God. May He help us to see and understand.

CHAPTER XI

THE YOUNG RULER

One thing thou lackest.

MARK 10:21.

It seems to us as though Jesus never said a more startling thing to any man who came to Him than this, "One thing thou lackest." Yet whether the "one thing" be much or little depends wholly upon what it is. Some five or six years ago, in an American city, as I stood upon the platform and gave out my first hymn in a series of meetings, I heard the weak tones of a small reed organ, notwithstanding the fact that there was a very fine organ in the building. Turning to my friend, the minister of the church, I said to him, "What is the matter with the great organ?" He replied, "Nothing." "Why is it not being played?" I asked. "It lacks only one thing, and that is a player," he replied.

One thing lacking! An instrument, fearfully and wonderfully made, constructed to catch the wind and transmute it into music—silent, no harmony, no symphony—why? There was one thing lacking, a master hand to sweep the keys and bring the music out. Which is a parable, helping us to see what Christ meant. "One thing thou lackest."

In order that we may understand what this lack really was, I am going to ask you first to look carefully at this young man. I want to say three things about him. I shall say nothing about his wealth; nothing concerning his position in the nation, except incidentally, for a man's wealth and position are nothing when you are measuring him by the standards of eternity, or looking upon him in the light of spiritual things. Let us see the man as he was in himself.

The first thing I say concerning him is that he was a man of fine natural temperament. This is revealed in his whole attitude toward Jesus Christ. That he was discerning is revealed in the fact that to Christ he said, "Good Master."

He was also a man of courage. He was a ruler, and so belonged to a class which had been critical at the commencement of our Lord's ministry, but now were openly against Him. Notwithstanding this fact, when this man saw goodness, he confessed it, daring to say, "Good Master."

He was moreover, a man of humility, for when he came into the presence of Jesus he knelt. You may tell me there is nothing more in that than the Eastern method of salutation. It was not the method by which a ruler saluted a peasant, even in the East. Peasants knelt to rulers. It was as strange a thing then as it would be for a ruler to kneel in the presence of a peasant in London. Jesus was most evidently, to the seeing of His own age, a peasant. Yet here is a man, who is a wealthy ruler, who dared to kneel in His presence.

At this man, discerning, courageous, humble, Christ looked, and said, "One thing thou lackest."

He was more than a man of fine temperament, he had a clean record. Never allow any man, be he prophet or priest or preacher, to tell you there is any value in pollution. Let no man make you believe there is no value in having a clean record. Even if you are not a Christian man, there is value in it. This man had a clean record. Jesus flashed upon him the light of six commandments from the decalogue, not the first four, which indicate the relationship which ought to exist between man and God, but the last six, which condition the relation of man to his neighbor. "Do not kill, Do not commit adultery, Do not steal, Do not bear false witness, Do not defraud, Honor thy father and mother." One light after another flashed upon the inner, hidden, secret life of the man, and he looked back into the face of Christ and said, "Master, all these things have I observed from my youth." Now, it has been declared that this was an empty boast, that this man said to Christ a thing that was not true. I do not believe it. I believe his statement was the simple, honest truth. I belive that standing there, confronting Jesus Christ, and looking into the eyes of incarnate purity, here was a man who was able to say concerning these ancient commandments which forbid a man violating the true relationship between himself and his neighbor, "All these things have I observed from my youth." Immediately the evangelist tells us that "Jesus looking upon him, loved him." I do not mean to infer by that statement that if he had broken the whole six Christ would not have loved him. There is, perchance, a man in this building, hiding away from the crowd, who has broken the whole ten. Christ loves that man, and can save him if he will let Him. It is noticeable, however, that at this point the evangelist declares He loved him. I do not think you will ever find it declared that Christ loved a hypocrite or a liar. There is a sense in which he loved even them, but never in the act of hypocrisy or lying. Christ's anger was white-hot in the presence of all lying and hypocrisy. This young man said, "Master, all these things have I observed from my youth." He was a man of clean record.

Once again, he was a man of true aspiration. What is this question with which he comes to Christ, "Good Master, what shall I do that I may inherit eternal life?" Let us be careful here in order that we may catch if possible the real thought in the mind of this man. What is the meaning of this phrase, "eternal life"? We have used it constantly in the Christian Church as though it were a phrase indicating continuity of existence merely. I do not deny that this is partially the meaning of the phrase, but there is much more in it than this. Age-abiding life is what he was seeking. This is not merely life which continues; it is life which contains. It is perfectly evident that in his own soul he was conscious of a present lack. All his wealth could not purchase that something which he needed. He was a man of position, but his position could not command that which his soul was supremely seeking. It was life that he needed, more life that he was seeking. He was conscious of the infinite, and yet could not grasp it. In the midst of all the things of time and sense he heard the echoes of the eternal and spiritual. His clean record did not satisfy him. His power of discernment left him still hungry. His courage had behind it an ache and an agony. His very humility did not bring his inner soul into the realization of that for which it was perpetually asking. He wanted life, he desired to take hold of that which can satisfy the deepest in a man. He heard the call of the infinite sighing its way up through his own nature. He knew he was more than flesh. He knew he was more than that which could be fed with the things which were all about him. Life! Let us state the truth at once. This cry after life is the cry of the lost offspring of God after the Father God. He was seeking God, seeking life, and all this before Christ met him. His meeting with Christ, as we see it in the Gospel narrative, simply brings out into clear relief these facts concerning him, a man of fine temperament, a man of clean record, a man of true aspiration, and to that man Christ said, "One thing thou lackest."

Let us proceed at once to ask what Christ meant. What

did he lack? The popular, and I had almost said, the superficial interpretation of the story declares that he lacked poverty. Nothing of the kind. If you leave your story there you have not listened to it, you have not caught the meaning of Christ's strange question at the beginning, "Why callest thou Me good?" If when Christ told this man to sell all that he had and give to the poor, He meant that what he lacked was poverty, then there is no application to the vast majority of us. That surely is not the last word. I am not going to lose that. It has its place in the story. The fact that Christ told this man to sell all that he had and give to the poor is not to be omitted, but it is to be placed in its right relationship. What is the word of Christ to this man? "One thing thou lackest," and then as a preliminary the Master Physician puts His hand upon the one thing that stands in his way. Christ will deal with some of you tonight, but He will not say to you, sell all that you have and give to the poor. He will say something else, put His hand upon some preliminary thing, something, which if you do not abandon you will never be able to obey Him in the ultimate and supreme command. He is moving toward the heart and center of man's need, and it is necessary in doing so to clear out of the way the things that stand between him and the realization of his own life. What is the final word, "Come, follow Me." That is the man's lack. You say to me, Then do you mean to say that what the man lacked was following Christ? Yes, finally, that is what this word really means. Look at it from the standpoint, first of all, not of the Person of Christ, though there we must end, but from the standpoint of the man's real condition. What did this man lack? He lacked a center of authority. He lacked a dominating principle in his life. He had never found his King.

Will you patiently for a moment keep that statement in

mind, while I come a little way from it in order to get back to it. Another of the New Testament stories reveals the principle. A Roman centurion once said, "I also am a man under authority, having under myself soldiers." When he uttered these words he did not intend to state a principle, but he did so. He was speaking out of the natural order of his own life. Remember, he was a centurion. In that sentence of his is revealed the whole system of true government. "I also am a man under authority, having under myself soldiers." No man ought to have soldiers under him who is not himself under authority. No man—to put this now, not in its application to soldier life, but to all life—no man can reign who does not serve. No man can wield a scepter who has not kissed a scepter. No man can enter into and possess the kingdom of his own life who has not first of all recognized that he is part of a larger kingdom, and has submitted himself to control. "I also am a man under authority, having under myself soldiers," is a true philosophy of life. This young ruler coming to Christ said, "What shall I do that I may inherit eternal life," that I may enter into it and possess it, that I may reign in life. Christ said to him, "One thing thou lackest." You have never found your King. You have never bent before the supreme will, even in your religion. In your seeking and your planning you have been self-centered, self-governed. You cannot find life until you have found a King, external and superior to yourself.

Let me take you a little further back for a moment. This man first came to Jesus and said, "Good Master, what shall I do that I may inherit eternal life?" Jesus said to him, "Why callest thou Me good? None is good, save One, even God." I do not believe that was an idle question. I do not believe that it was spoken carelessly. I think that when our Lord asked the question He desired to arrest this man and to leave an impression upon his mind to which presently He would return. Hear the question, and think of it quite simply. "Why callest thou Me Good? None is good, save One, even God." I know there are different interpretations of that question. As a matter of fact, it is one of the sayings of the New Testament which Professor Schmiedel acknowledges to be true, and he tells us it is true because in it Christ evidently discounts Himself, that He evidently meant to say to this man, Do not call Me good. There is none good save God, and I am not God. Did He mean that? Look at the question again. When Christ said, "Why callest thou Me good? None is good, save One, even God," He meant one of two things. He either meant I am not good, or, I am God. I do not think you can escape the alternative. You may escape it by denying the accuracy of the story. If you accept the view that He denied Deity, then if He were true in His philosophy that only God is good, He denied goodness. I do not believe that here Jesus denied good, He denied goodness. I do not believe that He claimed Deity. Looking into the face of this man, He knew that what he wanted was a Master. Man has only one Master, God. There is only one King able to realize the kingdom of human life, and that is God. If a man shall bow the knee to any human teacher, and submit himself to him, he is in peril of his soul, of his very life. There is only one scepter we must kiss, it is the scepter of the Most High. There is only one King Who can govern your complex mysterious, far-reaching life, and that is God. When Christ asked that question, it is as though He had said to the man, You are after life. Your discernment is great, because you have linked life with goodness—"Good Master, what shall I do that I may inherit eternal life?" You come to goodness to inquire the way into life. Why do you call Me good? Think what you are saying. If you have seen goodness in Me, you have seen God. If you have recognized goodness as you have looked into My face, watched My deeds, and listened to My words, your life has come into the light of the Divine, into the light of God Himself.

Presently we read, "One thing thou lackest. Go, sell whatsoever thou hast, and give to the poor . . . and come, follow Me." That is to say, He confronted this man and said in effect, Fine is the temperament, clean is the record, true is the aspiration, but in order that all these things may be brought to fruition you must find your King Who is God, "Follow Me." He called the man after Himself. This again is one of those stupendous, appalling, overwhelming claims of Christ which either demonstrate Him God in very deed and truth, or prove Him to have been devoid of honesty, purity, and meekness. Standing confronting this man, He says, You need your King. Your King is God. Behold your King. Follow Me!

How is this man to follow Him? What stands in the way? All the things that have ministered perpetually to his own selfish life. Now, says Christ, put them all away. Do not dream for one single moment that if you are really bent on finding your life, and if you are coming after your King, that you can do so by manipulating the things that have ministered to the self life. By drastic, daring, courageous heroism, make an end of them. That is Christ's method with the man, "Sell whatsoever thou hast, and give to the poor." There is a touch of fine, sweet satire in Christ's terms, "and thou shalt have treasure in heaven." You will lose your treasure for a moment, and grasp it for the ages. Christ recommends this man to invest his money in such a way that rust cannot corrupt it, and thieves cannot steal it. Postpone the possession to increase it, that is all. Put out of thy life all the things that minister to selfish desire. Be at the end of them. "Follow Me."

What happened? I do not know. Alternatively I do know what happened. The story is left at a point full of sadness, full of suggestiveness. You have no right to say that this man never found his way to Christ. You do not know. This you know, "he went away sorrowful for he was one that had great possessions." "Sorrowful" is the most hopeful word in that statement. I make no dogmatic declaration about the actual issue in his case, but I will tell you absolutely what happened as between one of two things. He had heard the voice which spoke to his inmost heart and soul. From the lips of poverty he had heard the language of the infinite wealth. All the light of spiritual truth flashed and flamed about him, and he knew it. Why was he sorrowful? Tell me, did you ever read anything so strangely contradictory if you measure it by the philosophy of this age or any other age. "He went away sorrowful, because," that is the real force of it, "because he was one that had great possessions." You say, men do not go away sorrowful because they have great possessions. Oh, yes they do, if they have stood face to face with Christ and have heard Him calling them to abandon them, and they do not do it. He had stood in the light and had seen the power of the life which he was seeking. He had come nearer than ever before. For years, I believe, there had been a sighing, groaning, sobbing, agony in the soul of this man after life. He had been close to it, had seen it, had heard its music, had heard its demands, and he went away sorrowful. What happened? One of two things. He got back presently to his own home, a home of ease and luxury, doubtless, for he was a man who had great possessions, a home which in all probability the merchants of Damascus had made beautiful. I see him go back to his own house. I follow him home. There came a moment presently when he said: I can no longer bear it, I have seen life and I must have it. Call in my steward, render an account of my possessions; it is drastic, terrible, I shall suffer lack, but sweep it all out. I must find Him again, the Man of the seamless robe, the lowly Stranger Who looked into my eyes and flashed the very light of life upon me. If he did that, sold all, obeyed Christ, and swept away the power and authority of his past life, he found the age-abiding life. If not, he said to himself, That was a strange thing I did yesterday. I cannot imagine what possessed me to kneel to that peasant. I thought I wanted life, and that He could say something about it—and the conscience says, He did say something about it. But no, it was a mere phantasy. Thus gradually he would argue himself out of the thing. If that were his action, the day came when he laughed at the weakness of the moment when he knelt in the presence of Jesus. Not long ago a Member of Parliament laughed in the presence of a great meeting as he told them that he was nearly born again in a great revival meeting years before. When a man has stood face to face with Christ, as that young ruler had done, it is higher or lower, it is either an ascent by the way of the cross, or a descent by the way of selfishness and luxury and sin. I do not know which it was in the case of this young man. Men tell us that tradition has it that this was Lazarus, the brother of Martha and Mary. I do not know. It has been said that this may actually have been Saul of Tarsus. I do not know. I do not think so. I know this. From that hour he was never the same. Either the sorrow with which he turned away from Christ was turned into joy when he obeyed Him, and found his life, or else the sorrow passed to numbness and deadness, and he became, to use the terrific word of the writer of the letter to the Hebrews, "hardened." That is the one condition of all others against which we need to pray.

My brothers and sisters, the story needs very little application. You tell me it is an old story. It is as fresh as this Palm Sunday. You tell me it is Eastern. It is Western. You tell me it happened long ago. I tell you it is happening here and now. There are those of you in this house who have a fine temperament. I do not undervalue it. Your friends love you. You are generous and kind and discerning, frank and courageous. Some of you have a clean record, so far as the vulgarities of sin are concerned. You have right aspirations. You will not be angry with me if I say that your presence here proves it. You do not come here for entertainment. You have heard the undertone of the eternities in your lives, and you have paused this Sabbath evening for a little to listen once again to a man who will speak to you only of Christ and of your relation to God, and you knew it when you came.

There is in your soul the sob after life. Even now the Christ is confronting you. What is He saying to you? I do not know as to the preliminary. I do know as to the ultimate. I cannot say whether He is telling you to go and sell all you have. I do know that He is saying, "Come, follow Me." He is saying "Go"—but what else, I do not know. You say, I wish you would tell me. I cannot tell you. God in heaven give us two or three minutes of honesty! There is no man here tonight who has not yielded to Christ but knows what stands between him and his Lord. "One thing thou lackest, Go,"—and I cannot fill in the gap. If I gave you one illustration, or two or three, what are they in a crowd like this? Scores of men and women would say, These things do not refer to us, therefore we are all right. Listen, not to me, but for the Voice which makes no mistake, "One thing thou lackest. Go——" You know the thing that stands between you and the "Follow Me." What stands between? Right hand? Right eye? Cut it off. Pluck it out. Brother? Sister? Father? Mother? Wife? Child? Man, you know what it is. Fling it out, and then, "Follow Me." Now one would like to begin to preach again. I am not going to. Oh, that "Follow Me." No man ever did it but that he found his own life, found its meaning, found its unfolding, its realization. "Follow Me." Here is my last word to you, my brother, you cannot reign in life until you have found your King. There are no words I have ever heard sung that have rung in my soul more than these:—

> Make me a captive, Lord,
>   And then I shall be free;
> Force me to render up my sword,
>   And I shall conqueror be.
> I sink in life's alarms
>   When by myself I stand;
> Imprison me within Thine arms,
>   And strong shall be my hand.
>
> My heart is weak and poor
>   Until it Master find:
> It has no spring of action sure—
>   It varies with the wind:
> It cannot freely move
>   Till Thou hast wrought its chain;
> Enslave it with Thy matchless love
>   And deathless it shall reign.
>
> My power is faint and low
>   Till I have learned to serve:
> It wants the needed fire to glow,
>   It wants the breeze to nerve;
> It cannot drive the world
>   Until itself be driven;

> Its flag can only be unfurled
>   When Thou shalt breathe from heaven.
>
> My will is not my own
>   Till Thou hast made it Thine;
> If it would reach the monarch's throne
>   It must its crown resign;
> It only stands unbent,
>   Amid the clashing strife,
> When on Thy bosom it has leant,
>   And found in Thee its life.

That is the meaning of our story. Anything that stands between you and the crowning of Christ, I beseech you, sweep it away. You will never be just the same again after this hour, but higher or lower, to the throne or to the dungeon, and that of your own choice and action in the presence of the Christ. May God in His great grace help us to crown Him and follow Him and find our life.

CHAPTER XII

JESUS AND SINNERS

This man receiveth sinners.
LUKE 15:2.

THESE WORDS WERE UTTERED IN CONDEMNATION OF JESUS OF Nazareth, and yet to us they contain an inclusive statement of the truth concerning Him as the Saviour of men. It is a very interesting thing to notice in the reading of the Gospel stories how the wonderful personality of Jesus transmuted things spoken in condemnation into declarations of commendation. Indeed, it may fairly be said that one might gather from these Gospel narratives a selection of passages which would constitute a fifth Gospel, and we might call that the Gospel according to the enemies of Jesus Christ. They said of Him, with disdain in every tone of their question, "Is not this the carpenter?" By which they meant, "We know all about Him. He is one of us. Who is He that He should set Himself up as a teacher in the Synagogue at Nazareth, where He has wrought at the carpenter's shop?" Today we are asking the same question about Him, in another tone, knowing that by the lowliness of the long years in the carpenter's shop He came into close comradeship with all toilers forevermore. They said of Him upon one occasion, "By Beelzebub the prince of the devils casteth He out devils," and thus came very near to the confines of unpardonable sin. Yet even that has come to be in some senses a truth, for He has overcome the prince of ill, and compels him into the service of perfecting the saints by testing. Said they of Him in that dark and overwhelming hour of His supreme agony, flinging the cruel taunt into His face when He was all alone in His sorrow, "He saved others; Himself He cannot save." In that sentence, all unknowingly, they uttered the deepest truth about that death. Had He saved Himself He never could have saved others; but because He could not save Himself He is able still to save all who come unto God by Him. Among all these statements none is more wonderful, because none is more simple, than this statement of my text, "This Man receiveth sinners."

Let us endeavor to understand this criticism. First of all, I pray you mark that it is a criticism. The first word of this chapter links it, and indeed the great and glorious threefold parable which follows, with all that immediately preceded. Jesus had been saying some strange and hard things in the listening ears of the multitude. I do not hesitate to say that they were strange and hard things. I do not hesitate to declare that many of you who are children of God never read these words without somehow, in the deepest of you, half wishing He had never said them. I do not defend the wish. I know that when my heart rises in half rebellion against some of the words I have read tonight it is because of some evil thing that abides in my life. Even today, though nineteen centuries have demonstrated the imperial dignity of the Christ, and though this whole worshiping congregation is prepared to acknowledge His Lordship, still, when He stands confronting us and says to us that unless we hate father, mother, wife, brethren, sisters, and our own lives, we cannot be His disciples, we are startled, we are afraid, we are half inclined to draw back from every attempt at discipleship. Yet Luke tells us of that strange thing, which has been repeated ever since, and is being repeated still, that when Christ said His severest things the greatest sinners crowded to Him. Severity which on other lips would have repelled, attracted, for there was something besides severity in the tone of His voice, something in Himself which, in spite of the fierce scorching fire of His severest word, drew men to Him. "Now all the publicans and sinners were drawing near unto Him for to hear Him." The Pharisees observed that when these people came to Him He received them, He received them in friendliness, He received them in the very spirit of comradeship. He did not stand aloof from them notwithstanding that He had said such severe things. He was even prepared to sit at the table and eat with them. "And both the Pharisees and the scribes murmured, saying, This Man receiveth sinners, and eateth with them." This exclamation of criticism was a revelation of their sense that His action was not in keeping with His teaching. The severity of His ethic did not seem to harmonize, as they looked at Him, with the looseness of His friendship for these men.

I go one step further, and ask you to notice that what they said of Him was perfectly true, had He been such as they were. They meant to say that no man can take fire into his bosom and not be burned. They meant what some of you remember being told when you were children, You cannot touch pitch without being defiled. They meant, if this man becomes the friend, the comrade, the companion of sinners, he will be contaminated. I think there was a tone of genuine disappointment in their voices. They had hoped great things of Jesus—and that is no piece of imagination, for you cannot read these stories without seeing that at the commencement of His public ministry the rulers, the men in authority, the teachers, were interested in Him, followed Him, listened to Him, invited Him to their houses. As they watched Him receiving sinners they said to themselves, This man is going to spoil His career. He is going to cut the nerve of His influence. They were quite right, if He had been such as they were. There is a young man in this house, perchance, who quite recently came up to the great city. Show me his friends and I will tell you what he will be in half a dozen years. If he is making his first friendships with sinful men, he will be spoiled, ruined by his comradeships. He cannot escape it. I should say with keen and bitter disappointment of some young man, full of promise, who made his companionships among sinful men, "This man receiveth sinners, and eateth with them." Yet nineteen centuries have passed away and a Christian congregation gathered together in the heart of this city hears this text, and to all such as know Christ it sings the one anthem that is worth singing. "This Man receiveth sinners." How are we to account for this fact?

The text is a great text, because the Person concerning Whom the statement was made was a great Person. The text has become an Evangel because of the unique personality of the Man at Whom the Pharisees were looking. They did not understand Him. They did not know how He stood at infinite distance from themselves and from all other men. They did not understand how when He received men to Himself, instead of being contaminated by the pollution which He received, the men were uplifted and healed by the purity which He communicated. It is by that distance which is yet nearness, and by that nearness which is yet distance that my text is made a great Evangel.

Let us, then, consider two matters: first, the Person referred to, and then the pronouncement.

Reverently, then, let us attempt first to see "This Man." I am going to speak of four things about Him; of two in which He is in close association with all of us, and of two in which He stands at infinite distance from us. Before naming these, let me say it is not by the things of identification that I am helped or saved, but by the things of separation is it made possible that I may come near to Him and find all the virtue and healing of His life made mine.

First, the two things in which He is identified with me; He was a man of probation, and He was a man of sorrows. Then the two things in which He stands far away from me. He was a man of victory, and He was a Man of atonement. If I find Him near to me as I think of the first two, I shall yet by the contemplation of what He was in these first two respects discover how unlike Him I am; the very likeness will reveal the unlikeness, the very nearness will create a sense of infinite distance. It is when I see Him in the twofold fact of His separation and distance that I shall begin to hope that I may indeed come into a fellowship with Him which is age-abiding.

A Man of probation. He was a Man Who lived His human life upon the same level on which I have to live mine. He was a Man of toil. He was a Man of temptation. He was a Man of trust.

He was a Man of toil. This is an old story, full of beauty, yet it is well for us to think of it for a passing moment. I do not think that in this particular Jesus Christ entered into limitation or suffering. Toil is the proper lot of humanity. God did not intend that any human being should live apart from toil. I know there are very many people who read the Genesis story, and imagine that man commenced to work after the fall. But that is not the Genesis story. The story of Genesis is that God put unfallen man into the garden "to dress it and to keep it." There are some very curious ideas about the garden of Eden. Half the things which men attack in Genesis are not in it. Some people have an idea that the garden of

Eden was a garden something like those which we see as we travel through this beautiful land of ours, with flower beds carefully laid out. I do not so read my Bible. I think the garden of Eden was a mass of potentiality, waiting for development. The Lord God planted it, filled it with possibilities, and man was put into it to bring out what God had put in. It was a garden waiting for the touch of man's hand in order that there might come out of its russet commonplace the flaming beauties of all the flowers. Man was made for toil. This Man was a toiler. He knew what it was to have to face a day's work in order to win a day's bread. God have mercy upon the man who does not know what that is! I care not whether it be with sweat of brain or brawn, every man should earn his living, or cease to live. I want that some of the comfort of the contemplation should come to you. Some of you are almost sighing as you think of tomorrow morning. Remember this Man is your comrade tomorrow morning, just as much as He is your Lord here and now. When tomorrow morning comes, if your calling is an honorable and holy calling, you are in fellowship with Jesus just as much as you are in the holy place.

A Man of temptation, He felt the force of temptation keenly because of the perfection of His humanity. I think that is a statement with which some of you, at first, will be inclined to join issue. There is a popular conception in the world that the proportion in which a man is morally weak is the proportion in which he feels temptation. Not so. It is the strong man, physically, mentally, spiritually, morally, who feels the full force of temptation. A man weakened in his moral fiber by sin is weakened in his sensitiveness in the presence of temptation. No man has had anything to do with young life as it turns to Jesus Christ without having had this question asked, "How is it that since I gave myself to Christ and began the Christian life I have been more tempted than I was before?" The answer is, You are not more tempted, but the very life of Christ in you, strengthening you, makes you keen, quick, sensitive to the force of temptation. In the perfect man temptation has a larger area of attack. The Perfect Man, "This Man" was a Man Who felt temptation as it came against Him through every vulnerable point of His being. The story of the temptation in the wilderness is not merely the story of one hour, one event, one lonely incident, it is a story which reveals the lines along which temptation always comes. Temptation is first directed against the physical, then against the spiritual, then against the vocational, and it has no other avenue of approach. In proportion as a man is physically strong he feels the force of material temptation. In proportion as a man is strong spiritually he feels the appeal of the spiritual assault. In proportion as a man sees clearly his vocation, and earnestly desires to fulfil it, he feels keenly the suggestion that he should reach it by a short cut and an easy road. He was a Man of temptation, and there is no temptation that assaults my soul but that He felt its force.

A Man of trust, He lived a life of dependence upon the highest. He received His messages, His words, and His life from Another. He was a Man Who lived so far the limited life of humanity that He could say, "I do always the things that are pleasing to Him. . . . I do nothing of Myself, but as the Father taught Me, I speak these things." He was a Man of probation, living upon my level, toiling, tempted, trusting.

Yet in some senses He comes nearer to us when I say that He was a Man of sorrows, entering into all the experiences of human suffering. The sorrow of poverty, the sorrow of loneliness, and that most terrible sorrow of all to sensitive souls, the sorrow born of sympathy.

The sorrow of poverty. I know there are those who very glibly tell us that poverty is a blessing. Who said so? Whoever said so, it is a lie. No one ever said so, it seems to me, save such as live apart from poverty, and contemplate it from a distance. I know perfectly well that there have been many souls who have been poor in this world's goods, who have recognized that God was overruling the pain of poverty for the making of character. That is quite another matter. He transmutes the base into the pure, but poverty is no part of God's provision for the race; it is a part of man's mismanagement of what God has provided for the race. This Man was poor. You can tell all the story of His human poverty in a very few sentences, tragic sentences. Chapter one, There was no room for Him in the inn. Chapter two, "The foxes have holes, and the birds of the heaven have nests; but the Son of man hath not where to lay His head." Chapter three, What shall we do with Him? He is dead. Bury Him in a charity grave in a rich man's garden. Do not imagine that so keenly sensitive and fine a soul as that of Christ was not conscious of the limitations of poverty.

But there was the sorrow of loneliness. Think how lonely a Man He was. No one ever understood Him. The rulers were interested in Him, but they never understood Him, and at last became His enemies, hunting Him to death. His mother never understood Him. I for one am inclined to pause in the presence of that and think, for if a man's mother does not understand him, he is generally unutterably alone. I think we of the Protestant Church have made a great mistake in our neglect of the virgin mother. I believe that in very deed and truth she is to be held in high and holy honor. We will not worship her. That is sacrilege and blasphemy, but we will hold her in high honor, highly favored amongst women. Yet she never understood Him. Her misunderstanding was the misunderstanding of love, but it was misunderstanding. The souls who came into closest touch with Him were the souls of such as did the will of God first, last and always. Did they understand Him? "They all forsook Him, and fled." His pathway became more and more lonely, until at last there was no eye to pity, no heart to sympathize. Moreover, He was a Man of sorrows in that final and most terrible way, of the keen sensitiveness of soul and spirit which gathers all the pain of others into its consciousness. I am now saying something in which perhaps you do not follow me or agree with me at once. I make my appeal to the fathers and mothers. Tell me, when do you suffer most, when you yourself are in physical pain, or when your child is in physical pain? If you have ever stood by the side of some suffering loved one, you have felt honestly that you could have sung for joy if you could have gathered that sorrow and pain into your own life and freed your loved one from it. Forgive that low level of illustration, and come into the presence of this Man of spirit so perfectly poised and so full of sensitiveness that every tear fell upon His heart like a storm. Among all the stories there is nothing which so beautifully illustrates this as the story of how He wept in the presence of the tears of Mary. There is something about that story very difficult of interpretation. Commentators—I make my apology to them—have been busy trying to account for the tears of Jesus. Read the story simply, and you will know why He wept. He wept out of sympathy with Mary's tears. But, you say, that can never be. He knew that within an hour he would unlock the tomb and give her brother back to her. There, again, you are measuring Him by yourself, as the Pharisees did. I am not criticizing you. I would say the same thing. If you were in great sorrow and I came to see you in your home, and knew that by some act I could remove the cause of your sorrow,

I really do not believe I could weep with you in your sorrow, I should be so eager to bring you the joy. He will give to you, His trusting ones, heaven presently, but he weeps with you today in the midst of your sorrow. He knows perfectly well that out of all the darkness He is bringing light, but in every pang that rends the heart the Man of sorrows has His part. We read that little phrase, "He was moved with compassion," very carelessly. His whole inner life was shaken and swept as by a tempest in the presence of human need and human sorrow. What the ancient prophet said of Him long ago was literally true, "His visage was so marred more than any man." He was a Man of sorrows.

As we have contemplated the things of His nearness to us we have all been conscious that we are away from Him. A Man of toil. How have we failed in our toil! A Man of temptation. How have we yielded thereto! A Man of trust. How have we trembled in trust! A Man of sorrows! Oh, heart of mine, was there ever sorrow like His? He is near to me, and yet away from me in the very facts of His nearness.

So I come necessarily to other things. He was a Man of victory. There is the difference. I have already hinted at it, now I declare it. Along this way of the probationary life in the midst of these sorrows that have come to me, I have failed. I have failed in my toil and done it meanly, ah me, how often! I have failed in temptation, yielding to the seducing allurements of evil. I have failed in trust. But this Man never failed. This Man never failed in toil. When He made yokes in which the cattle should plow the plains of Bethshan, He made them perfectly. When He, the house-builder, erected a house upon the rock He knew, that which Michaelangelo learned from Him, that angels of God saw the hidden things, and they were perfectly wrought. I have failed: He never. In temptation He refused every seduction of evil and trod the lonely way of truth and uprightness, even though it was a way of suffering and of shame. He was a Man of victory. Victory over circumstances, victory over sin, victory over sorrow, victory over all the forces that were against Him, moving in quiet, kingly dignity against all difficulties, until at last He stood in the midst of a group of men and said to them, "All authority hath been given unto Me in heaven and on earth." Here is the difference between this Man and myself. It is not the ultimate difference. It is not the final distinction, it is only the first, but it is so great as to make me know that I am other than He, and He is other than I. He is the one Man in all the centuries Who by common consent of the Church, and of the world, so far as it has thought, is the sinless, Perfect, victorious Man, climbing to the throne of the mightiest, not upon the policy of cunning, or the force of arms, but upon integrity of character and perfection of ideal in thinking and speaking and doing. How far am I away from Him!

Finally, this Man became the Man of atonement, the One Who was able at last to ransom His brother, the One Who by dying entered into an experience which had no true place in the story of His life save as in it He was dying in the stead of another. This Man, and I cannot so end the story: I feel as you feel that when I approach this final fact I am in the presence of something which demands a new term, a new explanation. A Man, yea, verily, a Man of probation and of sorrow, yet a Man of victory, and of such victory that I am compelled to say that He is infinitely other than Man. A Man through Whose heart it is possible for God to outwork into human vision infinite and eternal things. A Man Who has become the perfect instrument of the Divine speech and of the Divine working, and of the Divine heart of Love. A Man into the presence of Whose death I come, and say with the old

Roman centurion who saw more that day than he had ever seen before, "Truly this was the Son of God." This Man, ye Pharisees of old, ye have mis-measured Him, and ye philosophers of today, ye do not know Him. This Man, so near that I can touch His warm flesh and call Him Brother, so far that I cannot see the ultimate height of Him, or encompass the full blaze of His glory. This Man, if we see Him thus, of the race and apart from it; kin of it and King of it, near to it and far away from it, immanent, transcendent, then we shall hear the Gospel. "This Man receiveth sinners."

Now for a closing word concerning the pronouncement. What is this that they said of Him? Let us dismiss them. We have no more to do with the Pharisees. What is this that we are saying of Him? What is this the Spirit of God says of Him? What is this the Bride says of Him? "This Man receiveth sinners." "Receiveth" here means infinitely more than we sometimes mean by the word. I shall do no violence to the thought behind this word "receiveth" if I translate it thus, This Man *receiveth unto Himself* sinners. This Man does not patronize sinners. He takes them into His comradeship, makes familiar friends of them, takes them to His heart. That is the Gospel. He is not high seated on a throne bending down to you and offering you pardon if you will kiss His scepter. He is by you in the pew, He is close to you in your sin, and He will take you as you are, with the poison and the virus within you, put His arms about you, and press you into a great comradeship.

These men said, If He does this He will be contaminated. What was the fact? He received them, and never a dimming of His white purity, but rather an ending of their scarlet corruption. He took to Himself Mary of Magdala, possessed of seven devils, embittered, hot, worldly, evil in her temper and disposition, and she became the lone watcher through the night of His burial, the first preacher of the resurrection. Down in the quiet village outside Bedford is a tinker, and he swears and blasphemes so that even the low and the lewd are ashamed of him. "This Man receiveth sinners." He received this tinker, wrapped him to His heart, communicated to him His own purity, opened his eyes, and he became the celestial dreamer.

Those are far distant examples, and if I stay in the Gospel story you feel the distance. You are not sure even about Bunyan. Then there are witnesses here tonight. Here is a man who was a low-down, lost drunkard in New York streets, and was brought into the old Hippodrome in the days when Dwight Lyman Moody was preaching this Gospel there. "This Man" took him to His heart and the passion for drink died and the man was remade. Let the preacher tell his story, at least in such sentences as he may utter. "This Man" has received him also. Not yet is the work all done. Much is there yet to do, but I bear witness in your presence tonight that the tides of His life have quenched fires of passion, stilled tempests of upheaval, and are leading me out toward the ultimate. "This Man receiveth sinners." This is the Evangel. This is the Gospel. There is none other.

You never can be such as He in that respect. You never can be a Saviour, receiving other men, communicating your purity. You can share the fellowship of His sufferings, not as you bring men to yourself to save them, but as you lead them to Him that He may save them. "This Man receiveth sinners."

CHAPTER XIII

THE GREAT APOSTLE

I am not a whit behind the very chiefest apostles.
                              II CORINTHIANS 11:5.

THIS CLAIM OF PAUL OCCURS IN THE MIDST OF WHICH HE was evidently ashamed, but which was necessary in defense of truth. There is no surer sign of modesty than the absence of mock modesty. When a man is able to boast in vindication of his appointment to service by his Lord he proves his humility.

The greatness of Paul as an apostle is now conceded, yet during his exercise of the apostolic vocation he had perpetually to defend his right to the title. In his letters, sometimes with a touch of satire, he defended his apostleship against the misunderstanding—that is the kindest word to use—of the other apostles. In the Galatian letter he declared that he went up to Jerusalem and gained nothing from them. He referred to those whom he found there as persons "who were reputed to be somewhat," then absolutely denied that they ministered to him in any way, either by original authority, or subsequent counsel. He received his Gospel from his Master. He received his commission from his master. He did his work under his master's immediate direction. He remitted his case and cause to his master's judgment.

In defense of his apostleship he always adopted two lines

of argument. First, he insisted upon his Divine appointment. Second, he claimed that the fulfilment in his ministry of the true apostolic function proved that Divine appointment.

Wherein lay the greatness of this apostle? The simplest and most inclusive answer to that inquiry is to be found in a statement of the deepest facts of His life in its relation to Christ. I desire now to make that statement quite briefly and only by way of introduction, for I propose another method of approaching the subject. I cannot, however, entirely pass over these fundamental and inclusive matters.

The greatness of the apostle was created in the first place by the absoluteness of his surrender to. Jesus. On the way to Damascus, surprised, startled, and stricken to the earth by the revelation of the living Christ, he in one brief and simple question handed over his whole life to Jesus. "What shall I do, Lord?"

The greatness of Paul as an apostle is further to be accounted for by his attitude, consequent upon that surrender, toward all the things of his former life. "What things were gain to me, these have I counted loss for Christ."

Finally, his greatness is to be accounted for by the resulting experience which he crystallized into one brief sentence, "To me to live is Christ."

These things being stated and granted, I desire to consider certain attitudes of the mind of this man which reveal the strength which made him the great apostle, the pattern missionary for all time. These attitudes of mind are revealed, not so much by the formal statements of his writings, as by the incidental and almost unconscious utterances thereof. I particularly desire to make clear my own discrimination between these two things. In his letters there are certain paragraphs which are formal statements concerning himself. I do not propose turning to these for this reason—I say this with all respect to Paul, and with recognition of the fact that these are inspired writings—men do not reveal themselves in their formal utterances half so clearly as in their incidental words.

I have recently been going through the writings of Paul, and gathering out some of the incidental things he uttered concerning himself. I propose to take seven of them, without any set sequence or order, hoping the effect may be cumulative, helping to an understanding of the attitudes of mind which made this man a great apostle.

The deepest thing in human personality is not mind, but spirit. The spiritual life of Paul commenced when he said, "What shall I do, Lord?" was continued when he said, "What things were gain to me, these have I counted loss for Christ"; was perfected as Christ was formed in him and shone out through his life. That is the spiritual fact. I desire now to deal with the mental, that is, with the attitudes of mind which were natural to him, and which were baptized by the Spirit into life and fire and power.

I

In the midst of his classic passage on love, he declared, "*Now that I am become a man, I have put away childish things.*" Comparing love with knowledge, and showing how knowledge passes away, the richer and fuller forevermore making obsolete the smaller and the incomplete, by way of illustration he wrote, "Now that I am become a man, I have put away childish things," or, more literally, "I have *made an end* of childish things." In that declaration there is revealed an attitude of mind, consisting of a sense of proportion. It is a recognition of the fact that the ways of a child are right for a child, but that the ways of a child are wrong for a man. There are men who when they become men do not put away childish things. There are people who make advance in certain directions, and carry up with them into the raw region of their life things which ought to have been left behind. Should the butterfly cling to the shell in which it had been but a grub, what disaster! When it became a butterfly, it put away the things of the former life. "Now that I am become a man, I have put away childish things." That is to say, toys gave place to tools. Playtime was succeeded by worldtime. Instruction began to express itself in construction. This is a principle of greatness in all Christian service, and lack of it is inimical to progress. It is a sense of proportion and readiness to answer new conditions whenever they arise.

II

My second illustration is taken from the Galatian letter, "*I conferred not with flesh and blood.*" That is a revelation of the sense of spiritual compulsion. He had already declared that he had received a double unveiling of Jesus Christ. Mark the twofold fact. Christ was unveiled to him, and in him. He had seen a vision of Christ external to himself on the way to Damascus, and he had seen a vision of Christ as part of his inner, deepest and profoundest life. That vision, that unveiling of Jesus Christ, became the master principle of his life. In a moment all the lower motives were canceled. The spiritual truth breaking in upon his soul by the revealing of Christ to him and the revealing of Christ in him came not only as light but as fire, not only illuminating, but destroying every other motive that existed within.

Now mark the fine scorn of his word, "I conferred not with flesh and blood," that is to say, material motives at their very highest and best were forevermore out of court and out of count. "I conferred not with flesh and blood," quite literally, I did not take advice from flesh and blood, I did not take counsel with flesh and blood, did not seek the guidance of flesh and blood. First, his own flesh and blood. He never took counsel with his material life from the moment when God revealed His Son in him. He took counsel with the revealed Son. He did not take counsel with the apostles of flesh and blood. He took counsel only with the spiritual truth which had broken upon him through the inner and spiritual conception of Christ.

III

Turn to another of these declarations, "*I know how to be abased and I know also how to abound.*" That is a sense of detachment from circumstances. Did ever apostle pass through more varied circumstances than this one? Was ever man less affected by them than he was?

This is not the detachment of absence. That is the ascetic, monastic ideal which is anti-Christian. The man who says, I will escape the possibility of abasement, the possibility of abundance by hiding myself from the commonplace affairs of life, is not realizing the apostolic ideal, which is ability to stay in the midst of circumstances of abasement and to dwell amid abundance.

Neither is it the detachment of indifference. It is not the stoicism of the Greek which steels the heart and says, Abasement shall not affect me, abundance shall not appeal to me. Far from it.

It is rather the detachment of mastery and of use. "I know how to be abased, and I know also how to abound." I am not afraid of abasement. I will not escape from it. I am not afraid of abundance, I will not avoid it. I do not imagine that in the hour when my Lord gives me abundance there is something wrong in my inner life. "I know also how to abound." I know how to suffer hunger. I know how to suffer need. Abasement without dejection. Abundance without tyranny. That is one of the greatest sentences Paul ever wrote as revealing his absolute triumph in human life. It is the picture of a man so absolutely detached from all the circumstances of his life that he was able to take hold of them and press them into the making of his own character, and, what is more, into the service which his Master's will had appointed. This is one of the statements of Paul of which I hardly dare to speak, so little do I know it personally, so difficult do I find it to be. Where was the secret? How was it this man could say such a thing. Follow right on and he tells you. "I can do all things in Him that strengtheneth me." It is the Christ-centered life. That is the spiritual fact. I refer to it only that we may find the secret of this mental attitude which is so difficult, nay impossible, to cultivate, which can come only as Christ within becomes in very deed the Master of the whole life. Whenever Christ does become the Master of the life you will find a servant who says, I cannot hurry from abasement, "I know how to be abased." I do not fear abundance, "I know also how to abound." You cannot turn my feet out of the way of His commandment by hunger, I know how to suffer hunger. You cannot quench my zeal for His service by giving me fulness. I know how to be filled. I am so detached from circumstances that I can master them.

IV

I come now to the very heart and center of the references which reveal his greatness as an apostle. In that wonderful Roman letter—introducing the subject of the salvation of God—he made three personal references within the compass of a few phrases. *"I am debtor . . . I am ready . . . I am not ashamed."* "I am debtor," the Gospel is a deposit which I hold in trust. "I am ready," the Gospel is an equipment so that I am able to discharge my debt. "I am not ashamed," the Gospel is a glory, so that if I come to imperial Rome, sitting on its seven hills, I shall delight to preach the Gospel there also. In each case the personal emphasis reveals the sense of responsibility. "*I* am debtor." Here you touch the driving power of the man's life. Here you find out why he could not rest, why the very motto of his missionary movement was "the regions beyond," why he traversed continents, crossed seas, and entered into perils on perils. He felt that while anywhere there was a human being who had not heard the evangel, he was in debt to that human being.

"*I* am ready." I suppose you have all read what Artemus Ward said about the American War Between the States. He said he had already donated several brothers and cousins to the war, and he was prepared to donate a few more. How many of you have donated other people to missionary enterprise? Paul said, "*I* am ready." "*I* am not ashamed." You tell me we must cancel the capital "I." Yes, nail it to the cross and let it emerge in resurrection glory.

V

In the same letter I presently find this man writing another revealing sentence. "I could wish that I myself were anathema from Christ." I do not know that there is anything other than silence possible in the presence of that. There have been endless attempts made to account for it, and to explain it, usually to explain it away. It has been said that the Apostle did not really mean that he wished he were accursed from Christ. Then, in the name of God, why did he write it? If language means anything, he meant exactly that. "I could wish that I myself were anathema from Christ for my brethren's sake, my kinsmen according to the flesh." How is this to be accounted for? It can be accounted for only by declaring that it is the mental attitude which grows out of the fulness of spiritual life, of which Christ is the fountain. Again, go back in memory over the argument. He had stated the great doctrine of sanctification. He had climbed up out of the unutterable ruin of human sin until he had come to that height at the close of the eighth chapter in which he said that nothing can "separate us from the love of God, which is in Christ Jesus our Lord." Immediately the shout of personal triumph merged into the cry of a great sorrow, "I could wish that I myself were anathema from Christ for my brethren's sake." How are we to account for it? Only thus, he is now speaking with the tongue of Christ, feeling with the heart of Christ. He is a man surcharged with the Christ-life. It thrills and throbs through every fiber of his being. If that be so, I have no further difficulty, for He Who knew no sin was made sin for me. Here is a man in whom His life is dominant, in whom the Christ passion is moving and burning. What is the mental attitude now? Utter and absolute self-abnegation. "I could wish that I myself were anathema from Christ." It is the sense of compassion.

VI

I turn to another passage which stands in almost brutal contrast to the one at which we have just been looking. "*I resisted him to the face.*" Who is this that he resisted to the face? Peter. Why did he resist Peter to the face? Read the story carefully. Not because Peter had been preaching a false doctrine. He had done nothing of the kind. Peter, to whom first had come the commission to preach the Gospel to the Gentiles, having come down to these Gentile Christians, had sat down at the table with them quite naturally. But there came down certain men from Jerusalem, and when they came Peter declined to sit down with the Gentiles. Paul calls his action by the right word, dissimulation, positive dishonesty. I pray you notice carefully what this means. Paul saw that Peter insulted truth in the commonplaces. He would never have insulted truth in a great crisis. Peter argumentatively and theologically would have defended the liberty of the Gentile quite as eagerly as would have Paul, but under stress of conventionality he conformed to the false thinking of the Judean visitors by refusing to sit down with the Gentiles. Paul's anger here is a finer revelation of loyalty to truth than any lengthy treatise. I will put that in another form. His attitude toward Peter is the supreme vindication of the honesty of the Galatian letter. Had he written his Galatian letter, a powerful treatise in defense of the liberty of the Christian, and yet had lightly passed over Peter's dissimulation, I would have been compelled to doubt his sincerity. Here, again, I remind you of the principle enunciated at the beginning of this study. A man is revealed in the commonplace thing, not in the crisis. Paul, when he saw Peter violating truth in the commonplace, resisted him to the face, because he was to be blamed. An apostle violating truth in the commonplace is not to be excused because he is an apostle. In all probability Peter was one of those to whom Paul referred as those who were "reputed to be somewhat." The "somewhat" that he seemed to be could not save him in the presence of this man in whom the truth reigned supremely, who would not deviate by a hair's breadth from loyalty to it. No man is great who excuses the violation of truth in the commonplaces of life. "I resisted him to the *face*."

VII

One more illustration, "I must also see Rome." That was not the feverish desire of the tourist. He was himself a Roman citizen, and was conscious of the far-reaching power of the Roman empire. He knew full well how the influence of the capital city spread out over all the known world. He was perfectly well aware that the Roman highways extended in every direction, and Roman rule was everywhere. It was the strategic center of the life of his age. "I must also see Rome." I must go to Rome, and from that great center send forth this self-same evangel, this Gospel message.

It is exactly this sense of method which the Church has so perpetually been in danger of losing. Take one illustration of what I mean from home missionary work, and another, a living one at this moment, from the foreign field. The home illustration is to be found in the perpetual habit the Church of God has had of abandoning some building at the center of a vast population. When the Church of God abandons some strategic center it is because she has not the apostle's sense, "I must also see Rome," I must be at the heart of the world's movements, I must take this Gospel into the very center where the tides of life are throbbing, and from which the influences which make or mar men are proceeding. Take the other illustration, from the foreign field. If the Church of God did but know its day and opportunity it would fasten its attention at this hour upon Japan. China is waking from her long, long slumber, and the question of the politician is not the question of the Christian. The question of the politician is, "What shall we do with China?" The question of the Christian is, "What will China do with us?" for I believe the Christian man climbs to the highest height and sees things more clearly. That is the question of the future. Remember, finally, China is not going to be influenced by us. If she desires Western civilization she will certainly choose to take it from her neighbor and kin, Japan. If we did but know the hour of our visitation and opportunity, we should evangelize Japan, and especially in the centers of learning, for from them are going forth the men who will presently effect the molding of China. The Church today ought to be restless through all her missionary societies, and her great cry ought to be, "I must see Japan." It was a great sense of method. It was the word of a man who thought imperially in very deed and truth, and who knew that to be at the center of empire with the message of the Gospel was to affect the uttermost part of the earth.

Let me gather up in brief sentences these sayings and their values. First of all, I find a sense of proportion which made Paul willing to pass on into new light and new conditions and forget absolutely the things of the past. "*Now that I am become a man, I have put away childish things.*" Then I find the sense of spiritual compulsion which made him magnificently, even satirically, independent of the counsel of flesh and blood. "*I conferred not with flesh and blood.*" Then I find that splendid detachment from circumstances which meant mastery of circumstances. "*I know how to be abased, and I know also how to abound.*" Then I find that sense of personal responsibility which made him say, "*I am debtor . . . I am ready . . . I am not ashamed.*" Then I find that overwhelming sense of compassion which made him say, "*I could wish that I myself were anathema from Christ.*" Then I find the sense of stern loyalty to truth which made him resist Peter to the face—"*I resisted him to the face.*" Finally, I find that sense of method which made him put into a sentence the burning desire of his heart when he said, "*I must also see Rome.*"

Truly this was the great apostle, the great pattern for all time of those who would desire to be apostles, messengers, missionaries of the cross of Christ.

Yet I am compelled to return to the fundamental statements with which I began. If these are the mental attitudes, what is the spiritual fact? "To me to live is Christ." So that as I look at Paul, the apostle, the missionary, the last thing I have to say is not of the great apostle, but of the great Christ, the One Who took hold of this man, and revealing Himself within him, unveiling His glory to his inner consciousness, drove him forth, and made him such as he was. Christ diffused through Paul will not help us. It is good to see Paul, to know what Christ can do; but we must indeed get to Christ Himself if we would enter into fellowship even with Paul. If the vision of the great apostle shall drive us to his Lord, then how great and gracious will be the result. If we will but make his surrender, "What shall I do, Lord?": if we will take up this attitude toward the things we have counted best, counting them but loss that we may win Christ: if we will but enter into the experience which he expressed in the words, "To me to live is Christ"—what then? First, He will not make us Pauls, but He will make us His own. Though He may never send us over continents and among such perils, all that matters nothing, for it is local, and incidental merely. He will send us where He would have us go, and He will make us what He would have us be, and through us—oh, matchless wonder of overwhelming grace—the light of His love may shine, and the force of His life may be felt.

We cannot have this Christ-life within us without having clear vision, and without having driving compassion, and without having the dynamic which makes us mighty. We cannot have Christ within us and be parochial. Christ overleaps the boundaries of parish, society, and nation, and His clear vision takes in the whole world. If Christ be verily in us we shall see with His eyes, feel with His heart, be driven with His very compassion.

"If I have eaten my morsel alone!"
The patriarch spoke in scorn;

What would He think of the Church, were He shown
    Heathendom, huge, forlorn,
Godless, Christless, with soul unfed,
While the Church's ailment is fulness of bread,
    Eating her morsel alone?

"I am debtor alike to the Jew and the Greek,"
    The mighty apostle cried;
Traversing continents, souls to seek,
    For the love of the Crucified.
Centuries, centuries since have sped;
Millions are famishing, we have bread,
    But we eat our morsel alone.

Ever of them who have largest dower
    Shall heaven require the more.
Ours is affluence, knowledge, power,
    Ocean from shore to shore;
And East and West in our ears have said,
Give us, give us your living Bread.
    Yet we eat our morsel alone.

Freely, as ye have received, so give,
    He bade, Who hath given us all.
How shall the soul in us longer live,
    Deaf to their starving call,
For whom the blood of the Lord was shed,
And His body broken to give them Bread,
    If we eat our morsel alone?

CHAPTER XIV

CHRIST'S VISION OF JERUSALEM

And it came to pass, when the days were well nigh come that He should be received up, He stedfastly set His face to go to Jerusalem.

LUKE 9:51.

EVERY CONTEMPLATION OF THE LAST MONTH, AND WEEKS, and days in the life of our Lord fills the soul with a sense of solemn and almost overwhelming awe. Through all those movements which culminated in the Cross and resurrection, He stands out, awful in His loneliness, magnificent in His heroism, supreme in His revelation of the highest possible in human life, and of the greatest in God.

This determined setting of His face to Jerusalem is worthy of our closest attention. A superficial reading would leave the impression that the value of the statement is exhausted geographically. This is by no means so. Jesus had just left the mount of glory, and set His face toward the valley, and the multitudes, toward the sin, the sorrow, and the suffering. And "when the days were well nigh come that He should be received up, He stedfastly set His face to go to Jerusalem."

This declaration, as a revelation of His outlook, and in the light of the teaching which immediately followed, is of supreme value to all such as bear His name and share His toil.

I shall ask you to consider first this attitude of Christ, and then the things concerning discipleship, which are chronicled for us immediately after this declaration of Luke concerning the Lord.

In consideration of His attitude notice first His vision of Jerusalem, "He stedfastly set His face *to go to Jerusalem*"; second, the consciousness that created the stedfastness, "The days were well nigh come that He should be received up"; and, finally, His action, "He *stedfastly set His face to go* to Jerusalem."

What, then, was the vision which Jesus had of Jerusalem? First of all, it was that of a city utterly and absolutely hostile to Himself. He was drawing near the end of His ministry. He had walked the streets of Jerusalem, had taught in the courts of the temple, had held intercourse with the leaders of the people, and He knew right well that the whole city was hostile to Him. The religious leaders, the political parties, the multitudes who were city folk, were against Him.

The religious leaders were against Him because His spiritual teaching had been directly contradictory to all for which they stood. There were two great religious parties at the time, which we may broadly describe as rationalistic and ritualistic. There were the Sadducees, and the Pharisees, diametrically opposed, and yet both of them against Jesus Christ.

The Sadducees did not believe in angel, or spirit, or resurrection. That is to say, they were the rationalists in religion, the men who were attempting still to retain the religious ideal, while yet denying all the supernatural element therein. These men were against Christ necessarily. He had ruthlessly swept aside their views by speaking of angels, by referring to the Spirit, by declaring that God was not the God of the dead but of the living.

The Pharisees stood for ritualistic practice, were eager

and anxious about the tithing of mint, anise, cummin, and rue; while neglecting the weightier matters of the law. They would not eat with unwashed hands, but were content to stand before the altar of God with filthy hearts.

The political parties were against Him. None of them had been able to capture Him. He had dictated the terms of righteousness to all as they had come to Him with subtle questions, but He had stood aloof from them, not uninterested in the affairs of city and nation, but speaking to His time the things of God alone.

The Jerusalem multitudes were against Him, for I think there is a sharp line of distinction to be drawn between the simple folk of Galilee and the city dwellers. It has been said that the people shouted, "Hosanna!" and within a week shouted, "Crucify!" I do not think so. I think that they were two quite different multitudes. The Galileans who had come with Him shouted, "Hosanna." The people of the city were priest-ridden, and king-enslaved, and they were all against Him.

Jesus had had His day, His opportunity. He had delivered His message. He had unburdened His soul. He had flashed upon them the light of the Divine Kingdom. His message was refused, and they were against Him; and subtle and devilish intrigues were busy, waiting for the opportunity to lay hands on Him, and hand Him over to death. All this He knew, and yet "He stedfastly set His face to go to Jerusalem."

But then He had another vision of Jerusalem. Not only did He see it hostile, He saw it doomed. At last, with a sigh and a sob, He pronounced that doom. "O Jerusalem, Jerusalem . . . how often would I have gathered thy children together," and He saw Jerusalem doomed by the inevitable sequence of wrong. False shepherds and scattered sheep. False prophets, and deluded people. False priests, and degraded religion. He knew perfectly well that Jerusalem was doomed by the deliberate rejection of its own opportunity. "How often would I!" That was the desire of His heart. "And ye *would not*"! That was the choice of their sin. He knew perfectly well therefore that the sentence must be carried out. "Behold, your house is left unto you desolate." Nevertheless, "He stedfastly set His face to go to Jerusalem," the hostile city, and the doomed city.

He had another vision of Jerusalem, and I have dwelt only upon the first two that I might lead you to the third. He saw Jerusalem hostile. He saw Jerusalem doomed. But He saw Jerusalem rebuilt. He saw through all the mists and the darkness and the opposition and the doom to something beyond.

The men of faith had ever been men of vision, looking "for the city which hath the foundations, whose Builder and Maker is God." When Abraham turned his back upon Ur of the Chaldees, and went out seeking a city, he did not go to seek a heaven beyond the earth. His passion, the passion of all the men of faith, and supremely the passion of Jesus, was not that men should pass through earth and win heaven; but that there should be established on the earth the city of God. The vision which had kept the Hebrews a people through all the processes of their failure, was the vision of the ultimate. Read the ancient prophecies carefully, and amid the thunder of denunciation you will constantly hear tones that tell of coming accomplishment in the world, of the day when "the knowledge of the glory of the Lord" shall fill the earth, "as the waters cover the sea"; of the day when "they shall not hurt nor destroy in all My holy mountain." All these men had looked toward the building of a city. Cities had been built, but the hopes and aspirations of seers and psalmists had never been realized.

Jerusalem as Jesus looked at it was the home of evil things, and yet it was "the city of the great King," and through it He saw the city of God established, "the holy city, new Jerusalem coming down out of heaven from God," the ultimate accomplishment of that which is in the heart of God, not merely in individual life, but in civic life; the setting up of the Kingdom of God in the world, and seeing that, "He stedfastly set His face to go to Jerusalem."

Let us gather up these thoughts. When the time was coming that He should be received up, He stedfastly set His face toward Jerusalem. What Jerusalem? The Jerusalem hostile to Himself, waiting to arrest and murder Him. What Jerusalem? That Jerusalem over which hung the sword of God, upon which the judgment of God must soon fall. What Jerusalem? The Jerusalem beyond all this, that which the hostile and doomed city must yet become in the economy of God, a city established, "the joy of the whole earth," because the home of "the great King," and the center from which His government was to go forth to the ends of the world. Jesus saw the city, and deliberately set His face toward its hostility, its doom, and its ultimate triumph. He had a vision of the immediate, but He had that more wonderful vision which sees through the immediate to the ultimate. Beyond the gathering storm clouds settling over Himself and the city He saw the morning without clouds, the ultimate and final victory, when the last stone will be brought on to the city of God, and all tribes of the earth will rejoice in the setting up of His government and the accomplishment of His will. He saw through the process of pain to that ultimate for which He taught us to pray, for the day when God's name shall be hallowed, His Kingdom come, His will be done in earth as it is in heaven. And he set his face toward the Jerusalem of hostility, because He saw through it the Jerusalem of ultimate achievement.

Notice, in the second place, the consciousness which created the vision. "It came to pass, when the days were well night come that He should be *received up*, . . ." He is coming down. He has just turned His back upon the mountain, and has set His face to the valley, and has immediately cast the devil out of the boy, and is still moving down to the valley of darkness. No, that is not the story. That is only part of it. He is moving toward the day in which "He should be received up." Here the declaration is an incidental one, but in the Gospel of John we find how perpetually our Lord looked upon His mission in its entirety. "I came out from the Father, and am come into the world: again, I leave the world, and go unto the Father." He saw the Cross, but He saw the resurrection. He saw the travail, and shrank from it, but He saw the triumph, and hastened to it. He saw the hostility in Jerusalem, the cruel, brutal hostility. He knew exactly what was awaiting Him, but He saw beyond the hostility to the crowning and the victory, and the position He was to occupy when He was received up. He was going down, but the descent was the preliminary to an ascent. The setting of His face toward the darkness was the lifting of His face toward the light, and although He set His face stedfastly toward Jerusalem, and the sorrow, and the shame, and the pain, and the dying, He set His face toward the victory, and the joy, and the triumph. To Him the Cross was the way of ascent to the throne. To Him all the travail that waited for Him was the very process that made possible the triumph upon which His heart was set. From the glorious height of the Transfiguration Mount He had seen the mists as they lay along the valleys through which

He must pass—the strange and chilly mists of death; but He had seen them from the height of glory, and they had been purple as the light shone upon them. Men are going to nail Him to a Cross, and taunt Him as He hangs there; "If Thou art the Son of God, came down from the Cross." But He knows perfectly well by the way of the helplessness of that hour of His dying that help is to be laid upon Him for all who put their trust in Him, and by the way of that mystery of descent He is moving out toward eternal ascent. He is to be received up.

What, then, was the effect of this consciousness upon Him? That hostility could neither hinder nor anger Him. I wish I knew how to say that so as to arrest you. Is there anything more wonderful in the story of His coming than the fact that hostility never hindered Him? We speak of Gethsemane and the shrinking there, but we must remember that the shrinking was not from human hostility, but from something far more deep and mysterious, into the meaning of which you and I can never enter. But the hostility in Jerusalem never hindered Him, and never angered Him. Is there anything in human history and literature that begins to compare with the patient, unprovoked spirit in which this Christ of ours set His face toward Jerusalem, or in the majestic and exhaustive language of the ancient prophecy, "As a sheep that before her shearers is dumb; yea, He opened not His mouth." The vision of the glory beyond the hostility made Him such a One as could set His face toward the city, and be unhindered and unangered by its hostility.

Again, the doom which He Himself must pronounce upon the city could not thwart Him, could not dishearten Him. Could there be a greater triumph than the triumph of One Who saw through the ruined, doomed city, a greater city, and was not disheartened by the doom?

Yet there is another thing which must be said. He saw Jerusalem hostile, He saw Jerusalem doomed, He saw Jerusalem certainly to be rebuilt; but the vision of the ultimate, the assurance that God must win, did not make Him careless. He did not say because this victory of God must be won in the long run of the centuries, I may turn aside and leave it. He set His face toward the pain, and toward the suffering, and toward the strife. Jerusalem hostile, He is to be received up; but He will go through hostile Jerusalem. Its hostility cannot hinder him. Jerusalem doomed, He is to be received up; but He cannot be disheartened about the doom of Jerusalem, for He knows through what He will do amid its darkness He will create a new day for it. Jerusalem is to be rebuilt, ah, yes, but He must go through the midst of its darkness to turn it into light; through the midst of its sin to take hold upon it and make possible that which He sees in the economy of God.

As I read this word about my Lord, I stand in His presence overawed. "He stedfastly set His face to go to Jerusalem," because He was to be received up. That is suffering transfigured by the light of the victory which would result from it. The only thing I fear now is that a multiplicity of my words may hide the vision. Behold the Man of Nazareth. There He stands at the foot of the hill where He has been transfigured. The multitudes are all about Him. In the city all the forces are against Him. Over the city hang the dark thunder clouds of the Divine judgment. But beyond is Jerusalem the golden, God's own perfect city! He stedfastly set His face toward the hostility, toward the doom, caring not for the one, gathering the other into His own soul, looking ultimately toward the glory and toward the victory.

Turn now to the things which immediately follow, for they are full of significance for us. What is the next thing that Luke tells us? As He set His face toward Jerusalem they came to a Samaritan village, and the Samaritans would not receive Him. Why not? Mark it carefully, because His face was toward Jerusalem. See how people may put a narrow and local interpretation upon a broad and infinite truth. They simply saw Him as a Jew traveling toward Jerusalem, and because Jerusalem was the objective of His journey, they would not entertain Him. The narrowness of the Samaritan was manifest there. That which was His purpose of blessing for them was the reason of their anger with Him. As He set His face toward Jerusalem it was not for Jerusalem merely, but for Samaria. Presently, having been to Jerusalem, having been smitten to the death in Jerusalem, having been raised from the dead, He will stand among these disciples who wanted to call down fire upon the Samaritan village, and He will say to them, "Ye shall be My witnesses both in Jerusalem, and in all Judea *and Samaria*, and unto the uttermost part of the earth." His vision had not been the vision of Jerusalem only. It had been the vision of Samaria won and redeemed, of the uttermost part of the earth brought into right relationship with the government of God. And that is why His face was set stedfastly toward Jerusalem, and these Samaritans are against Him because He was going to Jerusalem. All unknowingly and ignorantly they were angry with Him, because of the purpose which was in His heart to bring blessing to them.

Then notice the disciples' anger. They requested that they might call down fire to destroy this village. They respected His person, but they were quite ignorant of His purpose. They were standing outside the great circle in which He lived and moved. They had not the vision of the ultimate as He had; and, consequently, while loyal to Him, and angry because He was not hospitably received, they rather hindered than helped Him.

Now look at the Lord. Mark the patience of His purpose. He rebuked the disciples, and quietly went to another village. The village that would not entertain Him He left, not in anger, but in patience. And yet there is a touch of impatience here in Christ. It is only a great patience that ever can be purely impatient. What impatience is there? Impatience with His own disciples. There is no impatience with the Samaritan village that had not understood Him. There is a touch of impatience with His disciples because of their blindness. Ah, methinks sometimes He must be impatient with some of us. He was moving toward the city, with all the glory filling His vision, and He rebukes the disciples, and yet is patient with Samaria.

Let us read on. On His way three men came to Him. One of them said impulsively, "I will follow Thee whithersoever Thou goest." I always love that man. I like the man who speaks out what is in His heart even though impulsively. Christ did not rebuke him, but He flashed before him the truth, "The foxes have holes, and the birds of the heaven have nests; but the Son of Man hath not where to lay His head."

Jesus looked at another and said, "Follow Me," and the man answered, "Lord, suffer me first to go and bury my father," which does not mean that his father was dead. Dr. George Adam Smith told me, talking about this very story, that when he was in Palestine he very particularly desired to get a certain man to act as guide in one of those wonderful journeys of his into the unknown regions, and was startled when the man said to him in actual words, with the Eastern salaam, "Suffer me first to go and bury my father." His father was alive and hale and hearty. What the man meant was, I have home ties and responsibilities, and I cannot break them. And that is what this man in the Gospel story meant. The word of Jesus is more severe than it seems. "Leave the dead to bury their own dead; but go thou and publish abroad the Kingdom of God."

A little further on another man said, "I will follow Thee, Lord; but first suffer me to bid farewell to them that are at my house." To him Christ said, "No man, having put his hand to the plow, and looking back, is fit for the Kingdom of God."

Now reverently I bring the three men together, and I look at the Lord. His face is set toward Jerusalem. Mark the answers. "The foxes have holes, and the birds of the heaven have nests." What is that? Detachment from all that prevents progress to Jerusalem. And what next? "Leave the dead to bury their own dead." What is that? Abandonment of the nearest earthly tie in the interest of the heavenly purpose. And what next? "No man, having put his hand to the plow, and looking back, is fit for the Kingdom of God." "Looking back." Mark it! His face set toward Jerusalem. "No man looking back." The face set. *The looking back.*

Christ speaking to these men unveiled His own attitude. It was first that of detachment from everything that prevented progress to Jerusalem. I want to say this most reverently, and carefully. Do not pity Him because He said, "The foxes have holes, and the birds of the heaven have nests; but the Son of Man hath not where to lay His head." Rather pity yourself if you have something left in your life that makes it hard to go with Him to Jerusalem. It was a declaration of the splendid detachment of Christ from all the things that prevented the progress. I have not where to lay My head. All personal property is abandoned that I may reach Jerusalem, the hostile and the doomed, and make it Jerusalem, the city of God.

Then mark the next word. "Leave the dead to bury their

own dead." Abandonment of the nearest earthly tie in the interest of the heavenly purpose. And was not that true of Him? Did He not say upon one memorable occasion, when they said, "Thy mother and Thy brethren stand without, seeking to speak with Thee," "Who is My mother? and who are My brethren?" When Jesus asked that question He was not speaking disrespectfully of His mother. In the last consummating agony of His life, when all the sins of the world were sweeping in anguish over His soul, He was able to think of His mother, and provide for the days remaining to her, "Woman, behold, thy son! . . . Behold, thy mother!" What, then, did He mean? He meant that even so dear a tie as the tie of relationship between son and mother must be swept aside in the interests of getting to Jerusalem the doomed and turning it into Jerusalem the glorified!

And then, again, "No man, having put his hand to the plow, and looking back." How they tried to persuade Him to look back! How the devil tried, how His own disciples tried! But He never looked back. He put His hand to the plow, and the furrow was lone and long, but, blessed be God, it was straight; and He reached the ultimate goal, because He never looked back.

Brethren, if this is the revelation of Christ's own heart, and I think it is, then if I am to go after Him, I must come this way. If I am to have anything to do in the building of God's city, it must be by detachment from all that prevents progress to Jerusalem. Oh, soul of mine, what hast thou of thine own that hinders thy progress toward Jerusalem with Him? And I have come in hours of meditation almost to feel myself filled with envy for the men who can say, I have not where to lay my head, I have not a thing that stands between me and this one supreme purpose.

I must also abandon the nearest earthly tie that prevents.

I must remember that to look back from this enterprise is to make myself unfit for the Kingdom.

But let me thus conclude. Every city is Jerusalem for the purpose of my application. London is Jerusalem, hostile, doomed, and yet possible. London is as hostile to Jesus Christ as Jerusalem was. And therefore it is as surely doomed as Jerusalem was. Yet it is for Christian men and women in London to see through, to see to the ultimate, to see the purpose of God. And if it be impossible for us to take in the larger whole, take the local, take the thing close to you. Take the hostility that abounds all about the place where you live and serve and work. How much there is of it! And take the fact that doom is writ upon everything that is hostile. It does seem to me sometimes we want to remind ourselves of that. Are we not tempted sometimes to think that all these hostile things are going to win? Never! God's verdict is found, and His sentence passed, and all hell cannot prevent the doom of the thing hostile to Jesus Christ. Yes, but, brethren, you and I are to look through, and are to see the possible and God's ultimate.

And if it be true that every city is Jerusalem, in this sense of application, then I will say another thing, and it is this. His face is still toward Jerusalem, stedfastly set toward it, coming to it even when it is hostile to Him. Has it never occurred to you that it is an amazing wonder that He has not turned His back upon London long ago? He has not. His face is toward it. Tears are upon His cheeks even now. Call it figurative language if you will, but remember the fact is finer than the figure. His heart is still moved with compassion toward the city. He knows men will bruise Him, and are bruising Him, but He is coming toward it always. The Cross is not over. It is in His heart today, the infinite passion that was manifest on the green hill is there yet.

> The Son of God in tears,
>   The wondering angels see.
> Be thou astonished, Oh, my soul!
>   He shed those tears for thee.

That is His attitude toward us today.

Now, this is the question. Who is with Him? How many see these things as He saw them? How many can see through to the light and the victory? It is the men and women whose eyes are illumined with His love to see through who are prepared today to tread the pathway of shame and suffering. It would be so much easier to do something else.

> I said, "Let me walk in the fields."
>   He said, "No, walk in the town."
> I said, "There are no flowers there."
>   He said, "No flowers, but a crown."
>
> I said, "But the skies are black;
>   There is nothing but noise and din,"
> And He wept as He sent me back:
>   "There is more," He said, "there is sin."
>
> I said, "But the air is thick,
>   And fogs are veiling the sun."
> He answered, "Yet souls are sick,
>   And souls in the dark undone."
>
> I said, "I shall miss the light,
>   And friends will miss me, they say."
> He answered, "Choose tonight
>   If I am to miss you, or they."
>
> I pleaded for time to be given.
>   He said, "Is it hard to decide?
> It will not seem hard in heaven
>   To have followed the steps of your Guide." *

May God set our faces toward Jerusalem!

* From "Obedience," by George MacDonald.

CHAPTER XV

THE ALL-SUFFICIENT GRACE

My grace is sufficient for thee.
                    II CORINTHIANS 12:9.

THIS PHRASE FORMS PART OF A STORY IN THE LIFE OF ONE man. It is, however, a great word, revealing a profound philosophy of life, unfolding the deepest truth concerning God; in the knowledge of which life finds the place of peace and rest; and becomes powerful and influential in service. It is remarkable how these words have taken hold upon the heart of humanity. I think that as a general rule it is not wise to differentiate as to the value of particular portions of God's Word, and yet there are outstanding passages which all men seem to know and love. These passages are those characterized by simplicity of statement and sublimity of meaning. This is one of them. "My grace is sufficient for thee." Upon that great word many a weary head has rested; many wounded hearts have been healed by it; discouraged souls have heard its infinite music and have set their lives to new endeavor until they have become victorious. Yet, in common with other passages of a similar quality, I believe that multitudes have been helped and comforted by this word who never have discovered its deepest meaning; for in proportion as the soul trusts in God, God communicates to that soul strength and comfort, even though His promise be not perfectly apprehended intellectually.

All of us, with perhaps some very rare exceptions, accept the truth of these words. If I thus admit that there may be some who are a little doubtful in the deepest of their heart about the strict accuracy of this declaration, I am perfectly sure that such doubt arises from some present sorrow, some overwhelming pain, some deep and profound consciousness of perplexity. It is especially for such that these words are precious. In order that they may see it and know its truth, let us examine the statement carefully.

May I first of all briefly remind you of what the text does not mean. Perhaps I ought to put that a little more carefully. Allow me to remind you of something which does not exhaust the meaning of the text, though it may be contained therein. This word came to the apostle as a veritable word of God, quieting his life, making all its turmoil pass into peace. It means far more than as though God had said to His child, The circumstances in which you find yourself are very hard and very difficult, and very trying, but I will help you to bear them. It does not for a single moment suggest that the adverse circumstances are outside the Divine government. The meaning of the grace of God here is far profounder, far more startling, and full of comfort. God is not saying to His servant, It is very hard and very difficult, and very trying: if it could have been avoided it would have been better, but seeing that it cannot be avoided, I am with you, I am going to help you, to strengthen you.

Is not that what we have thought this text meant? Even if it meant only that it would be worth while trusting it; but that is not the fulness of it, that is not the simplest of it; therefore it is not the sublimest.

The text means this, if I may put it broadly first and then

examine the accuracy of the interpretation afterwards. That stake in the flesh, that messenger of Satan, is in My grace. It is part of My method. The stake in the flesh is sent. The messenger of Satan is My messenger. This is not something that is against you, but for you. This hard and difficult and trying circumstance is not something outside My province, My economy, which you must overcome with My help: it is of My purpose, it is in My plan. I am high enthroned above all the powers of darkness, and to the trusting soul Satan himself is compelled to be a means of My grace. All your suffering is in My economy. I have poised in My own hand the weight of your burden and know it. Everything that is imposed upon you is under My control. "My grace is sufficient for thee." It is enough for you to know that what you are suffering is part of My discipline, evidence of My love.

In order that we may see that this is indeed what Paul meant when he wrote this word as being God's message to him, first notice the context. Concerning the apostle's experiences as here described there are a great many questions which I do not propose to answer. It is always unwise to attempt to understand things which we are told cannot be understood. It is not very long ago that someone asked me, half incredulously, Do you really believe that Paul was caught up into the third heaven? My answer was, Certainly I believe it. Well, but how? You do not expect me to know how, when he did not know himself. He distinctly wrote, "Whether in the body, or apart from the body, I know not." The things of which he was perfectly sure were that he was caught up into the third heaven, and that he saw and heard, and that upon his lips the seal of a solemn and necessary silence was set. He did not know how, but he knew the fact.

Again, there has been great curiosity as to what he saw and what he heard, notwithstanding the fact that he tells us he heard things "which it is not lawful for a man to utter." There is a book of the visions of Paul, and we are told that in the house of Saul of Tarsus there was discovered a marble casket in which was a writing declaring the things he saw and heard. I hope and believe we have grown out of all such foolishness as that. They were unutterable things. The value of them was undoubtedly manifest in his after life.

Probably the experience came to him at Lystra, for he was there about fourteen years prior to the writing of this letter. They stoned him with stones and left him for dead, and it may be that when the men had left him for dead, bruised and battered by their dreadful stones, the Master caught him up and gave him visions. I do not know. I dare not say that it was so. It may have been so. But how he went, or what he saw, and what he heard are not revealed things; consequently they are not for us. They are among the secret things that belong to God.

And yet again many people are attempting to discover what this stake in the flesh was, and again I say to you that if we were meant to know, that also would have been told us. His word is that it was a stake for, rather than in, the flesh. The thought is really that of crucifixion, of suffering in the flesh, and actual and positive physical affliction. It was a stake for the flesh, and it was a messenger of Satan to buffet. There you have the two ideas of abiding affliction, the thorn, the stake in the flesh, and the repetition of trial, the messenger of Satan to buffet. Physical and mental affliction. Then we are told by the apostle why this stake in the flesh came to him, why this messenger of Satan came to buffet him. It was in order that he should not be exalted overmuch by reason of the revelation which had been granted to him in that great hour when he was caught up into the third heaven and saw and heard things which it was impossible for him to utter.

There is a specific purpose, and will you notice that when Paul wrote his letter he knew this.

Then he tells us how he "besought the Lord thrice that it might depart" from him. That prayer was finally answered by the voice of God in his soul, speaking the words, "My grace is sufficient for thee." When the prayer was answered he wrote, "There *was given to me* a thorn in the flesh, a messenger of Satan to buffet me, that I should not be exalted overmuch."

While the apostle was praying for the stake in the flesh to be removed, and for the messenger of Satan to be withheld, I do not think he could possibly have written, "There was given to me a thorn in the flesh." When he wrote these words he had come to understand that the thing he wanted to get rid of was part of the Divine purpose for him. The writing of that sentence, "There was given to me a thorn in the flesh, a messenger of Satan to buffet me," was subsequent to the great answer of the text. The purpose is now clearly revealed, a thorn in the flesh for a specific purpose. His prayer for its removal has issued in his understanding of this fact, that whatever it was, it was sent, given, appointed; that whatever form the buffeting of the angel of Satan took, it was part of God's appointment, something that God Himself had sent to Paul.

But we must get behind to the consciousness of the apostle ere he understood the meaning of the stake in the flesh, ere he understood the meaning of the buffeting of Satan's messenger. There he was, having seen a great vision, yet suddenly depressed by pain and suffering, both physical and mental. Out of the consciousness of his pain, out of the very fierce agony of His suffering, he cried to God and asked that this might be removed from him, that he might be delivered from the stake and from the angel messenger of Satan who buffeted him. To that condition of mind this word of God came, "My grace is sufficient for thee: for My power is made perfect in weakness."

Now, notice the effect of the word. "Most gladly, therefore, will I rather glory in my weaknesses, that the power of Christ may rest upon me." It is so easy to read and so difficult to enter into that spirit. "Most gladly, therefore, will I rather glory in my weaknesses, that the power of Christ may cover me." Heart of mine, attend these words. "Wherefore I take pleasure in weaknesses." He does not say, I endure them, I bear them, I suffer them, I am resigned. No, "I take pleasure in weaknesses, in injuries, in necessities, in persecutions, in distresses, for Christ's sake: for when I am weak then am I strong." This is a change from complaint and petition for the removal of these things to a song of triumph in the midst of them, and over them. I see, first of all, a man pleading with great earnestness and great sincerity that he might be delivered from the pain and burden and unrest. Suddenly, I find a man who no longer asks that these things be taken from him, but says, "I take pleasure in weaknesses, in injuries, in necessities, in persecutions, in distresses." I take pleasure in these things, not in the fact that power is given to me to bear them but in the things themselves. I take pleasure in my suffering. I rejoice in my weakness. I sing a song of gladness because of the injury. This is something infinitely beyond the experience of the man who is thankful because God helps him to bear the thing which cannot be escaped. This is the expression of a philosophy that is infinitely removed from that which expresses itself in the words, "*What cannot be cured must be endured.*" Somehow, this man has come to say concerning the thing he wanted to be rid of, I ask no longer to be rid of it, I glory in it! The stake in the flesh is no less painful, but I am glad of the pain. The buffeting of Satan's messenger is no less terrible, but I rejoice in the buffeting. Here is a man who has seen in his pain something of value, who has discovered that the very cross from which he would have escaped is of value, something that he cannot afford to be rid of. "I take pleasure in weaknesses, in injuries, in necessities, in persecutions, in distresses." Notice, he begins with "Wherefore," and the "wherefore" drives me back to the preceding word, "Most gladly therefore will I rather glory in my weaknesses," and that drives me back to my text. It is this vision of the purpose of the stake and of the messenger of Satan as the apostle declares it, the vision resulting from the word spoken in the text, that sends me back to the text itself that I may ask, What does this mean?

What was it that turned this man's dirge into a song? What was it that changed this man from a good man praying to be delivered from pain into a man singing a song of gladness because he suffered pain? Here is the answer. "He hath said unto me, My grace is sufficient for thee." I submit to you that must mean far more than that God said to him, This thing cannot be avoided, but I will help you to endure it.

Let us take the simple word of the text and look at it. "My grace." What is the meaning of this great word? Who shall answer that question? The word runs through all the New Testament. We see it everywhere, first shining and flaming in revealed glory in the face of Jesus Christ, and then proving to be that root principle out of which the ultimate glory will blossom, the grace of God. Who shall exhaust it? Let us take the word itself. The root idea is that which is pleasing to God. The thought lying at the back of the word is that of the Divine complacency. When grace becomes a river flowing from the throne of God over the life of man it is a beneficent, healing river always, because it is a river which, coming from the throne, accomplishes the will of the throne, and brings into the ordinary life of man the purpose and thought of God which is forevermore a purpose and thought of love. The grace of God. If we accept the old theological definition of the word, that grace is unmerited favor, remember that is only a partial definition. That is the definition of what grace is in activity toward man. Grace exists before it becomes a favor given to anyone. Grace is the fact of the heart of God. You may spell it in the four letters which give you the great word "love." It is essentially the truth concerning God. He is the God of all grace, and we need to remember that as well as to remember that the thing which helps and blesses us is the grace of God. Grace means that which gives pleasure to God, the thing that delights Him, the thing that gives complacency to God Himself. Nothing gives the heart of God pleasure except that which is an activity of love for the blessing of others. God finds His delight forevermore in loving, and in the presence of need, in healing and restoring and blessing, so that the essential grace of God's character becomes a river of healing and of life wherever it flows forth.

"My grace," that which pleases Me, that which comes to you out of My heart, that which reaches you through My love, as a part of its process.

"My grace is sufficient." That is to say the region of the Divine complacency is the region of power forevermore. If a man be where God loves to have Him, he is in the place of power even though at the moment it should be the place of pain.

Let us take two illustrations from the Scripture. I go back to Nehemiah. Ezra had been reading the law of God. Its sense had been given, the interpretation given, the meaning and method explained to the listening people, with what result? The people were filled with sorrow and grief, and the voice of lamentation was raised, and we hear the voice of a people stricken and afflicted. For that there were two reasons: first, the severity of the law, and, second, their consciousness of sin and failure. These people were listening to the law of God—do not miss this—and as they heard it read and explained, they wept and were sorrowful. "Then he said unto them, Go your way, eat the fat, and drink the sweet, and send portions unto him for whom nothing is prepared; for this day is holy unto our Lord; neither be ye grieved; for the joy of the Lord is your strength. So the Levites stilled all the people, saying, Hold your peace, for the day is holy; neither be ye grieved. And all the people went their way to eat, and to drink, and to send portions, and to make great mirth, because they had understood the words that were declared unto them" (Neh. 8:10). Mark the change. The people heard the law and wept; but when Nehemiah said to them, "The joy of the Lord is your strength," they went away full of mirth. "The joy of the Lord is your strength." Do not let us spoil a great word by superficial exposition. Nehemiah did not mean to say to them, If you will but be happy, you will be strong. He meant to say, Do not be afraid of this law of God. The thing that gives God satisfaction, the thing that makes His heart glad, is your strength—your strength lies in the keeping of His law, and as you give Him joy, you get His joy and so you will become strong.

Take another illustration from the Old Testament of the same great principle, the strange and somewhat startling statement of Isaiah 53:10. "It pleased the Lord to bruise Him: He hath put Him to grief: when thou shalt make His soul an offering for sin. He shall see His seed, He shall prolong His days, and the pleasure of the Lord shall prosper in His hand." It is a somewhat difficult passage, and one that certainly cannot be interpreted to mean that God took any personal delight in the suffering of Messiah. "It pleased the Lord to bruise Him" means that it was part of the Divine economy, it was a thing that was necessary, it came into the operations of God, a necessary part of them, that the Son of His love should be bruised, so it pleased the Lord to bruise Him. Out of that bruising came the victory of Messiah so that He prolongs His days and sees the pleasure of the Lord prosper in His own hands. To the Messiah—I say it reverently, and yet it is true, for here we touch the profoundest illustration of our text—to the Messiah the joy of the Lord, which was represented to Him by pain which He endured, was His strength through His realization of the fact that in the midst of the tragedy of His pain He was co-operative with God in the victory by which He leads the long procession of trusting souls into liberty and into light. It was not that He was helped in the Cross to endure something which was outside the Divine economy. It was rather that in the mystery of the Cross He was having the most perfect fellowship with God, dwelling in His pleasure, in His love, in His provision.

To go back from that supreme height of illustration to the actual word of the text, "My grace is sufficient for thee." It is enough for you to know that you are in the place that pleases Me, in the place of My joy, in the place of My appointment. Someone says, I cannot understand how God could be pleased in the suffering of His servant, or how God could be pleased or have joy in the thorn in the flesh and the messenger of Satan. He had such pleasure because He knew that through the process of pain there should come the very power for which His servant was seeking. He had His watchful eye fixed upon the ultimate issue, and He delighted in the processes because of that which was to come out of them. It was that in the great word which He spoke to Paul which turned his dirge into song, his complaint into thanksgiving, his restlessness into perfect peace, without the removal of the actual pain. It was the consciousness that this pain also was part of his Father's tender provision for his own making and his own perfecting which created the comfort of the message, "My grace is sufficient for thee."

Let us now turn from the examination of the text in its context to consider what it teaches us. First is this truth, that "God is love." He is a God of grace, therefore His arrangements for my life are all of love and are all of grace. Every pain that comes to me is a part of His economy, and therefore it is precious pain. The apostle says that the stake in the flesh was given him, that the messenger of Satan was sent not of Satan or of human malice, but of his Father. Until he saw that the pain came from his Father he prayed, naturally and rightly and beautifully, that it might be removed; but when God had spoken in his soul, and he came to understand that the pain also was part of the Divine provision, he sang in the midst of it, he triumphed over it, he rejoiced in it. He made the very suffering the reason for song. Therefore the supreme anxiety of every life should be to be in God's grace, that is, in His will, in His law, in the place that pleases Him. The joy of the Lord, the thing that satisfies Him, is for me the place of my strength whether it be pleasant or painful, rough or smooth, dark or light. Whatever His will appoints is manifestation of His grace, and in that will is the realm, the region, of my strength. Consequently, there should be no anxiety in the life of trusting souls other than that of finding out where God would have us be. The grace of God may be for you, for me, who knows, the stake in the flesh. It may not be that. It may be quite other. The grace of God for some of us is not the thorn, the process that is a lingering agony in the life, but the rose blossoming and blushing in beauty. Do not imagine that God's only method of grace is the method of the thorn. I think it is more often the method of the flower. Do not imagine that God's only method is the method of the storm. I think it is more often the method of the sunlight. I think nature, even in our own land, is often a parable to us of God's method. We are always complaining of the rainy days: but count them and you will find that they are fewer than the sunshiny days. I am not saying we are to seek for pain, that we are to inflict pain upon ourselves. That is the devil's method of stirring up a sensual spirit, not of creating a spiritual sense. God's grace may be a thorn. It may not. It may be cloud. It may be sunshine. It may be a rough pathway. It may be a smooth pathway. It may be through a sea tempest tossed, or it may be by the still waters and through green pastures. The thing we are taught by this word is that the fact that it is His grace is sufficient. I am to rest in His provision, to rest in what He appoints for me, to sing my song, not because I am free from pain, but because He wills that I should be free from pain. If I can sing the song of health and strength and freedom from pain and care, then presently, if for some reason other than I know, He sends me the stake in the flesh and weakness, I shall be able to keep on singing. The reason of man's gladness must be that he is where God would have him be. Delight in your circumstances and they will soon change and your delight will vanish. Delight in the will of God and the darkest day cannot shut out the light from your life.

Reverently let me say this. Suppose before the apostle had discovered this word of God to him, suppose his prayer had been answered and the stake had been taken away, and the messenger of Satan had come no more. What then? When the stake in the flesh was removed and the messenger of Satan came no more, the ministers of God's grace would have been absent.

Somewhere in this house there is a broken, bruised soul. Have you, oh, brother, sister mine, been crying out that God would deliver you from this pain? May God help you to learn the deeper lesson. Do not think the preacher is telling you that he has learned it. I do not know that I have, but I am praying God to teach it to me. It may be, dear heart, that in the very pain which is laid upon you is the thing which is making you as nothing else could. Miss Ellen Thorneycroft Fowler, in one of her little poems, reminds us that the gates of heaven are gates of pearl, and she says:

> A pearl is found beneath the flowing tide,
>   And there is held a worse than worthless thing,
> Spoiling the shell-built home where it doth cling—
>   Marring the life near which it must abide.
> The everlasting portals are of these,
>   To teach us that perchance some heavy load—
> Some cross 'gainst which so sorely we have striven,
>   That seems to mar our lives and spoil our ease—
> May bring us nearer to the saints' abode,
>   And prove at last the very "Gate of Heaven."

Do you tell me this morning, dear bruised and broken heart, that your life is spoiled by pain and suffering, physical or mental? God speaks to you and says, "My grace is sufficient for thee." God's fires never harm God's saints. They purify the saints. The pain into which he brings me is pain, a stake for the flesh, actual suffering, a messenger of Satan to buffet and bruise; it is real suffering. "My grace is sufficient." What His will appoints is best. There are many instances of people having prayer answered not for their blessing. I read in the Psalms, "He gave them their request, but sent leanness into their soul." It is possible to have an answer that is not a blessing.

Jesus lay asleep in the hinder part of the vessel. A storm of unusual violence arose. Even the men who were accustomed to storms were afraid, and they wakened Him and rebuked Him, saying, "Master, carest Thou not that we perish?" What did He do? Heard their prayer and answered it. He came to the edge of the boat and looked out over the troubled waters and said, very literally, "Be muzzled." Was not that an excellent thing to do? It was an excellent thing if these men could not climb any higher, but there was something better they might have done. They might have said, Let Him sleep on.

> No waters can swallow the ship where lies
> The Master of ocean, and earth, and skies.

It is easy to criticize them. Most probably I should have wakened Him, but that does not prove that it would have been right. He rebuked the winds and the waves, and then said to the men, "Why are ye fearful? Have ye not yet faith?" I would rather weather the storm and miss His rebuke. I would rather come through the storm without disturbing Him. I pray Him to teach me the lesson. I want to be able to say, Thy grace is sufficient, and if Thy grace is storm or pain or weakness, then that, and not escape from trouble, is the better way. I would hear His voice saying, "My grace is sufficient for thee," until I can say, "Most gladly therefore will I rather glory in my weaknesses.... I take pleasure in weaknesses."

My last word is not to those who are in sorrow, but to those who are not. It is a word I have already said, and I would repeat it with emphasis. Do not say, I cannot be a saint unless I have a stake in the flesh. The philosophy of this text for you is this, that you are to live in the sunshine and sing among the roses. Rejoice, young man, in thy strength. If it is His will that yours should be a flowery pathway, pluck the flowers and live among their fragrance, and when presently the sun is o'ercast and the last rose of summer fades, if you have learned how to abide in His will in the sunshine you will be triumphant in the shadow.

CHAPTER XVI

FAMINE FOR THE WORD OF GOD

Behold, the days come, saith the Lord God, that I will send a famine in the land, not a famine of bread, nor a thirst for water, but of hearing the words of the Lord. And they shall wander from sea to sea, and from the north even to the east; they shall run to and fro to seek the word of the Lord, and shall not find it. In that day shall the fair virgins and the young men faint for thirst.

AMOS 8:11-13.

TECHNICALLY, THE PROPHET AMOS WAS AN UNTRAINED man. He declared, "I was no prophet, neither was I a prophet's son; but I was an herdman, and a dresser of sycamore trees." In the language of our age, he was a layman. Yet Amos was a prophet in the one and only sense of the word, as again his words indicate in the verse following the one just read, "And the Lord took me from following the flock, and the Lord said unto me, Go, prophesy unto My people Israel."

His prophecy as preserved for us is unique in its method. None other of the Hebrew messengers adopted exactly his plan. He spoke finally to Israel. He began, however, far away from Israel, and gradually came nearer, until he spoke directly to Israel. His first message was concerning Damascus. Then in turn he spoke to Gaza, Tyre, Edom, Moab, and Judah. At last he came to Israel, and if his words had been burning words to the nations lying about, they were scorching, flaming words when he spoke to Israel.

The message of Amos had for the men of his time a twofold significance in addition to its direct words spoken to them. First, it revealed the fact that God maintained His government of all the nations, and not merely of Judah and of Israel. In the second place the message of Amos made it perfectly plain to those who had ears open to hear, that privilege creates responsibility, for the mildest things he said were said to Damascus, the farthest away, and the fiercest things were said to Israel.

The words of my text constitute the final statement of the judgment that is falling upon Israel. There is to be a famine, not of bread or of water, but of the Word of the Lord. There is to be consequent upon this famine a great restlessness. Men will travel from sea to sea, from north to east, striving to find the Word of the Lord, and will not be able. There is to be as the issue of this restlessness the absolute failure of the finest and best in the life of the people. "The fair virgins and the young men faint for thirst." This is a new word in the prophetic message. Judgment has been described oftentimes as the coming of a sword, as the coming of a plague; but this man sees more deeply, and announces judgment which is no longer a material judgment, but a spiritual one; speaks to them no longer of the locusts and the fire and the plague and the sword, but of the lack of the Word of God. That, according to Amos, is the final fact in God's judgment upon a guilty people. Not the thunder of cannon, not the march of armies, not the devastation of lightning, and thunder, and hail, but of famine of the Word of God.

We shall think of three things: first, the famine suggested; second, the restlessness ensuing from the fruitless search; and, finally, the issue in the fainting of the fair virgins and the young men.

First of all, then, this famine of lack of the Word of the Lord. I think, brethren, we need to be very careful in reading this message to understand its true meaning, or we may fall into an appalling mistake upon the very margin of our consideration. The prophet did not mean to say that there would be on the part of God a capricious withholding of His Word. He did not mean to say that the famine would be because God did not speak, or because God had nothing more to say to men. That is a surface interpretation, and I believe it to be as false as it is pernicious, and as pernicious as it is false. His description of the famine indicates rather a condition of man in which he is incapable of discerning. The difference is essential and radical. Not that God ceases to speak, but that man loses his power to hear. Not that God withholds His Word from men, but that men hear it, and never hear it.

What, then, is this condition of being without the Word of God? No message from the unseen that man hears or recognizes, or believes in. No word speaking to the deeps in a man's life. No authority laying its command upon the life. That is famine of the Word of the Lord. Think of these things in separation from the line of our study for a moment, and ask whether any men are in that condition. Are there men who say there is no message from the unseen, men who never hear the voice that speaks to the deepest and profoundest thing within them, men who live upon the surface of things? If so, they are men living in the midst of a famine of the Word of God. No consciousness of the infinite, no ear that catches its music, no heart that feels its thrill. That there are multitudes of such it is impossible to deny. What, then, is the reason?

In the case of this message of Amos, what was the cause

of the famine? "They that swear by the sin of Samaria, and say, As thy God, O Dan, liveth; and, As the way of Beer-sheba liveth; even they shall fall, and never rise up again." The sin of Samaria was the worship of the calf. The men who swore by that calf and said, "As thy God, O Dan, liveth," were the men who passed into the place of famine for the Word of God. The substitution of the creature in any form for the Creator, constitutes incapacity to receive the Word of God. If a man shall substitute nature for God, a priest for God, a ceremony for God, then, though the Word of God be speaking to him by a thousand voices, he hears none; though the light of God flash on him from every point of the compass, he walks in the darkness; though all the mystic influences of the Divine immanence are about him; he is unconscious of them. No voice, no virtue, no vision, no victory, a famine of the Word of God, because a man has stayed with something short of God. It is possible there is someone in this congregation who is living in the midst of a famine for the Word of God. It may be even as I attempt to deliver the message there is nothing in it for you. Words, empty words, a meaningless occasion, an opportunity for curiosity. You are in the midst of a great famine, famine for the Word of God; and the reason is that you have compelled the capacity in your life which ought to take hold of God to cling to something short of Him. As Paul puts it in writing to the Romans, you have substituted the creature for the Creator, and having fastened your life upon something short of God you have become hardened to the touch of God, unconscious of the fact of God; and though His Word is living and quick and powerful, and sharper than a two-edged sword, it fails to affect you.

The sealing of the Bible always follows idolatry, and the issue of such idolatry is famine, and the result emaciated, emasculated humanity. I am sometimes told that the Word of God has been sadly neglected for many years—and, alas, I am sure it is true, but it is declared that the reason is that men outside the Church and within the Church have been indulging in what we speak of as Criticism, Higher and Lower. Nothing of the kind. The thing that has sealed the Word of God to the believer is the believer's unbelief and disobedience and idolatry. If we could rid ourselves of our idols, the famine would be over, and the Word of God would be living to us again. It is our own idolatry that robs us of the consciousness of the living sustenance of the Word of God.

But follow on, and notice how the prophet describes the fruitless search. He says, "They wander from sea to sea, and from the north even to the east; they shall run to and fro to seek the Word of the Lord, and shall not find it." How does that apply in our own day? You may make the statement in another form. Wherever a man has lost his capacity for the Word of God, cannot discern it, does not hear it, does not appreciate it, almost ceases—hear me carefully in this apparent contradiction—almost ceases to desire it, wherever that is true, there results in the life of that man, woman, community, a great ceaseless searching restlessness; and I believe that the restlessness of our own age is due to the fact that our age is in the midst of the famine of the Word of God, a famine following upon its idolatry, national, social, and individual.

But is there such restlessness? Think with me for a moment. I maintain there is an ignorant restlessness. By that I mean a restlessness that does not understand itself in any measure, and I believe that that ignorant restlessness which is unconscious of the meaning of its own fruitless search is that of nothing less than a search for the Word of God. Men do not know it. They would not so name it; but every attempt to satisfy the life without God is in the last analysis an attempt to find the Word of God. I suppose the old illustration, the most familiar perhaps, the most sublime in Scripture, is the natural one that comes to the mind at this moment. Paul's great word to the Ephesians, "Be not drunken with wine, wherein is riot, but be filled with the Spirit." What did the apostle mean? Why link these two things together? Because they are bound together, because in the underlying meaning of the attempt to get some kind of satisfaction out of wine is the cry of the soul after God. And all the restlessness of this ignorant age is the panting of the human heart after the Word of God. There are men and women running from north to south—from north to east, to be true to the figure of my text—from sea to sea, from land to land, in ceaseless, roving restlessness. What do they want? Ask them and they tell you, some new sensation, some new thing, some new thrill. What do they really want? They want the Word of God, they want God Himself, communicating to them through the Word that they may find the sustenance of their spiritual life. Oh, the restlessness of the worldling in London, as understood from the upper spaces, is the panting of the heart, in ignorance, after God. In such ignorant restlessness God is not recognized, and no sin is admitted. God is not talked of. It is a little out of date to talk of God among such people. They dismiss the word. Religion is taboo! God is not named, and sin is never mentioned. There is a great famine in the land.

But then there is a semi-conscious restlessness in this age, and you will find it in all the attempts to substitute something that is seemingly religious for God, and the Word of God. We are hearing a great deal about the new thought in religion. The whole movement, including Theosophy and Christian Science, what is it? It is a fruitless search after something to put into the place of God. It is the cry of the soul after God.

It is semiconscious; but do you want to know wherein lies the radical famine of all these new things? I will tell you in two sentences. God without government. Sin without guilt. God, oh yes, we believe in God, but not in the God of the throne, and the God of the white light, and the God of holiness, and the God of government, and the God Who is of purer eyes than to behold iniquity, and the God Who can by no means look upon sin, and the God Who claims the whole strength and mind and passion of a man. Not that God, but some sickly, sentimental ideal which is the God of these new movements; and the supreme revelation of their idea of God comes in that second sentence of mine, sin without guilt. Sin, oh, yes, it is the under side of good! It is the necessary shadow cast by light! It is a process in the evolution of the race! It is an infirmity, and the man who is a sinner is more to be pitied than anything else. Sin, oh, yes, but no guilt. The man is not to blame. There is to be no terror in his heart as he thinks of God. There is to be no shame in his face as he thinks of sin. And all these things are the false substitutes of a semi-ignorance, and they leave the heart hot and restless, wandering in the deserts, seeking for the Word of God. But I want to say to you tonight that a doctrine of God that leaves out government never gives the heart rest, and a doctrine of sin that does not admit guilt never heals the open sore of humanity's wound. There is no rest. It is a fruitless search.

But I am afraid I am bound to go further, and say that there is a conscious search after God which yet finds no answer. Our age is full of the lust of people who call themselves spiritual for new things. New preachers, new movements, new setting of truth, forsooth! God is honored with the lip, but not with the life; and even among these people sin is lightly, slightly treated. You say, "What do you mean by that?" I mean this. I know some people who would have me think of them as being pre-eminently spiritual, who are marvelously particular about the tithe, and mint, and anise, and rue and cummin, who have signed pledges not to touch everything they do not care much about, and yet who are forevermore neglecting love and charity and rightness, and the things which are the things of the holy God. And I think this last state is the worst of them all, because there is more light and less obedience among these people. In the midst of the famine they finger the Word of God, they do despite to it by making it minister to their own preconceived notion, never hear its deepest note, never catch its profoundest sound, never measure their lives by it. It is a poor business, and they are living in the midst of the famine, a famine for the Word of God.

Do you hear what Amos says: "They shall run to and fro to seek the Word of the Lord, and shall not find it"? This is perfectly true. Materialism is a perpetual lust, an unanswered agony of desire. Sensualism is a deadly opiate. Novelty is a pernicious irritant. It is a fruitless search. There is no substitute for the Word of God, directly heard by the spirit of man and obeyed. Restlessness is fever. Fever is a destroying fire.

I turn, finally, for a moment to the last thought. What is the issue of it all? The prophet speaks of the fair virgins and the young men; and you see at once, beloved, that that is a superlative method of treating his subject. He does not say a word of the effect produced by the famine of the Word of God upon the full-grown man, tending toward arrest of development. He does not say a word concerning the effect of the famine upon the aged, merging toward the shadows where the light ceases. He chooses the fair virgins, the young men, those who are the strongest and best, the most hopeful, those most able to endure. He takes them as illustration, and he makes his illustration absolutely superlative by his choice. Not, I repeat, the man who is in the midst of the battle, and presently expects to lay down his weapons. The prophet does not speak of the effect of the famine upon this man or upon the age, but upon the fair virgin, with the bright and beautiful cheek, and the lustrous eyes, and the light of hope. The young man with the strength and vigor of his young manhood upon him, the youth for whom the fingers of morning are ever busy, laying on their gold and vermilion. These, what of them in the day when the Word of God fails, what of them? They shall faint for thirst. If I may venture with all reverence to put the statement of the prophet into another form it is this, that the best without God fails, that the finest capacities lacking their true inspiration faint and pass and perish. It is a superlative illustration, a daring one, an arresting one, one that has appealed to my own heart as I have prayed and thought of my message.

Follow the issue naturally. If this be true of them, what of the rest? Where the Word of God fails, what happens? Morning is overcast, noon is a tempest, and night is starless. And yet—oh, the terror of it!—we tremble if we hear of the possibility of an army's invasion. We blanch with fear if we think that plague is about to visit our shores and our cities. We are afraid of the failure of the harvest. But when we speak of the famine of the Word of God, even we who name His name are in danger of being interested and nothing more. And yet the greatest disease that can come to a nation, the final judgment of a nation, the thing that presages its decay and disintegration and downfall, is famine of the Word of God. Find me a nation largely composed of men and women and little children who do not hear the voice, or see the vision, or feel the touch of God, and I will find you a people marching to ruin, despite their armaments and their policies, and their banners and their boastings. "Lest we forget." It was a prophetic word. "A famine of the word of God," carelessness about what He says and thinks, with a restless search after something, which does not understand the meaning of its own endeavor, and ends only in the hectic flush and the devouring fever. I am bound to say that I think we, as a nation, are living right there. There has been a famine of the Word of God.

Now hear me as I utter my final word. The prophet of today, like Amos, cannot, if he climb the mountains of vision and see from God's standpoint, be blind to the sins of other nations; for he can never forget that God is the God of all the nations. The prophet of today will see quite clearly the cruelty of Russia, the frivolity of France, the rationalism of Germany, the civic corruption of America. But the prophet cannot forget the relation of privilege and responsibility, and he cannot forget the fiery, burning, searching words of his Lord, that it is to be more tolerable for Sodom and Gomorrah in the day of judgment than for the cities that heard His voice, Capernaum, Chorazim, and Bethsaida. Russia will have a far better chance in the final judgment of the nations than England, because England has had infinitely more light. Feeling as I do that the thing rests almost as a burden on my heart night and day that we are living in the midst of a great famine, not of bread, but of the Word of God, what is this famine? It is a curse upon our idolatries. Do not forget that, like all the curses of God, it is an effect following a cause. God never curses capriciously. The curses of God are the harvests of man's own wrongdoing. If we have lost our sense of the Word, and our love for the Word, and our confidence in the Word, and our appreciation of the Word, why is it? It is God's judgment, but it is an effect following a cause. To turn from the cause will be to disannul the effect.

And how shall we turn from the cause? By turning from our idolatries to the living God. You notice the emphasis I am inclined to put upon this, which I think is the prophetic emphasis. I am not saying we must turn to the Word of God to be corrected from our idolatries. I do not think that is the order. We must turn from our idolatry to find the Word of God. If we are gathered to study the Word of God we had better begin by putting our idols away. The Word of God will be a sealed book to me, though I desire to teach it, unless my idols are set aside. Granting, for the sake of my argument, that the teacher himself has defined his relation to God, and the idols are broken down, and God reigns in the life, he cannot teach it to you if idolatry remains in your life. Holiness guards the wicket gate to the Word of God. As it is true that if iniquity be in my heart, God will not hear me, it is equally true if iniquity be in my heart, I cannot hear God. The first condition for the study of the Word of God, the fundamental condition, the absolute condition is not the intelligence of the schoolman; it is the clean heart, and the pure soul, and the temple in which no idol lives or hides. If the idols are broken down, if we are governed absolutely in the temple of God by the will of God, then there is no famine in the land. God's Word flames with light, and thrills with power, and is food for the hungry soul as much as ever. But you can read it, study it, analyze it, tabulate it, and remember it, and die for lack of it if in your heart the idols remain, and the impure thing abides. May God in His infinite grace and mercy and power take His own message out of all my words, and speak it to your hearts.

CHAPTER XVII

THE STUMBLING-BLOCK OF THE CROSS

The stumbling-block of the Cross.
GALATIANS 5:11.

THE AUTHORIZED VERSION READS, "THE OFFENCE OF THE Cross." The apostle was arguing that if he would but preach circumcision, he would no longer be persecuted; if he would conform to the method of those Judaizing teachers whose influence he was combating, the stumbling-block of the Cross, that in the Cross which offends, would be done away, and consequently persecution of himself would cease.

Perhaps a third translation of the passage may be permitted, "the scandal of the Cross." This would undoubtedly shock our sensibilities, and yet it is really in harmony with the thought of the writer. The Greek word *skandalon* indicates a stone of stumbling, something over which men fall, something that does not aid progress, but rather prevents it. There can be no doubt from the whole context that the Apostle was referring to a prevalent antipathy to the Cross itself, and especially to the Cross as the center of a religion. The offense of the Cross, the stumbling-block of the Cross was, as I have already said, even more literally and bluntly, the scandal of the Cross. In the early days of Christianity a stigma attached to the followers of the Nazarene, particularly on account of the Cross. It was something so utterly and absolutely unheard of that religion should be centered in a Cross; and whether to the Jew, the Roman, or the Greek, the Cross was a stumbling-block, a scandal, an offense, something utterly and absolutely objectionable. To the Jew the Cross meant disgrace, for it had been associated with the breaking of law, and its penalty: "He that hangeth is accursed of God." To the Roman the Cross was an indication of defeat, and there was no crime in Rome equal to the crime of defeat. To win was everything. To lose was disgrace, and the proud patrician Roman, looking upon Jesus crucified, held Him in supreme contempt because He was beaten. And to the Greek the Cross was the utterest degradation. To the Greek who stood for the perfecting of individualism, for the ideal man, in form and feature and fashion—for every man aimed at perfection—for a man to be nailed to a Cross, and to be mauled in his death, was disgusting. To preach the Cross to the Jew was to preach the instrument with which the lawbreaker was punished. To preach the Cross to the Roman was to preach to a victorious people the instrument of defeat. To preach the Cross to the Greek was to preach to people who were seeking for perfect individual culture, the most disagreeable and disgusting method of death and failure. A stigma was attached to the religion of Jesus because at its very heart and center stood this Cross.

And yet, brethren, all this was superficial and sentimental objection. To understand the real meaning of the offense of the Cross we must inquire why this Man of Nazareth was nailed to it. I propose, then, to speak about this offense of the Cross: first, as to its real meaning in those olden days; and, second, whether the offense of the Cross has ceased, whether the age has really outgrown its objection thereto.

First, then, let us look back. Standing in imagination on

THE STUMBLING-BLOCK OF THE CROSS 219

the green hill outside the city wall, and looking upon the Man of Nazareth Who hangs upon that Cross, we ask this one question, Why have they crucified Him? And I think we shall find that the deepest offense of the Cross existed before the Cross, and that the Cross was the outcome of it. That in Jesus against which Hebraism, calling to its aid Roman power, flung itself in fury existed before they erected the Cross, and the Cross was the most logical outcome of the offense.

Let us look carefully. The Cross of Jesus, viewed from the human side, was man's answer to all that He was, and all that He taught. Jesus of Nazareth was the most revolutionary Teacher the world has ever seen, because He was the supreme Voice and Life in the proclamation of the truth of Divine government and Divine order. In His return in life and teaching to the first laws and principles of God's humanity He was a perpetual protest against the then existing order of things; and to the men of His own age there was but one alternative, either to accept His teaching and economy, and reverse theirs, or to murder Him and silence His voice, and be rid of Him. It was the offense which His conception of things gave to their conception of things that erected the Cross.

Did you ever quietly sit down alone to ask yourself the question I have propounded? Why did they crucify Christ? Have you ever considered that it was an infinite puzzle to the Roman procurator? He came to his own conclusion after a while, and he shrewdly approached the truth. He came to the conclusion that for envy they had delivered Him. He did not reach the deepest meaning of their determination to crucify Him when Pilate said that. Their envy grew out of something deeper. In public examination and private interview Pilate attempted to understand the meaning of the malice that was manifesting itself in hounding this Man to death, and he signally failed. In his failure there is cause for our closer investigation. Why did they crucify Him? We must find our answer in His teaching. He spoke out of the sense of eternity to the capacity for eternity in the heart of man. You may characterize the teaching of Jesus by borrowing a great phrase from the Old Testament and applying it in a new connection, "Deep calleth unto deep." When men heard Him they did not understand Him perfectly, but they felt, somehow, that He had spoken to the very depth of their personality. When He came down from the mountain multitudes followed Him, and were astonished at Him, for they said, "He taught them as One having authority, and not as their scribes."

What, then, was the difference between Him and the scribes? He spoke out of the sense of the relation of the infinite and the spiritual to the finite and the material. He set the measurement of eternity upon passing time. Wherever He went He said, "Repent," which meant, Change your mind, your thinking is wrong, your action is wrong, you have departed from the center of things, your measurements are false, your balances are evil, your judgments are perverted! He flung against the materialized age the force of His spiritual conception. He made heaven's light break upon earth's darkness. The voice of God sounded again in the deeps of human nature, and o'er all the region as He passed, men felt the atmosphere of heaven enwrapping them, and they hurried after Him, for never Man spake as He spake. That is the deeper secret in the ministry of Jesus. He was a voice from God, nay, the very Word of God incarnate, speaking in the syllables of human speech, and yet with all the force of infinite truth. What are men to do with that truth? My brethren, then as today, men standing in the presence of Christ have but one alternative. They must do one of two things. They must either crown Him or crucify Him. There is no middle course. And if you ask me why they crucified Christ, I tell you it was because they declined to submit themselves to the spiritual conceptions which He proclaimed, because they would have none of His views of things, because in their deepest heart, notwithstanding all their religiousness, they were godless. And when they silenced that voice, they silenced the voice of the infinite. When they took that Man to the Cross, they flung out the One Who had offended them by revealing the fact that all their thinking and all their life were false.

And yet again. The Cross of Jesus viewed from the Divine side was the logical issue of His own teaching. He Who might have summoned the legions of heaven to His side submitted to the Cross, and so by a mystery of healing love transformed the world's curse into God's benediction.

> The very spear that pierced His side
> Drew forth the blood to save.

All this was utterly beyond their comprehension. All this they could not answer, nor did they see the faintest gleam of its light. They were scandalized in Him, and crucified Him; and the Cross became the stumbling-block, the offense, the scandal of the age.

This is a very general statement. Let us try to look at it a little more closely. I must content myself with a mere summary of the cardinal truths that He came to reveal to men in His teaching and life. He came, first, to reveal to men the character of God. He revealed to man the truth that God is love. And, my brethren, let no one misunderstand that statement. May I not take it for granted that there is no need for me to say that when you have said that you have said everything, and having said everything, nothing must be omitted from the thinking? When I say that He came to reveal God as love I do not mean to say He revealed the fact that God is tender, and pitiful, and gracious, and compassionate at the expense of holiness and righteousness and truth. There is no fiercer fire burning in the universe of God than the fire of God's love; and if you could for one moment persuade me that God was merely a God of pity, then you would persuade me that the whole fabric of the universe is unsafe. He came to show men that God is love, and He revealed the love of God not merely in the tender, sweet, and gentle words that perpetually fell from His lips, but in the fiery, white-hot scorn that He poured forth as a lava flood against some, for you never find Jesus angry but that if you track His anger back to its source you will find His anger proceeded from His love. Perhaps the simplest illustration is the best. He was angry—do not forget it, my masters, He was angry when He said, "Suffer the little children, and forbid them not, to come unto Me: for of such is the Kingdom of heaven." We nearly always repeat that word as though it was some soft sweetness falling from His lips. Put the thunder in the next time you repeat it, or you miss something. The disciples were preventing the children. The disciples imagined He could have no time for children, and He was angry when He said, "Suffer the little children, and forbid *them* not," and there was thunder in His voice. Why was He angry? Because a little child was to be kept away from Him, and the thunder was as much an expression of His love as the sweet winsomeness of the permission given to the children to come. When I see Him with those bairns in His arms, and His dear hands upon their heads, and His face wreathed in laughter as He looked into their eyes, I see His love no more than when He rebuked the disciples for preventing their approach. Or when He said, "Woe unto you, scribes and Pharisees, hypocrites!" I listen and I hear Him finish His sentence, and I find the reason of the thunder, "Ye shut the Kingdom of heaven against men." At the back of all the anger is love, and He came to reveal God to man as the God of love in all the fulness of the word.

In His teaching moreover, He revealed the fact of God's actual and positive and present interest in all the affairs of human life. Men had relegated God in their thinking to the position of an abstraction that formed the basis of a creed, but He brought Him back into the position of continuous conduct. He said, God clothes lilies, and is with the dying bird; He is everywhere, He knows all you have need of, and He is holding His court of investigation in the deepest thinking of your life. He taught us the immanence of God, and the activity of God, and the government of God in the last detail of human life.

Then He taught men the truth of the supremacy of character. In the great Beatitudes of His great Manifesto He pronounced no single blessing on any man for having anything, or doing anything. All the Beatitudes are chaplets placed upon the brow of character.

Again, He came to reveal to men the true social order. He revealed the whole fact of the social order in half a dozen sentences. I think I may say in one of them, and that will be quite sufficient for our illustration. "Whosoever would be first among you shall be your servant." It is well that we should think in the presence of that in order that it may sink into mind and heart. If we would be great we must strip ourselves of our purple, and gird ourselves and serve somebody else. That is radical. It goes to the roots of things, and drags down the man high and lofty in the dignity of position, and makes another man great and mighty because he is serving someone else. Build your social order upon that conception, and you will have found the golden age for which men long have been looking, but which has not yet arrived.

Notice still further how He defended the dignity and the rights of men against all forms of tyranny and oppression. Listen to His Woes. He began His ministry with "Blessed." He ended it with "Woe." Over against the eight Beatitudes are the eight curses. It is an interesting study. But listen to the Woes. They are all hurled against men who tyrannize and oppress; and the whole teaching of Jesus concerning man is that a man has no right to bind himself beneath tyranny and be content. The teaching of Jesus is that there may be a good deal of incipient blasphemy in the popular idea that a man should stay in the position wherein he was born, and be content. The teaching of Jesus is that every man has inherent rights, and any man who comes between the individual and the throne of God is to be dealt with drastically, and the Woe that falls from the lips of incarnate purity is pronounced against him.

These were some of the things that Jesus taught. Now, for a moment look at the time in which He lived. It was a time characterized by the degradation of religion. There was a clouding of the Divine by the false interpretation of the men who professed to understand the Divine. The high priest was a Sadducee. The Sadducee was a rationalist in religion. The Sadducee, to take the Bible definition, was a man who did not believe in resurrection, or in spirit, or in angel. And the high priest was a Sadducee, and the men associated with Him were either Sadducees or Pharisees, men who were professing to interpret God, and all the while were hiding God, until all through that age there was a widespread infidelity, which was the revolt of the heart of man against the blaspheming of God that existed in high places. And into the midst of this age, hiding God by its very religion, Jesus came to unveil Him. Do you wonder that the religious leaders of the movement crucified Him?

Or move a step forward and see the age in the matter of government. Government was based upon expedience, upon policy. Far and wide, o'er all the earth the iron rule of Rome obtained, and the proud Hebrew was bowing his neck to that rule. Everywhere government was based upon might. Jesus came down into the midst of it all, and revealed the fact that the only government to which man ever ought to submit himself is the government that is based upon right, and that is the one and only government of God. He came and preached, as we have said, the supremacy of character in an age characterized by Pharisaism, which He described as being a whited wall, while within there was corruption and rottenness. In that age He came to preach the new order, the one social order of service, as the way to greatness, when all around vested interests were grinding men, and men were being taught that their only safety lay in their submission to the things that oppressed them. Around Him was an enslaved democracy, wickedly content, easily led. An enslaved people, and Jesus Christ came and exercised His ministry in the midst of it. As you look back at the age, and listen to the teaching, you are driven to the conclusion that the only place for Truth amid such conditions was the scaffold. The very genius of such a condition as existed in those days expressed itself in the Cross of Jesus.

And now I come to my second inquiry. Having seen the reason for the offense of the Cross, then we are inclined to say, Everything is changed now. That is what I want to ask, and my preliminary inquiry respects the Cross itself. Has the Cross altered in its essential meaning? Has truth changed? Has Christ gone back upon any positions of His earthly life and teaching? My brethren, I must apologize for these questions.

The very asking of them seems to me to smack of blasphemy. He is, as is God, unchangeable, "the same yesterday, today, and forever." Everything that He announced as truth when He was here is truth now. He has no new message to this age. I will not say if Christ came to London He would thus preach. It is a supposition I am always in revolt against. Christ is in London, and He is so speaking. Whether we hear or not may depend upon ourselves, but everything He said in the days of the Judean and Galilean and Perean ministry He is saying here and now.

Then my question must proceed a step further. Has the age altered? I am not proposing to discuss the age in any application other than that important to ourselves. What are the forces in the midst of which we are living today. There is still abroad the spirit of Sacerdotalism, which veils the face of God, and libels Him before humanity. I am not speaking of the Sacerdotalism of any section of the Christian Church, but of that general attempt, that cursed, and damnable attempt that is still prevalent, to stand between the individual soul of man and God. It is not the peculiar property of any one Church. It is to be found almost everywhere. You find it in Romanism. The very genius of Romanism, that with which I quarrel, is its dogmatic avowal that it interprets God to me. Personally I do not quarrel with the Romanist who wants candles and incense, and vestments. My quarrel is with the man who says to me, We represent God, and unless you see God this way, you cannot see Him. My quarrel with him is not merely because he makes such a puerile claim, but because when he tells me he is revealing God he is hiding God.

But there is not merely the Sacerdotalism of Romanism, but of Angelicanism, and also that of what is called Modernism in Biblical interpretation, the new priestism of scholarship, which tells the people that they must accept the views of experts on the meaning of its message, or whether it is true. All this is resulting in the veiling of the face of God.

And there is yet another form of priestism which I would speak of as Holinessism. Let no one imagine I am saying anything to undervalue holiness; but this movement which consists in a scheme of teaching, and a mechanical arrangement for blessing, interpreted by teachers who interfere in my life, and tell me what I am to do or not to do, is priestism clothed in a new garb. The terrible part of all this is that man is crying for an interpretation of God, and his crying is the result of his sin; and instead of turning to the one Interpreter, and one Priest, he will accept the view of anybody. We are in the midst of an age overshadowed by Sacerdotalism in one aspect or another, and men are not seeing the clear and open vision of God as they ought to see it.

And if you come to the question of human government, how many of us believe in God? There is not a government in the world at this hour that believes in God absolutely and utterly. There is not a government in the world at this hour that will not weaken in loyalty to righteousness at some point of policy. Where is the government that believes in God first and last? Do not let us waste time in discussing governments. How about ourselves? How far do we believe in God? How many business enterprises do we enter upon, purely upon the basis of profit and loss? My brethren, vested interests are still enthroned, and we will have it so. Men are still enslaved, waste and want abound on every hand. I need not stay with its description. What I want to say is this, that everything that Jesus stood for, and everything that the Cross really means as to deep underlying principle, is as unpopular today as when Jesus was crucified. The age is not Christianized.

Thank God, there are Christian people in the age, and, thank God, their influence has forced men to certain Christly acts in the age. But the thinking of the age, the planning of the age, the policy of the age are not Christian, and the scandal of the Cross has not ceased. This living Christ of God, dying on the Cross, is as much crucified in our midst today as He was of old. But the working out of a principle into human observation upon the green hill far away did not exhaust the principle, and the principle obtains at this moment.

If we have really any fellowship with Him, we stand where He stood. We stand for the things that He stood for. Identification with Jesus in the Cross does not mean that from the Cross I merely obtain the benefit which is to be an assurance against hell and insurance of heaven. It means that life is identified with Jesus in the protest against the veiling of the face of God, and in determined and constant unveiling of that face before men. Has He no voice today? Is there no way in which He can make Himself heard? It is His will that His people should speak for Him, and the only way in which they can do so is the way of the Cross. To speak for Jesus out of the midst of His Cross in experimental identification with Him therein will bring men to a Calvary of persecution and ostracism today as ever. But if it bring us there, our chief joy will be that in that ostracism we have touched the inner meaning of fellowship with Jesus Christ. Oh, that we may not only look upon the Cross as something outside ourselves, but that we may press to the heart of it, to be identified with all it stands for, and bear the offense, the shame, the scandal of it.

> I take, O Cross, thy shadow,
>   For my abiding place;
> I ask no other sunshine than
>   The sunshine of His face;

> Content to let the world go by,
>   To know no gain nor loss,—
> My sinful self my only shame,
>   My glory all the Cross.

It is for us to ask ourselves, How far in us are the things for which Jesus stood, and which led Him to that Cross, obtaining and being manifest in the affairs of men? For as the Cross of old set its doom upon selfishness and unveiled the face of God, and, blessed be His name, made it possible for every man to have free access to Him, so the Cross stands for these things today, and while in all the wooing tenderness of the mystery of love as therein revealed we call the wounded and the halt, and the lame and the burdened, and the oppressed to that Cross for healing, by that selfsame Cross we are to be the sworn foes of all the forces that are against God and against humanity.

CHAPTER XVIII

THE WORD BECAME FLESH

And the Word became flesh, and dwelt among us . . . full of grace and truth.

JOHN 1:14.

WHATEVER, IN THE COMPLEXITY OF PRESENT-DAY THOUGHT, may be our view of the method of the advent, it is impossible to deny that nigh two thousand years ago that happened which has absolutely and completely revolutionized human thinking and human life. The student of history is always interested in tracing great streams to their sources. The rise and fall of dynasties, great discoveries, revolutions, all of them are important and interesting, and yet in some senses all these things are related directly or indirectly to the one event described in the mystic language of this text.

In this advent of Jesus there was both a crowning and a comprehension of all that was excellent in the past; and the conception and initiation of all the ideas and movements which are lifting humanity ever nearer to God.

We come to this statement of John the mystic in order to consider what it teaches concerning the fact of the advent, concerning the revelation resulting from that fact, and, finally, concerning the values resulting from the revelation.

In order that we may see the simplicity of the statement, I have omitted the parenthesis. It is important. It states a truth concerning the Person Whom we are to consider from a slightly different standpoint. It lies in the heart of this verse by way of explanation and exposition, and yet it may be omitted without doing any violence to the thought. We consider, then, this simple and sublime statement, "The Word became flesh, and tabernacled among us . . . full of grace and truth."

The statement of fact which this verse contains can be understood only as we remember that in this prologue of the Gospel of John the verse in which the text occurs is intimately connected by way of declaration with the first verse of the chapter. The intervening verses constitute a parenthesis. Consequently we bring these two verses together in order that we may understand the facts declared in our text. I will read them in intimate connection. "In the beginning was the Word, and the Word was with God, and the Word was God. And the Word became flesh, and tabernacled among us . . . full of grace and truth." This is one continuous statement, and the fact that there is a great descent from the first statements to the second demonstrates the wisdom of inserting the parenthesis, for this helps us to see how great is the descent.

While the first and second statements present one complete declaration, they nevertheless constitute a perfect balance. The first three statements must be borne in mind as we consider the second three, for the second three need the first three.

There are three first statements: "In the beginning was the Word"; "the Word was with God"; and "the Word was God." There are three second statements: "The Word became flesh"; "and dwelt, pitched His tent among us"; and "full of grace and truth." Now, if we take these two series and bring them together, not exactly as one continued statement, but part to part, we shall see that the whole declaration tells how infinite and hidden mysteries came into the realm of finite and revealed things. "In the beginning was the Word" . . . "The Word became flesh." "The Word was with God" . . . "and pitched His tent among us." "The Word was God" . . . "full of grace and truth." Let us attempt an examination of these three couplets.

Taking the first half of the first, every phrase defies us. Every word is beyond our comprehension. "In the beginning"! We may at once reverently declare that the thought transcends the possibility of our understanding. It is one of those matchless sweeps of inspiration that go beyond all the thinking of man. "In the beginning." I lay my hand on anything in this world, and I begin to ask questions concerning its origin. I begin to track it through long and tedious processes back to the point of its initiation. No man has ever been able to do this successfully. We have never been able to say the final thing concerning origins by the processes of investigation and discovery, but we are always attempting to find them, and rightly so. Man has more than once formulated a philosophy, has more than once suggested a solution, but as surely as he has done so, within a decade, or quarter of a century, his philosophy has passed away, and his solution is found to be false. This phrase takes us behind all the processes, behind the fact of the initiation of all things material and mental, behind all the things of which man can be conscious, and we bow in the presence of the statement, and reverently declare that it transcends us.

Or if I take the other expression, "the Word," I am equally conscious of disability to comprehend its final meaning. I am personally inclined to think we get to the sublimest meaning as we take the simplest, and remember that a word is an expression. A word is that by which one person expresses his thought to another, so that the other may be able to understand it. A word spoken by one person to another is the revelation of something in the mind of the one that the other did not know, and could know only through that word. A word is a revelation made, a thought communicated. "The Word was in the beginning," a method of manifestation, a method of speech, that in and of God by which He made something of Himself known to those without Himself, apart from Himself, beyond Himself.

You inquire whether the Word was a Person, and I reply, What do you mean by a person? Until you have defined your term "person"—which, by the way, never occurs in Scripture—I cannot answer you. If you tell me that man is a person, I say, Yes, undoubtedly he is; but he is finite. Now, a finite person is an incomplete person, and therefore not a perfect revelation of what a person is. A perfect Person must be infinite also.

This at least is declared, that in the beginning there was an expression of Deity. But that is not helpful to us, for it was beyond our finite comprehension. "The Word became flesh," that is where the help begins. When the infinite Person—and I do not quite know what that means—becomes a finite Person Whom I can understand, I do pass into some new appreciation of the character and the value, and the fact of the infinite that transcends me, "In the beginning was the Word. . . . And the Word became flesh."

A few words only are necessary concerning the second of these couplets, "And the Word was with God." That which was the method of Divine speech and manifestation was with God, and again I freely confess to you here are terms, finite terms struggling to express infinite meaning, and failing even though they be the words of inspiration. Then I read, "He pitched His tent among men"; and the thing that has baffled me and perplexed me, and overwhelmed me in the realm of Deity, which is beyond my comprehension, becomes something I can look at within the realm of human life: "He tabernacled among men."

And then, finally, when I read in the great introductory word, "the Word was God," both with God, and God; both method of Divine expression, and that which expresses itself, again I am overwhelmed, I cannot understand. Again I feel that I have read a simple sentence that is so full of mystery as absolutely to defy my explanation. Then I read "full of grace and truth," and I have an unveiling of the nature of God, though perhaps no explanation of the method. I have seen One Who is flesh, and pitches His tent by my side in the valleys where I dwell, upon the mountains to which I climb, in the midst of the life I live; and in the life of this One grace and truth flash and flame in glory. I am told that that is God, and I feel, not that I have been able to encompass all the mystery of Deity by revelation, but that I have been taken through a wicket gate, and my eyes are gazing out upon light such as I had never seen. I have at least been able to look through a veil at that which unveiled would have blinded me: "In the beginning was the Word," and I do not understand it. "The Word became flesh," and it has come within the reach of my hand. "The Word was with God," and I cannot comprehend the meaning of the statement, but the Word "tabernacled among us," pitched His tent near us, and I at least may draw near and behold. "And the Word was God," and there is no more in the statement than there was in all the other things that men had said long before. But "full of grace and truth," and here are two essential facts concerning God which will help me.

Pass over this ground with me again. "In the beginning was the Word" . . . "the Word became flesh." What does this signify? Eternity, the ageless age, coming into time; expressing itself in the language of time, manifesting itself in the method of time. "In the beginning was the Word," the utterance of God; not letters, or syllables or words merely; not a literature which I can commence here, and finish presently, but the Word of God. Not only that which fills the whole fact of space so far as I can imagine it; but "the Word became flesh," that is, came to a locality; it came to a place to which I can travel; it came to a place to which coming, I can see.

"The Word was in the beginning," the infinite, but it became flesh, the finite. "In the beginning was the Word," the infinite Wisdom, the all-encompassing Wisdom, the Wisdom that lies at the back of all manifestation, the Wisdom of which the preacher sang long ago in the Proverbs. But "the Word became flesh," that is, Wisdom began to spell itself out in an alphabet. We sometimes quote the words of Jesus uttered to John in Patmos as though they were full of dignity. So they were, but they have another tone also. "I am the Alpha and the Omega, the first and the last." There is some sense in which in God there is no first, no last; and, consequently, that is not a figure of completeness intended only to create amazement and wonder. It is the symbol of simplicity, it is the figure of the alphabet. "I am the Alpha and the Omega," the alphabet which the little child may learn. Yet remember that all literature lies within the compass of the twenty-six letters of the alphabet. Do not talk to your children about a thing being as easy as A B C. It is the hardest thing we have to learn. You have forgotten the task, but it was such. You did not know it, but in that task you were beginning to climb up to that literature which you love, and all its vast reaches lay before you. So when the Word became flesh infinite Wisdom expressed itself in an alphabet. That began nineteen centuries ago. There had been attempts before, hieroglyphics before, but at last the mysterious hieroglyphics of the past found the key of interpretation in Alpha and Omega—the Alphabet. We must be little children to begin; but we never arrive at the infinite literature to which it introduces us until we have learned it. The Word, the infinite Wisdom, dwelt with God, and was the mighty Workman at His right hand when He created, by whatever process I care nothing. That Wisdom became an alphabet when a baby Boy lay upon His mother's breast in the Judean country.

But notice the next couplet of contrast. "The Word was with God." There are those who can explain it to me. I cannot. I make no attempt to do it. But I will attempt the next. He "tabernacled among us." This Person Who defies definition—for I do not know the meaning of "person," as I have already said—this Person "tabernacled among us," and John of the mystic vision had looked at Him, and warm-hearted Peter had gazed upon Him, and all the rest had seen Him. He "tabernacled among us." Now for the parenthesis a moment. "We beheld His glory, glory as of the only begotten from the Father." "We beheld," we saw that which was with God, and the statement overwhelms us. I love the other rendering of that, not accurate translation perhaps, but certainly correct interpretation. He pitched His tent by us, and came to live where we lived. He pitched His tent down by the side of my tent. It is the figure of the Arab nation, and of one who is going to take the same journey with me and be under the same rule with me. He "tabernacled among us." We are pilgrims through the world, coming out of darkness, and passing toward the darkness. He "tabernacled among us," put His tent down by the side of our tent.

Yet that is not all, and we must interpret this word "tabernacled" by the religious thinking of the man who wrote the words, by John's religious conviction and upbringing. If you do that you will see that this word "tabernacled" has its explanation in the religious mysteries of the past. I go back again to the kindergarten days of religion, to the hieroglyphics of the past, and I find the Tabernacle. You remember how in the Old Testament that word "Tabernacle" is written descriptively in two ways. Sometimes it is called the Tabernacle of witness, and sometimes it is called the Tabernacle of the congregation, and both are faulty. May I take the same ideas, and express them in other words? The Tent of meeting rather than the Tabernacle of the congregation. The Tent of testimony, rather than the Tabernacle of witness. That is to say, when in your Old Testament you read that the Tabernacle was the Tabernacle of the congregation, it does not mean that it was the place where men congregated for worship, but that it was the place where God and man met for fellowship. The Tabernacle of meeting was the place, God-appointed, where He met with man, and to which man came to meet with Him.

It was the Tent of testimony, which did not mean that it was the place where men proclaimed the truth of God. The Tent of testimony was the place where God spoke to men, and men listened. Now, wrote John, who had been brought up in that religion, and to whom that symbolism was always luminous, the Word pitched His tent among us. That was the Tabernacle for which we had been waiting, toward which we had been looking. He became at once Tent of meeting between God and man, and Tent of testimony through which God spoke to man. And so in this Word, the infinite and incomprehensive mystery of the eternities, Who became finite and comprehensive in time, by becoming flesh, I find my tent of meeting with God. He is all I am, but He is all

God is. And when I lay this hand of mine upon His hand, I have touched the hand of a man such as I am; but I have taken hold of the might of God. And when I look into the eyes of the Man Who pitched His tent among Galilean fishermen I have looked into human eyes all brimming with love, but through them I have looked out into the very heart of the Infinite God. He is the Tent of meeting. I find God in Christ, as nowhere else. I cannot find Him in Nature. I see His goings; I hear the thunder of His power; I mark the matchless beauty of the delicate touch of His pencil on the petals of the flowers; but I cannot find Him, I cannot reach Him. But here, as God is my witness, I come to the Christ— warm, sweet, tender, even yet:

> A present help is He:
> And faith has still its Olivet,
> And love its Galilee.

I feel in my spirit the consciousness of the human Christ; but enwrapping me all the fullness of the Godhead bodily. And because He pitched His tent by me, and pitches it by me still in all sympathy, I have found God, and if you take that away I have lost God. "He tabernacled among us," He pitched His tent by us. It was the Tent of meeting, and it was the Tent of testimony. Through that life God spoke so that I might hear; and to explain that I must use terms that seem to be contradictory, but the relation of which I am sure you will see. In Christ, the long, long silence became speech. But in Christ the thunder became a whisper. Silence became speech. Men had been waiting and longing and listening, climbing mountains for stillness, getting into loneliness to hear. They had heard, but they had never heard. They had heard the thunder of His power, but they had never heard all that they needed to hear. But in Him Who pitched His tent by the side of the fishermen, they heard. And the long silence and all the loneliness became the sweet speech for which men had waited; and all the thunder that had reverberated around the rocky fastnesses of Sinai became love whispers in the ears of listening individuals when He became flesh. "The Word became flesh, and pitched His tent among us."

"And the Word was God," and again I remit the mystery, "full of grace and truth." All that men saw and heard in Jesus was an unveiling of Deity. The attractiveness of His grace, the awfulness of His truth, were revelations to men of God.

If that is the fact of the incarnation, what is this inclusive revelation that it has brought to us? "The Word became flesh, and dwelt among us . . . full of grace and truth." Grace. You may express that in another way, in another phrase, in another sentence, of this selfsame writer. "God is love," "full of grace." Truth. You may express that also in another way. "God is light," "full of truth." Out of the grace came the redemption. Out of the truth was manifest the righteousness. The supreme revelation that Jesus made to men was not a revelation first of grace, or only of grace; not a revelation first of truth, or only of truth; but a revelation of the relation between "grace" and "truth."

Look at them in separation. Do not rob this word "grace" of its beauty by reading into it merely the ideas of a human system of theology. We behold him "full of grace," full of tenderness, full of gentleness, full of pity, full of all that winsomeness and attractiveness that made Him dear to children, and to needy men, and to sinning souls. We behold Him full of grace, full of grace to children, gathering them into His arms, putting them into the midst of His disciples; full of grace toward the afflicted, forevermore moved with compassion in the presence of any limitation. No cripple ever crossed the vision of Christ without Christ feeling the pain of all the cripple's limitation. Full of grace toward sinners. Take the New Testament and read it once more, and see if you can find one harsh thing He said to a sinner. Harsh things to oppressors and to sinners in that particular respect; but to someone taken in an act of sin, overwhelmed with the burden of sin, never an angry word. Full of grace, full of winsomeness, full of beauty. That is human. I am not dealing with all the infinite values of the word "grace," but with the simplicity of it as manifested in the life of this Man.

But "full of truth," capable of anger, capable of severity, capable of cursing as well as of blessing, with lips that could frame a "Woe" of unutterable terror as well as a "Blessed" of unutterable tenderness. Truth, and truth manifesting itself in anger against all selfishness, all tyranny, all sin. Grace acting in truth because it is grace. Truth acting in grace because it is truth. Here is the revelation that surprises. We have put these into two compartments. We often still speak of the grace of God and the righteousness of God as though they were poles asunder. They are never separated. They cannot be separated, and in the moment in which you deny truth, you deny grace. If there be no severity in God He is incapable of tenderness. Because there is love there is light, and it is love that will make no peace with the thing that spoils and harms and ruins. Grace and truth always go together. I have referred to His grace as manifested in His welcoming of the children. I have declared that truth could be manifest in anger, and these two things were operating at the same moment. When He said the most beautiful thing that men ever heard concerning little children, there was the tone of anger in His voice. The voice which was brimful of tenderness was vibrant with thunder. The disciples would have kept the children away. Why should He be angry for a small thing like that? It is not a small thing to keep a child away from Christ. It is a misunderstanding of God and the child; and the man who misunderstands God and the child is a curse to society, find him where you will. Jesus was angry, and through the tenderness of the welcome to the bairns throbbed the anger of truth against a false idea of dignity that excluded bairns. That is but illustration of grace and truth acting together, as they did from beginning to end. This was the revelation that came to the world.

So, finally, we see the values of this incarnation, truth concerning God and man, and grace joining men to God. In Jesus man found God. In Him man finds himself. These were the two things that men had lost, their knowledge of God and their knowledge of themselves. The great and final word of the teaching of one of the greatest Greek masters, Socrates, was, "Man, know thyself"; but men could not obey him, and Socrates had to say so. He confessed that it was not given to him to do anything but teach humanity to ask questions. He said some other teacher must come and answer the questions, and in that word he revealed how much of heaven's light he had in his own soul. Jesus came to answer the questions, and man found himself again, and realized the meaning of the mystery of his life, when the Word became flesh, and tabernacled, pitched His tent, by the side of him. And that tabernacling meant not merely truth concerning God and man, but triumph for God and man. It was God's highway to accomplish His purposes for man. It was man's highway unto the purposes of God.

Let me say in conclusion that we underrate the infinite value and meaning of this fact of incarnation when we speak of it as something in the past. The incarnation is an abiding fact, not something merely past. At this very hour that same

Person is at the center of the universe of God, the risen, glorified and enthroned Man. And if you tell me that that is to state something that cannot be believed because it transcends the possibility of belief, I tell you that it no more transcends the possibility of belief than does the fact of the historic incarnation. If He came into human flesh, and tabernacled among us, and if while there He could speak of Himself as yet in the bosom of the Father, and as yet being the Word with God, so remember that today He abides for manifestation at the center of the universe of God, the risen and glorified Man, at once a prophecy and a promise, hearing which we dare believe that at last He also will perfect us, and we shall see Him, and be with Him, and be like Him.

CHAPTER XIX

THE DEITY OF JESUS

In Him dwelleth all the fulness of the Godhead bodily.
COLOSSIANS 2:9.

IN THE MIDST OF MULTIPLIED SERVICE IT IS GOOD THAT WE should ever and anon remind our hearts of the central creeds which are the perpetual inspiration of service. No one, in thoughtful moments, can possibly undervalue a creed, a belief, a conviction, a certainty of the mind. I very readily concede that written creeds are encumbrances, imprisoning the mind, giving occasion for heresy hunting, and sometimes creating dishonesty on the part of such as profess to hold them. No written creed can suffice for a thinking man for long. But a creed is an absolute necessity. All service springs from belief. I do nothing save upon the basis of conviction, and the conviction which lies behind the conduct is the creed. Attempts have been made to differentiate between religion and theology, and I am quite conscious that there is a difference. But if we make the difference so marked as to entirely separate the two, then we have not understood either the one or the other. It has been said that religion is the life of God in the soul of a man, and theology is what a man thinks about God. I am prepared to accept that as correct definition, and yet I remind you that these two things are interdependent. A man's life is the outcome of his thought.

"As a man thinketh in his heart, so is he." And it is important to Christian life and Christian service that we should understand what our underlying creed is.

In Christianity creed has always to do with Christ. The Church is Christocentric, and all the differences among theologians are, in the last analysis, Christological differences. The difference between Trinitarian and Unitarian is difference in conviction about Christ. The difference between Calvinist and Arminian is difference in interpretation of the meaning of Christ and His work. Yes, and if you will let me come to a matter which some may consider to be of minor importance, the difference between what is known as the pre-millennial view of the advent and the post-millennial is, finally, difference in opinion concerning the Christ. So that if you take the minor differences, or the great differences which divide Christendom at this hour, they are all differences concerning Him.

From the writings of the Apostle Paul a very few sentences might be gathered as setting forth his own personal relation to Christ. As to experience, you would naturally select his word, "To me to live is Christ." As to the perpetual burden of his exhortation to Christian souls you would select his word, "Have this mind in you which was also in Christ Jesus." As to his conception of Christian service, of its nearest and furthest application, you would select the words, "I am debtor . . . I am ready . . . I am not ashamed of the Gospel." And, similarly, his Christology is expressed in this text. All that Paul wrote about Jesus Christ, and all that he believed concerning Jesus Christ, and all which he did in the name of Jesus Christ, finds here its simplest and sublimest expression.

This letter is the crowning one of his system so far as the glories of Christ are concerned, and it is co-related to the

Ephesian letter, in which he shows the Church in all its ultimate beauty. But in this letter he is dealing with Christ, and in my text you have the profoundest thing he wrote, the gathering up into one brief statement of all his conviction concerning Christ. "In Him dwelleth all the fulness of the Godhead bodily." This reveals his conception of Christ as to His purpose, as to his Person; and if we take it in connection with that which follows, we see what is his conviction concerning Christ as being the resource of His people: "and ye are made full in Him."

I propose an examination of the statement, an investigation as to its truth, and, finally, an application of it to ourselves and to our service.

Paul says: "In Him dwelleth all the fulness of the Godhead bodily"; and the first question I ask is one concerning the Person. Of whom is Paul writing? Is he at this point speaking of some mythical person? Has he lost his view of the Divine-human Christ at this point? He is evidently speaking of that Person to Whom he refers in the opening of this letter as "the Lord Jesus Christ." Who was this? I go back to the early history of Paul, and I find it characterized by his opposition to One of Whom he spoke as "Jesus of Nazareth." Upon two occasions does he so describe Him. Once when he declared that he had thought he ought to do everything in his power against the name of "Jesus of Nazareth," and again when he affirmed that Jesus so named Himself out of the excellent glory. In answer to his inquiry, "Who art Thou?" the voice said: "I am Jesus of Nazareth, Whom thou persecutest." So that in the earlier years of Paul he had known of One spoken of among men as Jesus of Nazareth. There had come into the life of this man a great change. How had the change come? It had come, according to his own testimony, on an occasion when there came to him a vision of this same Jesus and the sound of His voice. For him from that time this Person became infinitely more than he had dreamed. Saul of Tarsus had thought of this Man as of Nazareth. He may have thought of Him as perfectly sincere; but he certainly thought of Him as grossly mistaken, and he believed the things He taught were heresies, and that the claims He made could not be substantiated, and, consequently, that the men following Him were mistaken men. But that description of the Person dropped out of his vocabulary, and, instead of describing Him as Jesus of Nazareth, as the men of the age described Him, Paul came to describe Him as the "Lord Jesus," as "Christ Jesus," as "Jesus Christ."

Thus all this man's life and ministry after Damascus resulted from changed convictions about this Person. His opposition to the Person had been opposition to a Man Jesus, Who taught a new way, and Who had been put to death, and Who, His fanatical followers imagined, was alive again. His lifelong devotion was to the same Man Who had revealed Himself to him so as to change his entire conception of Him. What was the new conception that captured his heart, compelled his will, became the driving force in his life? We have it in my text. "In Him dwelleth all the fulness of the Godhead bodily." Paul's yielding of himself to this Man, Paul's surrender of himself, intellectually, emotionally, volitionally, was not the surrender of a disciple to a human teacher. It was the surrender of a man to his God. He had discovered in this Person all the fulness of the Godhead bodily. And when he made that discovery he saw the folly of his way, and ceased, with an abruptness that was volcanic, the whole of his antagonism to the followers of the Nazarene, dropped out of his vocabulary the purely human description, "Jesus of Nazareth," and spoke of Him ever after in words that indicated His infinite superiority and dignity as the "Lord Jesus," "Christ

Jesus," "Jesus the Christ." So that the Person to Whom my text refers is the Man of Nazareth. When Paul says here, "In Him dwelleth all the fulness of the Godhead bodily," he has not lost sight of the Man, he has not forgotten the One Whom he persecuted, Who revealed Himself to him on the Damascus road, the same and yet another. The eyes of the apostle are on that same Form which had appeared to him in glory upon the road, and his ear still hears in imagination that same human voice which, nevertheless, had in it the thunder of the infinite and all the accents of Deity. And of that One he says, "In Him dwelleth all the fulness of the Godhead bodily."

Let us look at these terms carefully. I begin with the word "Godhead." This word occurs nowhere else in the New Testament. We have in the Roman epistle, from the pen of the same writer, another word also translated "Godhead," where he speaks of that which man may discover of God by the light of nature. But the words differ in their etymology and in their use, and the difference is fairly accurately described in our own language by the difference between Divinity and Deity. The word in Romans may be translated Divinity; but the word here cannot be so translated. It has a deeper and profounder meaning, and we need most carefully to distinguish between these two terms, "Divinity," and "Deity." *Divinitas* was a common word in the Latin language. But the Latin Christian writers coined a new word—the word *Deitas*—from which our word Deity comes, and they coined that word to express the thought and meaning of this Greek word which occurs in my text. What, then, is the difference between the two? This particular word suggests absolute Godhead rather than manifestations of the attributes of Godhead. You find Divinity in every man, but you do not find Deity in every man. You can find Divinity through all Nature. There is not a blade of grass that has not something of Divinity in it; no flower that blossoms that has not some manifestation of Divine power, and Divine presence, and Divine beauty, and Divine glory. But you cannot take this word and use it in the same sense. There is not a single flower that blossoms, no fair tree that spreads itself in the forest, no mighty deep, in which you can discover absolute Deity. God can make nothing but that He puts something of Himself into it; and there are manifestations of God everywhere in Nature, but you do not find proper and absolute Deity anywhere in nature, nor in any human being. Now, mark what the apostle says here as to his conception of this Man of Nazareth. He says: "In Him dwelleth" not Deity merely, but "In Him dwelleth all the fulness of Deity."

That brings us to another word. The word "fulness" means the totality, the pleroma. Paul, in this Colossian letter, was dealing with the Gnostic heresy, and one of the favorite words of its exponents was pleroma, fulness. They were perpetually teaching the fulness of Deity, and that the fulness of Deity had its manifestations in a hundred ways. Said they, It is manifested through all men and all Nature, and the whole manifestation is the sum total of Deity. Paul takes their word and declares that the pleroma dwelleth in Him. He had seen the Man Jesus in the glorified form, had heard His voice. It was the same Man of Nazareth. Paul never dreamed that the One Who spoke to Him on the way to Damascus was any other than the One Who had spoken to men before. He had imagined Him to be a mere Man, child of His age, limited, ignorant, mistaken, blundering, murdered; but he found out that "in Him dwelleth the pleroma of essential Deity, the fulness of the Godhead." In the previous chapter, you remember those wonderful words in which Paul tells us of the three facts about this Lord Jesus

Christ. He first indicates His relation to Deity. To the Father He is "the Image of the invisible God," which does not mean something made like God, but the outshining into visibility of the actual and essential God. The only difference between Jesus and Deity was that Deity is invisible, and He was visible. Then he tells us the relation of this selfsame Person to creation. "In Him all things consist," hold together. He thus declares that the Man Who arrested him on the way to Damascus, Jesus of Nazareth, holds all created things together. He had found the Deity, Who spoke and it was done, and by Whose Almightiness the whole process of creation was held together, or was consistent. Finally, he declares the relation of this Person to the Church. By the way of the shedding of blood He had made reconciliation.

Jesus of Nazareth, the Image of the invisible God, Jesus of Nazareth, Creator of the whole universe and Sustainer thereof, Jesus of Nazareth, dying upon a rough Cross, God in passion for the salvation of a lost race. Everything brought down to the span of human observation, and yet "in Him dwelleth all the fulness of the Godhead bodily."

Now mark, I pray you, the other two words of the declaration: "Dwelleth bodily." "Dwelleth." Notice carefully the present tense, that perpetual present tense by which the apostle teaches that in Him, this Person toward Whom he is always looking, and concerning Whom he is forever writing, and Whom he is always serving, that "in Him dwelleth," the eternal and essential fact, a fact before incarnation. But the word in my text that arrests us, and is of value to us, is that final word "bodily." Do not read it as though it meant wholly. The word literally means corporeally, that this essential fact of Deity has been wrought out into permanent manifestation, that "in Him" is "all the fulness of the Godhead bodily." The Lord Jesus Christ, according to Paul, is God, essentially, absolutely, actively, corporeally; and the purpose of the bodily manifestation of Deity is that of intrusion into the consciousness of man. God came no nearer to humanity by the way of incarnation; but God did come into the consciousness of blind humanity by the way of incarnation.

Now, if you ask, How can this be? you will find no answer. It absolutely transcends explanation. But if you take away this corporeal Presence of Deity in the universe of created things, then what have you left? You do not explain the ineffable mystery of this Man's being and life. The fact is announced, and the mystery as it remains is the only satisfactory explanation of the great fact of the Christian religion.

That leads me to some words of investigation. I would that we could think of the Person of these records apart from many of the traditions in the midst of which we have grown up. We read the records, and we think of the Person as merely localized, and incidental, and of a past, and there results a subconscious impression which it is a little difficult to state in words, but which is incomplete, and therefore false.

Our need is the measure of our conception of God. It is by my lack that I have an idea of God. God is all that which I lack. By my emptiness I have a conception of the fulness of Deity. If I have no emptiness, if I am full and satisfied, then I lose my conception of what fulness means. Fulness is that which I have not. What are the things that man craves? First, life, and at the point where he knows he is limited, he thinks at once of the illimitable life, and he knows that is God. Man craves holiness, and at the point of his recognition of his own failure to realize holiness he thinks of the ineffable Holiness, of holiness, it may be, in the abstract, and yet as existing, and that is God. Strength man seeks after in every department, and at the point of his weakness he is conscious of the fact of strength that is not his, and that is God. Knowledge man is ever seeking; knocking at doors, demanding answers, prying into secrets, and forevermore he is arrested. But he knows that knowledge exists, that there is a knowledge that he does not possess, and that knowledge is God. If I have no sense of limitation I have no sense of God. God is to me that which is beyond my limitation.

In this Person of the Gospels I find One Who lacked the sense of limitation by which I think of God. There is not a sigh after life in all His words; He possesses it. He declares that He possesses it. He declares that He so possesses it that He can lay it down, and take it up by his Father's decree. Holiness? His one perpetual claim was that of sinlessness. He is not seeking after holiness. It is His. "Which of you convicteth Me of sin?" is His challenge to all the sinners of His age and every age. Strength? Throughout the whole of his life you see Him moving in conscious strength to the accomplishment of all the purposes of His Heart. Knowledge? He never asks questions; He never institutes inquiry. He is never learning. That was the supreme wonder of the men of His own age, not the wonder of the provincials of Nazareth, but the wonder of the metropolitans, of the scribes and Pharisees and rulers of Jerusalem. Listen: "How knoweth this Man letters, having never learned?" He was never learning, but He knew. So that all of Deity, of which I am conscious through my limitation, I find realized in Him; and the very things for which I am seeking He possessed. Life, holiness, strength, knowledge, and a score of other things, for these are but illustrations taken almost at random, are all in Him. The things that make up Deity to me, the fulness of Deity, I find in Him.

Take a step further. What have been the results of the presence of this Person in the world? As the result of His presence in the world, the world has intellectually realized

God as never before. God is holy, is loving, is self-sacrificing; but these conceptions of God had never been really understood until this Man lived amongst us. So also the world has had a new conception of man, as spiritual in essence, and as only able to realize the present life as his life has dealings with the infinite and the eternal.

But, practically, what has this presence in the world meant? Rest. "Come unto Me . . . and I will give you rest." This is the call of Deity to humanity, and humanity heard it, and has been coming to this Man ever since, and has been finding rest. And not only rest, but realization of all the forces of human life personally and relatively. These facts attest the truth of the doctrine which Paul teaches. Test the intellectual by all other teachers. Mohammed came to teach the world a great lesson, as Carlyle has shown in his book, *Heroes and Hero Worship*. Mohammed stood for two things about God which were absolutely true. First, *Allah akbar*—God is great; second, *Islam*—submission. And Buddha's idea of God, if one may venture to attempt in a sentence to state it, was the idea of God as Self-conscious; so that, as from His Being there emanated different castes according to whether men came from head, or hand, or feet, they went back into completion to Him, losing consciousness. What were the practical issues of these things? Look at Mohammedanism today. Look at India today. These men were prophets. I will grant that they were true men and sincere. But as human teachers about God, they took hold of thoughts of God and made them all the fact of God, and failed disastrously. But here came a Man into human life, a Man of wisdom, a Man of human friendship, a Man eating and drinking, and He so came into human life that, without enunciating great philosophies, speaking only simple things, He brought into the world's consciousness the conviction of God which is not a conviction of things about God, but a consciousness of God which lifts, and rests, and realizes, and puts upon the brow of every man who hears and obeys, the very glory of God Himself. This is not Man merely. "In Him dwelleth all the pleroma of Deity," and through the veil of His flesh Divine there flamed out upon human life infinite and eternal light, and as men have come to it, and walked in it, they have found God, and have been healed and helped.

Then I submit to you that these are the findings. The results demonstrate the truth, and they are the realization of God and the resultant finding of life. Wherever there have been departures from these conceptions of Christ, they have lived only while they have retained results, which were the outcome of these conceptions. Put Jesus back again where He was in Paul's thinking before Paul's life was changed. Make Him Jesus of Nazareth, a sincere and blinded and failing Man among men, make Him that, make Him only that, burn your Pauline writings, sweep out the whole catholic conception of Him, and in half a century Christianity will have lost its power of moral uplift, and fail to bring men into union with God.

A final word by way of application. What effect should this doctrine have upon personal experience? That is the main argument of the letter, and if you will read the context you will see exactly what I mean. "Take heed lest there shall be anyone that maketh spoil of you through his philosophy and vain deceit, after the tradition of men, after the rudiments of the world, and not after Christ." The first application is that I find in this Christ an absolute sufficiency. But I find in my relation to Him a great responsibility. What effect does this conception of Christ have upon our service as individuals and as a church? This is the deepest fact as basis for all our work. We are bringing men to God when we bring them to Christ.

But the cosmic passion is the expression of that. As He is Creator, and in Him all these things consist, anything out of order will make the heart of those who are His hot and restless.

A serious word, which one would speak with all carefulness and sincerity, is that there must be separation on the part of those who hold this doctrine concerning Christ from all those who hold any other. They may be perfectly sincere. We must grant their sincerity. We are not to ascend any throne of judgment and pronounce our final verdict upon those who do not hold this view of Christ. But I say, in all kindness and all honesty, there can be no agreement, and no fellowship, and no co-operation between the man who makes Jesus Christ a child of His age, a Man among men, sharing Divinity in common with the rest, and in no other degree; and a man who looks into His face, and says, "My Lord and my God," believing that "in Him dwelleth all the fulness of the Godhead bodily."

CHAPTER XX

HARDENED

But exhort one another day by day, so long as it is called Today, lest any one of you be hardened by the deceitfulness of sin.

HEBREWS 3:13.

"Hardened by the deceitfulness of sin."
The warning of the text is addressed to people familiar with the letter of God's word. Hence its applicability to such an audience as this. Most of us heard the first music of that motherhood which soothed our childhood, expressing itself in the songs of the sanctuary. The vast majority of us were first fascinated by Bible stories told us by those best of all theologians for children—our mothers. We know the things of God, and therefore there is for every one of us here a message of warning: "Lest any one of you be hardened by the deceitfulness of sin."

No more solemn warning was ever uttered by any of the apostolic writers. No words to which we ought to pay closer attention, and to which we ought to give more earnest heed, are to be found in the whole of the Divine Library. Yet is it not the fact that we listen to a text like this with something of curiosity, something of wonder, as to what can possibly be said concerning it?

Or if the text does indeed speak to the conscience, is it

not because the old word "sin" is to be found in it, which some men are dropping out of their vocabulary today? Yet the word that should startle us is the word "hardened." We are not afraid, I fear, of being hardened. There are people today who are terribly afraid lest they or their loved ones should become drunkards. Better be a drunkard than hardened! There is more chance for the man who is in the grip of some one specific sin, who still retains a heart and conscience, than for the man who is hardened, and yet commits no vulgar sin condemned by the age in which he lives. The peril is of the subtlest, and it is the peculiar peril of those who know the terms of the law and the Gospel. I very much question whether you could find me a person hardened in the sense of my text who is unfamiliar with the Christian evangel. There are many men in this city who are quite unfamiliar with its terms, and they are so vicious that you thank God you are not as they; but they are not "hardened." If we are not startled by the word, if it produce no blush of shame, no blanch of fear, the danger is that we are already becoming hardened.

Let us consider, then, first the peril, "hardened"; second, the cause, "sin"; and, finally, the method, "deceitfulness."

First, then, the peril: "Lest any one of you be hardened." The word suggests a change, indicates a process, and reveals a condition.

When I say that the word suggests a change, I mean that no human being starts life hard. No little child is hard. Human nature is essentially impressionable. If you take a child in its earliest years out of any set of circumstances, and put it into new surroundings, you can mold its life. There is no greater illustration of this truth than Dr. Barnardo's great work. For forty years the doors of that institution have stood open to any child, the only qualification for admission being destitution. Though the children dealt with for the most part were born with hereditary taint of evil, with an environment that gave them no chance morally, the percentage who have answered the touch of Christ through Christly influence, and have become pure, and noble, and beautiful, is amazing. Every child is impressionable; every child has its windows open toward the morning; every child indulges in romance, dreams dreams, sees visions, hopes, is capable of tears and laughter; every child is plastic. The man who is hard, and who boasts in his hardness, was not always hard.

If I could put my hand, my brethren, tonight upon your shoulders, and by some mysterious process drive you back through the years, I should bring you to a period of tenderness, to a moment when you also were soft, and plastic, and emotional. You tell me you are glad the day has gone? If you knew what it really means, you would begin to weep again tonight, because you have lost the power to weep.

"Lest any one of you be hardened." Because the word suggests a change it also indicates a process.

What is this process? Let us look at it in its symptoms. What are the symptoms of this hardening? We began to fight against tenderness as being childish, and then we silenced conscience as being inconvenient to success, and finally we questioned the verity of the things unseen. This is the process of hardening.

There was a time when some of you men would have wept over a dead canary. Tonight you do not weep over lost souls! The fountain of tears has been dried up. There was a time when you blushed awkwardly when you told a lie. Today there is no blush and no inward shame. There was a time when you believed in God. Today you are hardly sure of your own wife.

The hardening process has gone forward until at last the

condition of hardness is reached. It is the inevitable result of the stifling of tears, and the refusal to listen to conscience, and to believe. No tears, no conscience, no faith! Hard! Equal to dealing with business problems, but not equal to the commerce of eternity. Quite equal to touching and handling forces which are merely the affairs of this life, but not equal to laying hold on eternal life. Quite equal, in a word, to dust and the things of dust, but not equal to Deity and fellowship with God. Yet let me put this even more practically and personally. The moment comes when a man, who as a boy wept as he heard the story of Jesus, hears it without one thrill of emotion. The day comes when a man still listens to the terms of the law of God, but never trembles. The most difficult men and women to reach with the evangel are those who know it best, and are yet unmoved by it to tears, or high endeavor. "Lest any one of you be hardened."

But now, how does a man become hardened? I take you to the final word of my text, "sin." What is sin? It would be unfair to interpret the word "sin" in this letter in any other way than by the use of the writer. In every case, from first chapter to last, he uses it of unbelief. The whole argument of the letter is intended to strengthen faith, and the whole force of the writer's appeal against sin is an appeal against unbelief, and the sin that hardens is the sin of unbelief.

In order to explain that, let me first deal with what is meant by unbelief, for I can quite imagine that someone finds reason in rebellion against such a statement. It may be affirmed that a man cannot help unbelief, because a man cannot compel his belief. Such an objection reveals the fact that the meaning of unbelief is not understood because the meaning of belief is not understood.

What is belief? Belief is that which brings a man into personal relationship with Jesus Christ so as to save that man.

But what is the belief that saves a man? It is not an intellectual assent to a certain number of formulated truths. It is possible for a man to believe intellectually all the truths of the evangelical faith, and yet be lost for time and eternity. The fact that I am convinced of the truth of the Deity of Jesus, and of the atoning nature of His death, will not save me. These truths do not become dynamic simply by intellectual apprehension and consent. No man is saved by intellectual comprehension and conviction. All that may be a part of the process, but it does not save a man. What, then, is the belief that saves? Now let me go to a slightly different standpoint. What is the thing you really do believe? A man in church on Sunday recites a creed. I have great respect for his doing so. He says, "I believe in God the Father Almighty, Maker of Heaven and Earth." Does he? The fact that he recites the creed on Sunday does not prove that in the deepest of him he believes. I shall want to watch him on Monday to know whether he really believes in God. I shall want to live with him, and observe his business method, and his habits of speech, and the tone and temper of his disposition before I know whether, in the deepest of him, he believes in God. You say, "I do believe in God," and that is true intellectually, but that is not the belief that saves. The faith that saves is the answer of the will to the truth of which the reason is convinced, the handing over of the life to the claim of truth. If I believe in God the Father Almighty, not merely with my mind and heart, but also with my will, then I shall walk from Monday morning until Saturday evening, as well as upon the Sabbath day, as a man recognizing God's throne, seeking His law, endeavoring to find the way of His commandments, measuring all the activities of my life by His claim upon me. That belief saves, which compels the surrender of the whole life to the conviction of truth. The following of light is the faith that saves a man. I am always thankful to remember—and I pause to say this, though it is not part of my main argument—that the New Testament never asks me to believe in the atonement in order to be saved. I am not saying a man can be saved without the atonement. But the Scripture asks that I shall believe in the Lord Jesus Christ. The belief which saves is belief in the Person of Christ, which expresses itself in surrender to Christ, even though I may have to postpone the explanation of the mystery of His being, and the marvel of His atonement, and the miracle of His resurrection.

Therefore it becomes evident that unbelief is refusal to obey that truth of which I am convinced intellectually. To know the truth, and then refuse to obey it; to hear the message, assent to its accuracy, bow in the presence of its great demand intellectually, and yet not answer its claim, that is the sin which hardens a man. When a man so disobeys, he becomes hardened by the very truth that might have softened him; he becomes enslaved and debased by the very message that ought to have made him free indeed. In that sense the Gospel is a savor of life unto life, or of death unto death; and the unbelief that hardens a man is not his refusal to accept intellectually a statement of truth, but his refusal to obey the truth when it lays claim to his allegiance, and calls upon him to tread some definite pathway. "Hardened by the deceitfulness of sin."

That brings us to the central thought of the text. How is it that men commit this sin of unbelief? Brethren, is not that the mystery, the perpetual mystery? Is not every preacher confronted by it, every Christian worker conscious of it? Why is it men hear the truth and do not obey? Why is it that men, conscious that the Spirit of God is striving with them, even though they may not express the fact in these words, yet will not yield. Why are men guilty of unbelief? Here in my text is the word that shows that the writer of this letter understood perfectly the reason: "the *deceitfulness* of sin." The sin of unbelief is always the result of a false argument. When truth breaks upon a human soul and makes its claim, if the man does not obey, it is because he is deceived either intellectually, emotionally, or volitionally.

It will be easier now, I think, to illustrate than to attempt to state the case theoretically. Suppose that I should resolve this service into one of another kind, and some of you in honesty should tell us why you are not Christian people in the full sense of the word, what would be the result? You are familiar with the terms of the evangel, you have been nursed upon the songs of the Church, and yet you yourself are not Christian. It may be that once you made a profession, and once you companied with the saints, and once rejoiced in the vision of God, and once knew all the blessedness of fellowship; but things have changed, and you have become hard. Why? Because of your unbelief, your refusal to obey truth. But why did you refuse? Now, I say if we could have definite testimony, I think we should hear some things such as these. I will not imagine a single case, but will tell you actual things that have been said to me. One man tells me that he is not a Christian because he desires his liberty. There are thousands of young men in London tonight who in their deepest heart revere the Christian standard; but they are not Christians simply because they want to be free. Now, listen. "The *deceitfulness* of sin." Was ever unbelief more subtle than when it promises a man that if he will refuse to believe, in this evangelical sense of the word, he will be a free man. Do you not know, have you not yet discovered in your own experience, that the only free man is the man bound to the throne of God, that no man is free who is simply attempting to follow the lusts and desires of his own heart and life? Your freedom to do the things that you yourself desire to do, unchecked by law, is at this very moment weaving a chain. It may seem to be of silk, and you toy with it in its silken loveliness, and imagine you will presently snap it. But you will find that the chain about you is adamant. If you and I were talking together as man to man you would confess that already you have discovered that habit has so fastened upon you that you cannot break it. What is the story of the corruption of sin that abounds in our city? It is the story of men who have sought for freedom and have found slavery. It is the story of men who declined to have a master, and they have become the slaves of the worst taskmasters that ever held human beings in bondage.

Your own lust? Lust is not wrong. Jesus said to His disciples, "With *lust* have I *lusted* to eat this passover with you." I find it is written in my Bible, "which things angels *lust* to look into." At the back of every sin that curses humanity is a true desire. Sin is always the prostitution of right, the taking of a true capacity, and using it in an untrue method. If a man answer his desire without constraint, without instruction, without guidance, without mastership, he cannot fulfil it, and at last the desire becomes a burning, flaming thirst, a passion that nothing can slake; and he becomes the slave of the desire he answered when he refused to obey the light that came to instruct him how to answer the true desire within his own life. You want to be free, my brother. Come tonight to your Master Jesus. Hand in to Him your wholehearted surrender and allegiance. Say to Him as you stand before Him, "Here and now, O living Christ of God, spirit, soul and body, now and forever, in every fiber of my personality, and every power of my being, take me!" Then you will be free. Then you will find liberty. The Son alone can make you free. If you have refused to obey the voice of truth, and so have been guilty of the sin of unbelief, it is because you have allowed yourself to be deceived by sin's promise of freedom, while all the time it has been forging your chain.

Take another illustration. A man will say to me, "Yes, I know all that you say is true. I know that the pure is the beautiful. With my mind I admire its great ideal, but I want to see life. Oh, sometimes I wish I could give all my life to speak on that one theme to the young men and women of our cities. You want to see life? Yes, you say, I should have to give up so much if I became a Christian. What would you have to give up? I would be quite willing to stop preaching for a moment if you would tell me. Will you tell me what you would have to give up if you became a Christian, which I cannot keep, being a Christian? Or, rather, what can you have of life by not being a Christian which is denied to me because I am a Christian? If you will name anything that you can do, not being a Christian, which I cannot do as a Christian man, you will know immediately that the thing that you are clinging to, that you call seeing life, is the thing that passes sentence of death upon you.

What does a man lose that is essential to his manhood when he becomes a Christian? Freedom for intellectual pursuits? Nay, verily, Christianity has set the world's intellect free. The late Lord Salisbury said that it was a good thing to study large maps. So it is. When you want to know what Christianity has done for the world, take a broad outlook over the centuries and over the world as it is, and know this, that the crucifixion and stoning of a man for scientific investigation has been made impossible by the presence of Jesus Christ in the world. Jesus Christ has set man's intellect free, has said to men in effect, You may knock at every door and demand admission, and you may enter as far as you can. The only limit set to your investigation is your power of investigation. But then Jesus Christ also says, When you have come as far as you can along the line of investigation, never forget the revealed things are yours, and the secret things belong to God.

Christ has set the intellect free. What is it that you have to abandon? Music? I will not insult the intelligence of this congregation by arguing it. You have all heard the "Messiah," and after that there is nothing to hear. Art? Certainly not, save as art may be debased in order to suggest evil thoughts. Some pictures you are hiding, or showing clandestinely, you had better burn, and you know it! Amusement? What form of amusement must you give up if you become a Christian? No amusement that is recreation. That must be your philosophy of amusement, *re-creation*. Anything that destroys you, spirit, mind, or body, of course you must give up because Jesus is set upon making you perfect and beautiful, and He will not tolerate a retention of anything that stultifies you physically, or dulls you mentally, or blights you spiritually. In the name of God, I charge you do not hear me as a theorist, but come and see me, if you will, and tell me what you have to give up that I cannot keep. You dare not do it, my brothers, because you know that I should say to you, "What about it? Do you not think you had better give it up?" And you would have to say, "Yes." And yet you are being deceived by sin. You want to see life, and in the pursuit of life you are tracking the desert of death. Oh, the deceitfulness of sin!

Or, again, another man says to me, "Well, I am not a Christian because I am not fully persuaded of all the truths of the Christian religion." If you adopted that method in any other department of life, where would you land yourself within the next seven days? The perpetual law of life is that a man accepts the known fact and acts upon it, afterwards investigating the mystery that lies behind it. And yet there are men—I know them, I hear from them; they come to see me, and tell me they are not Christian because they do not understand the mystery of incarnation, or the mystery of atonement, because they cannot quite follow all the statements of the Bible concerning the methods of God. My brethren, Jesus Christ presents Himself to you, attested by tens of thousands of witnesses in the passing centuries, as the One Who gives you at once the highest ideal of life, and is able to communicate to you a sufficient dynamic to enable you to realize your ideal. Obey that, and postpone the rest! I know there are men who tell me they understand all the mystery of the Christian truth. I thank God with all my heart that Christian truth is so large that at present I do not perfectly comprehend it all. I thank God for its vastness, for the infinite reaches of it. This heart of mine, poor little restless thing as it is, is yet so big that it would rebel against a religion formulated and tabulated, in which the last thing could be recited in a creed in half an hour. It is the vastness of the reach; it is the sense that this thing is greater than I, that there are infinite reaches stretching out on every hand, that makes me thank God in the midst of the mystery. I have found foothold, and I have found it upon the rock of Christ, and from that vantage ground I may inquire.

Because of the mystery, in God's name do not refuse to obey what is no longer mystery, the plain fact of what Christ is, and what He can do for you.

Compare your present position with the past. Take your childhood, and put it into comparison with your present position. I do not say possession, material possession. I said your present position, the position of your own inner life. What is the difference?

> I remember, I remember,
> The house where I was born,
> The little window where the sun
> Came peeping in at morn;
> He never came a wink too soon,
> Nor brought too long a day,
> But now I often wish the night
>   Had borne my breath away.
>
> I remember, I remember,
> The fir trees dark and high;
> I used to think their slender tops
> Were close against the sky.
> It was a childish ignorance,
> But now 'tis little joy
> To know I'm farther off from heaven
>   Than when I was a boy.

Is that what you are saying? You have done wonderfully well, so the world will tell you. You have made a great deal of money, you lost yourself. When you lost your tears, you lost God's finest gift to you. When you lost your conscience, you lost the balance wheel of your life. When you lost your faith in God and man, you lost everything that makes life high, and noble and beautiful.

Ah me, there is another song that comes back to a man's heart tonight, a song which I wonder people can sing without catching its pathos and tragedy:

> Backward, turn backward, O time in your flight,
> Make me a child again, just for tonight.
> Mother, come back from the echoless shore;
> Take me again to your heart as of yore.
> Kiss from my forehead the furrows of care,
> Smooth the few silver threads out of my hair,
> Over my slumbers your loving watch keep,
> Rock me to sleep, mother, rock me to sleep.

I do not know who wrote it.* I do not know the circumstances but I tell you that is not the cry of a baby for toys. It is the wail of a soul after God. Listen!

> Tired of the hollow, the base, the untrue,
> Mother, O mother, my heart yearns for you.
> Many a summer the grass has grown green,
> Blossomed and faded, our faces between;
> Yet with strong yearning, and passionate pain,
> Long I tonight for your presence again.
> Come from the silence, so long and so deep,
> Rock me to sleep, mother, rock me to sleep.

My brethren, do not check that emotion. If those lines have touched a chord that has not vibrated for years, thank God for it. If there is a sob in your heart tonight, it is a sign of hope. Follow it; it is a gleam, and it is because long ago you refused to follow some gleam like it that you have become hard as the nether millstone.

But there is another word, and it is a word that the King James's translators and the revisers have written with a capital letter. What is it? "Today." "Exhort one another day by day, so long as it is called Today." That means to say that if you have become hard, you are still in the place you can be remade.

> Today! O blessed word of hope,
>   And laden still with heaven's own breath,
> The night is passed, and has not come,
>   Between the shades life conquers death.
> Light falls around the ruined soul,
>   The wind of God blows with new lust!
> Fling back the shutters! Swing the door!
>   Answer God's breath upon thy dust!

---

* The verse is from "Rock Me to Sleep," by Elizabeth Akers Allen.—Ed.

> Then day shall never end in night,
>   But night be merged in perfect day;
> And all the forces of God's life
>   Control thy life with mighty sway.

It is Today, and you may go from the sanctuary without word spoken to any friend, with all the fallow ground plowed up, and with the promise of harvest, and the blossoming of the rose where the desert has been. But, my brethren, in order to do that you must obey the truth you know. So believe with all the mind, and all the heart, and all the life, and you shall find the remaking of your life by the grace of God.

CHAPTER XXI

WITNESSES

We are witnesses of these things; and so is the Holy Ghost, Whom God hath given to them that obey Him.
ACTS 5:32.

IN THESE WORDS PETER WAS THE SPOKESMAN OF THE INFANT Church, and he was at once answering a challenge and declaring the solution of a problem. We can appreciate the words at their true value only by remembering the occasion upon which they were spoken. In the context a picture full of life and color is presented to the mind. Two groups of men are seen confronting each other. They constitute a striking contrast. On the one hand are all the men of light and leading and position in Jerusalem, "the high priest . . . and they that were with him . . . and the council, and all the senate of the children of Israel." On the other hand are men, not one of them known, save by virtue of their association with Jesus of Nazareth, toiling fishermen of the Galilean Lake, no schoolman in their number, no ruler, no priest. I leave it to your imagination to fill in the details, the magnificent robing of the priest and his friends, the phylacteries, and the faces with that fine expression that tells of culture and of strong and passionate conviction; and, on the other hand, the homespun and simple garments, the rough and rugged splendor of hard-working men, and all the light gleaming from eyes newly illumined.

The high priest has challenged these men, and is strangely perplexed. He has accomplished the death of the troublesome prophet of Nazareth, but a strange story is abroad, told first by the keepers of the grave, and then by the disciples who had been scattered by the crucifixion, that this Jesus is alive, that He has been seen. Of course, he considers it a wild and foolish superstition, but it is having its effect upon both the men who had followed Him in the days of His teaching and those who now heard their preaching. They had flung the ringleaders into prison, and in the morning had gathered together that they might deal with them judicially. The message had come that the prison did not contain the men, but that they were in the temple speaking "all the words of this Life."

And now the apostles stand arraigned before priest and rulers. The priest demands of them how they dare continue to preach in the name of Jesus. Peter speaking here, veritably *ex cathedra*, on behalf of the whole Church, declared in answer, "We must obey God rather than men." . . . "We are witnesses of these things; and so is the Holy Ghost, Whom God hath given to them that obey Him."

That was an answer to the challenge of unbelief within a few weeks after Pentecost. It is the answer to the challenge of unbelief today, or we have no answer. In this verse there is declared the function and the force of discipleship, the mission and the method of the Church. The function is declared in these words, "We are witnesses of these things." The force is announced in the words, "We . . . and so is the Holy Ghost." The mission of the Church, to witness to these things. The method of the Church, to act in perpetual co-operation with the Holy Spirit. Wherever the Church recognizes this as the function and force of discipleship, as the mission and method of her life, the same results follow as followed in Jerusalem. Wherever the Church wanders from this primitive ideal, the early results are wanting. Wherever the Church, and all the disciples that constitute the Church, remember that the main calling of the Church is witness, and that the one and only power of witness is co-operation with the Holy Spirit, then cities are filled with the doctrine, conviction of sin takes hold upon men. The Pentecostal result follows the Pentecostal method.

You will find in this picture, moreover, a contrast of mental attitude. On the one hand we see "the high priest . . . and all they that were with him (which is the sect of the Sadducees)." Who were the Sadducees? I think, perhaps, there is no safer way to answer the question than to take the Bible declaration concerning them. "The Sadducees say that there is no resurrection, neither angel, nor spirit." These were the men who challenged the apostles, rationalists, men who denied the supernatural element in religion. Resurrection, angel, spirit, they declared to be superstitions of a bygone age. On the other hand, a group of men who testified to the reality of these very things. Said the Sadducee, there is no resurrection. Said the apostles, Christ is risen. Said the Sadducee, there is no angel. Said the apostles, an angel opened the prison doors you shut, and let us out. Said the Sadducee, there is no spirit. Said the apostles, we have entered into partnership with the Holy Spirit. It was the beginning of the long struggle between rationalism and Christianity, the conflict between the affirmation of the spiritual as real and the declaration that there is no spirit, but that man lives merely in dust.

Rationalism is still saying there is no resurrection, not even of Christ; there are no angels, they belong to pictures, to art, and to little children's fancies; there is no spirit, the mind is everything. When you have said psychic, you seem to have said the last word of human intellectuality at the present moment.

On the other hand, the Church is still saying that Christ rose from among the dead; that angels are all "ministering spirits, sent forth to do service for the sake of them that shall inherit salvation," that men are essentially spirits, and that there is one Holy Spirit of God. These are the declarations of the Church, but how is she to demonstrate the truth of them? The text is answer. "We are witnesses of these things; and so is the Holy Ghost, Whom God hath given to them that obey Him." Then let us consider these two things, the Church's mission, and the method by which she is able to fulfil that mission.

The Church's mission is declared in that very simple sentence, "We are witnesses of these things." Where do you suppose Peter put the emphasis when he uttered these words? Let me say, first of all, that I am quite sure he did not lay it upon the personal pronoun. He did not say, "*We* are witnesses of these things." That is where he would have put it before Pentecost, and after Cæsarea Philippi. Not so now. The consciousness of personality expressed in the pronoun is lost in the sense of the importance of the witness to be borne. "We are *witnesses*."

I do not think we have yet reached the point of the true emphasis. I think if we had heard Peter that day speak we should have heard him lay the emphasis on *"these things."* What things? "The God of our fathers raised up Jesus, Whom ye slew, hanging Him on a tree. Him did God exalt with His right hand to be a Prince and Saviour, for to give repentance to Israel, and remission of sins." That is the Evangel! Christ is risen. "God . . . raised up Jesus": Christ was crucified. "Whom ye slew, hanging Him on a tree": Christ is enthroned. "Him did God exalt to be a Prince and a Saviour": Christ is at work, to give repentance to Israel, and remission of sins." The risen Christ, the crucified Christ, the exalted Christ, the working Christ. "These things." "We are witnesses of these things."

That is the Church's mission. The Church does not exist to entertain the masses. She is unequal to competition with the theater. The Church does not exist to educate the masses: she must be interested in education, but this is not her supreme vocation. The Church exists to witness to "these things," the risen Christ, the crucified Christ, the enthroned Christ, the living and working Christ. The world does not want the Church. The Church cannot save the world. The world wants the things that the Church testifies of.

Alas, we have been so anxious about the structure of the lighthouse that we have forgotten often to see that the light is burning. We have been quarreling so busily and with such absolute abandonment concerning forms and garments that we have forgotten the men who wear the garments. We have been more anxious about trappings than about triumph. Find me a man who calls himself a Christian and does not witness to the risen Christ, the crucified Christ, the exalted Christ, the living, working Christ, and he is of use neither to God nor man. Find me a church where the resurrection light is not shining, where the passion of blood is not proclaimed, and the enthroned Lord is not revealed, and the working Lord is not felt, and it is a tomb, an insult to God and to man. "These things," that is the Church's business. "We are witnesses of these things."

Yet let us think of the word "witnesses." A witness is more than a man who talks. Indeed a man may talk and never witness in the New Testament sense of the word. It has been repeatedly pointed out that the word here translated, and translated uniformly throughout the New Testament "witness," is a Greek word which we have anglicized into our word "martyr"; "We are martyrs of these things." What is a martyr? We have come to use the word of such as seal their testimony with their blood. It is a beautiful word for such. When we speak of the "noble army of martyrs," who through flame and fire, through blood and suffering, proved their loyalty to Christ, let us remember that the fires did not make them martyrs. The fires did but reveal them to be martyrs. They were martyrs ere the fires were lit, or they would never have submitted to them. Every day of fiery persecution has been a day when martyrs have been revealed. What, then, is a martyr? He is a confessor. A martyr is one who is first convinced of truth, and then yields his life to the claims of the truth of which he is convinced, and who, therefore, is changed by the truth which he believes, and to which he has yielded himself. So that, finally, a martyr is a specimen, an evidence, a sample, a credential, a proof, a witness. We are the credentials of these things. We are the proof of these things. We say Jesus is risen from the dead. We say the risen Christ is the selfsame Christ Who was crucified. We say this Christ is exalted by God. We say this Christ is at work giving repentance and remission of sins. How are we going to prove these things? We are evidences. We prove the accuracy of our doctrine by the transformation of our lives. The apostle did not merely mean, as he stood in the presence of that august company of rulers and priests, that they bore testimony in words, that they were prepared to argue. He meant rather to say, You deny the resurrection; you deny the value we declare to have been created by the dying of this Christ Whom ye slew; you deny that Jesus of Nazareth is on the throne of God; you deny that He is alive and working in

Jerusalem! Go back and think of us as we were, and behold us as we are. We are what we are by virtue of the things we declare. It is by the risen Christ Who was crucified, is exalted, and is at work, that we are what we are. Rationalism has no right to deny the accuracy of the supernatural claims of Christ until it can account for the wonders wrought in men and women who by Christianity have been changed from all that is base to everything that is noble, from being slaves to sin into being bond-slaves of Christ, from being men consumed by lust and passion to men consumed by zeal for the salvation of men and for the glory of God.

That is the supreme value of my text as it reveals the work of the Church. The Church confronts the age with living witnesses. If she has none, she is useless. If she has none, she has no argument. If she is not able to present to the age in all its rationalism and unbelief, men and women changed, remade, she has no argument to which the age will listen. Such a declaration as that reacts upon the heart and conscience of every Christian man or woman, or ought so to do. Am I a witness? I do not mean am I a preacher. Unless behind the preaching of my lips there is the testimony of my life, my preaching is blasphemy and impertinence. Unless my own life is changed and transformed and transfigured, a revelation of the fact of the risen, crucified, exalted, working Christ, my preaching is as tinkling brass and a clanging cymbal. So with all of us. Any recitation of creed is blasphemy unless the creed is alive in conduct. Your affirmation of the truth of the Christian facts is impertinence unless in the very fiber of your personality these things are wrought out and are shining through in revelation upon the age. "We are witnesses of these things."

I get back at last to the personal pronoun. "*We* are witnesses of these things." Who were they? As I have said, none of them counted at all by any of the ordinary standards of human measurement. They were fishermen. Do you not think that term was often used of them disdainfully in those days? These Galilean fishermen! Yet they were witnesses of such things as made them makers of empire, and revolutionaries who turned the world upside down! Not they, but the things through them. The very simplest of the men who answered the claims of the things, and became transformed thereby, became also a force. There is no man here so weak but that if these things are by him believed, and he by them is changed, he becomes appointed a witness in apostolic succession, in Christly fellowship, in actual co-operation with God, a part of the Divine movement for bruising the head of the enemy, and destroying the works of the devil, and bringing in the triumph of righteousness.

They were poor Galilean fishermen, of no account, of no value in themselves, but they live in the imagination of this age, while the priests are remembered by their garments and their phylacteries and their folly.

Yes, but how did they do it? "We are witnesses of these things: and so is the Holy Ghost, Whom God hath given to them that obey Him." The Spirit is witness of the things of Christ. Jesus ere He left His disciples instructed them concerning the days of His absence, and said of the Spirit, "the Paraclete . . . shall teach you all things, and bring to your remembrance all that I said unto you. . . . He shall bear witness of Me, . . . He shall glorify Me." He declared that the mission of the Holy Spirit would be the interpretation of Himself. For the sake of the truth being remembered let me try to condense that great doctrine of the Spirit into two of the simplest of all sentences, so simple that there will be the same words in both, but differently arranged for the revelation of a different value.

The Holy Spirit witnesses of Jesus only.
Only the Holy Spirit witnesses of Jesus.

Think of the first. The Holy Spirit witnesses of Jesus only. How we forget it as Christian people! Christian people constantly pray for the coming of the Holy Spirit, and wait for His coming. In their minds there seems to be the idea that when the Spirit comes to them in fulness they will be conscious of the Spirit. There is no evidence of any such teaching in Scripture. If the Spirit come to us in all fulness, He will make us conscious, not of Himself, but of Christ. "He shall not speak from Himself . . . He shall take of Mine and declare it unto you," said Christ.

I would like to stay with that in all tenderness, because I think there are sincere souls being misled by their own thinking in this regard. It is not long since a young man came to me and said, I do not quite understand my relationship to Christ. I am a little puzzled by it. I have long been praying for the fulness of the Spirit, and waiting for it, and longing for it, and earnestly desiring it. I have heard of others who have received it, but it does not come to me. I began to talk to him, and I found that he thought when the Spirit came in fulness there would be a flash of light and glory, and a thrill and enthusiasm, and consciousness of fire and of the Holy Ghost. It is not so. All the while, through the days, weeks, months of his sincere seeking, this thing had been happening in his experience, Christ was becoming more precious than He was, far more real! The Spirit was there doing His work, unveiling Christ, yet this man did not recognize that the Spirit was fulfilling His one great function. The Spirit comes to witness to Jesus only. Once, tongues of fire and a mighty rushing wind, evidence to the senses of the coming of the Spirit. From that moment, straight on through generations, He has hidden Himself. The Spirit comes to reveal Jesus only. He has no other message, no other work than the unveiling of the face of Christ, in which we see the unveiling of the face of God.

Take my other sentence for a moment and consider it. Only the Holy Spirit witnesses of Jesus. Does this seem to contradict Peter's declaration, "We are witnesses"? By no means. How did they become witnesses? In the hour when they crowned Jesus Lord. Listen, "No man calleth Jesus Lord save by the Holy Spirit." I cannot make you call Him Lord. I can speak of His Lordship, of the perfection of His life, of the passion of His death, of the power of His resurrection, of the program of His reign, and you will hear it all and intellectually consent to the fact that He is Lord, but you never can look into His face and say, "Lord," save as the Spirit of God has unveiled His glory and captured your heart. It is the Spirit of God Who first reveals to the soul the Lordship of Jesus. So these men became witnesses because on the day of Pentecost they had seen Christ as they had never seen Him before. Think of it. They had looked at Christ for three years and had never, never seen Him. They had felt the touch of His human hand and never, never found Him. When the day of Pentecost was come, and the Spirit came as fire and power they saw Him and they became witnesses. Have you seen Him? It is only by the Spirit's unveiling of the face of Christ that He is ever seen, or that men become His witnesses.

When once the Lord has been seen and crowned there is a progressive operation of the Spirit in the life of the believer. The Spirit reveals the Christ to you in some new aspect as you read His Word, as you meditate upon Him, and the moment you see Christ in some new glory, that vision makes a demand upon you. What are you going to do with it? Answer it, obey it, and the Spirit realizes in you the thing you have seen in Christ. Disobey it, and the Spirit has no other message to you until you return to that point of disobedience, and have become obedient. I wonder if you will be patient if for a moment I pass from advocacy to witnessing. I remember with clear distinctness how more than twenty years ago I read a passage in Matthew's Gospel that I had read hundreds of times, but in that moment it flamed and burned before my eyes. It was this, "When He saw the multitudes, He was moved with compassion." I cannot give you what I saw. No man can pass these visions on. You must only hear me patiently, for the lonely vision is for the lonely soul. In that moment to which my own memory goes back, and which lives with me now, I saw the very heart of the Son of God, I saw that compassion as I had never known it, although I had been saved by it. A vision like that is not merely an illumination of the intellect for the entertainment or delight of the soul that sees it. It is a clarion call, a trumpet blast! It said to me—If you are His, and you share His life, you must answer His passion and be willing to follow Him in service which is sacrificial service. Now, let me drop the personal; granted that any man see that as I saw it that night, two pathways open out before him. It is the Spirit's unveiling of the compassion of Christ to the soul. What will the man do who sees it? He can stifle it, admire it merely, and never answer it, until the vision dim and die away, and the Spirit will have no more to say to him. Or he can answer it, give himself to sacrificial service, be willing to die in service, and then the Spirit will lead him further on to higher heights and deeper depths. That is but one illustration. The Spirit is always unveiling Christ. Your responsibility and mine if we would co-operate with Him in witness is that we obey when He speaks. When Christ is seen in a new light, the light is calling you to obey its claim. Answer it and you will become the thing you have seen. Deny it and you will sink to lower levels. This is His method, line upon line, here a little and there a little, grace for grace, beauty after beauty.

Man, you have never seen Christ, nor have I. I have seen something of Him, like a blind man waking to his first vision I have seen men as trees walking. I have seen more and more of the beauty of my Lord as the Spirit has unveiled Him, but I have never seen all the glory. I could not bear it yet. So little by little the Spirit patiently leads us on. Our responsibility is that when light comes we walk in it. When the trumpet call of truth sounds in our souls we must answer it. The Spirit's office—and He never fails—is to reveal Christ. Our duty is to answer the revelation, and when we do so, the Spirit becomes more than illumination, He becomes dynamic and makes us that which we obey.

Soul of mine, answer the light. Obey the Spirit. Do not resist, do not grieve, do not quench the Spirit, and thou, even thou, poor broken man of the dust, shall be made like Him. What is heaven, I pray you tell? Seeing Him and being like Him. To that goal the Spirit leads.

Now hear me as I say this in conclusion. It is when I act in co-operation with this Spirit Who reveals Jesus only, Who only reveals Jesus, that I become His witness. That brings me back to the emphasis I placed a few moments ago upon the word "witness." I pray you now place the emphasis upon "witness" by linking it with that other Witness. The Spirit witnessing in me, I become the instrument through which the Spirit witnesses to the world. Where? Anywhere. When? Everywhen. God deliver us from the heresy of ever imagining that we witness only when we are in the pulpit, from the heresy of imagining that what the world wants is more preaching. Preaching is of no use save as it makes living witnesses. How have I failed, how awfully have I failed, God have mercy upon me, if I have simply held you and interested you for this hour. But if I have sent you back to your office tomorrow, back to your store, back to your home, back to your place in the government, to be more like Christ, I have hastened the coming of the day of God, I have done something to bring the Kingdom in. He gave some apostles, some prophets, some evangelists, some pastors and teachers—to preach men to heaven? No, no! What, then? To perfect the saints to the work of ministering. The truth I preach is of value in the ultimate issue only as it is incarnate in the lives of the men who listen. London is perishing for lack of living witnesses. The world awaits the evangel of transformed, transfigured lives. Will you be a witness? You say, How can I? The answer is in the text, "the Holy Ghost Whom God hath given to them that obey Him." You have looked into the face of the Lord Christ. Intellectually, you have seen Him and have acknowledged that He is Lord. Crown Him. Submit to Him. Trust Him. Do it with something of heroism, I beseech you. Do it with something of daring, I implore you. The influence of the Church is sadly hindered, the world is sadly hindered by dilettante discipleship. Crown Christ. Obey Him. Cut the last shore rope that binds you to the old life. In the moment that you crown Him the Holy Spirit will baptize you into unity of life with Him, and you will become His witness.

CHAPTER XXII

SAINTS

To the saints. . . . As becometh saints.
EPHESIANS 1:1 and 5:3.

IT WOULD APPEAR AS THOUGH THIS WERE AN UNWARRANTable wresting of texts from their context, yet it is not really so. I grant at once that nothing of the teaching of this letter can be gained from these isolated quotations; but if I may take it for granted that we are familiar with the whole letter as to its contention and intention, then I say that these phrases indicate its practical values.

In this epistle Paul reaches the climax of his great system of teaching. Perhaps it would be more correct to say that in this epistle, taken together with the Colossian epistle, he reaches that climax. In Colossians he deals with the glories of Christ as at the disposal of the Church, so that the supreme sentences are, "In Him dwelleth all the fulness," and "In Him ye are made full." In this letter he deals with the glories of the Church as realized through her relationship to Christ Who is the Head. In some senses it is one of the simplest, while in others it is one of the sublimest, of the apostolic writings. It is simple in its method. Paul first describes the Church as to its nature, as to its calling: in three chapters, as we have divided the epistle, dealing with predestination, edification, vocation. Then he turns to the application of this great calling of the Church to her present life with the words, "I therefore . . . beseech you to walk worthily of the calling wherewith ye were called"; and in the second three chapters he shows the walk that is worthy, as to the Church itself, as to individual and social conduct, and as to united conflict. There is no letter more sublime in its teaching. In its earlier chapters the apostle reveals—not in detail, but with sufficient clearness to leave an impression forever upon the mind of the student—that the ultimate vocation of the Church belongs to the ages to come. In the second part of the letter he shows what that means for the present life, how it is to affect all relationships; personal character and conduct; home relationships, husbands and wives, children and parents; household responsibilities, masters and servants. In brief, he first floods the soul with the vision of the heavenly calling, and then flashes that selfsame light upon personal conduct.

From this epistle, then, believing that the general conception of it is upon the mind of the Bible student, I take these two phrases. He is writing "to the saints"; and the great burden of his letter as to present, personal, and practical application is that they should live "as becometh saints."

Our theme, then, is saintship. Let us say at once that we are still suffering from mistaken ideas of what saintship really is. We are by no means free from the false interpretations of what we now sometimes speak of as the dark ages. We are still held in bondage to a far greater extent than we recognize by mediæval thinking concerning saintship. This you will discover, not so much by the art, or poetry, or Christian literature of the present day, as by the common converse of Christian people whenever they approach the subject of saintship. In the past saintship was misinterpreted in art, in poetry, in Christian literature of all kinds. The conception of a saint was that of a person separated from the ordinary and everyday life of his own age by some geographical, external, material separation. The idea of saintship was that of a vocation granted to a few rather than that of the calling of all who indeed belong to Jesus Christ. Of course, the simplest way to illustrate this is to ask you to think of the art of the past, and you will find in all the representations of saintship indications of this false conception. The saints that we see in pictures of the great masters are men separated from their fellow men by the very garments they wore. Raphael paints Galilean fishermen in ecclesiastical robes such as they never wore: and the great artists all suggested a holy sanctity by things added to the personality that are by no means connected with human nature. The monastic idea was false. It was based upon an excellent intention born of the passion of man for fellowship with God in seclusion and quiet, born of a strong desire to enter a life of separation; but it is utterly false in its philosophy. In the moment when you separate a man from the actual and everyday affairs of this life, you cut the nerve of his praying, and remove all the friction which is necessary to the perfecting of his saintship. Christianity is not an exotic, it is a hardy perennial. The symbolic language of Canticles, whatever it may have meant in its first intention, teaches this exquisitely: "As a lily among thorns, so is my love among the daughters." The lily of the Lord prospers in the soil which produces thorns. It is a hardy plant, not an exotic. You do not make a saint of a man the moment you take him away from the friction of the world; you put him in awful peril of losing the last trace of sanctity. The moment you take a man or a woman away from close contact with the sorrow and agony of human life you cut the nerve of prayer. If I am to pray for the world I must live in it and know it. If I am to be one of the saints of God, I must be a saint in the midst of all the ordinary and everyday life of the age. Sometimes we make use of the phrase "counsel of perfection." I wonder how many people know the history of that phrase. We say of something that is proposed to be done: it is an admirable proposition, but it is not practicable; it is a "counsel of perfection." That phrase has come to us from the Roman Church, in which "counsels of perfection" are instructions for such as devote themselves to the holy and saintly life. "Counsels of perfection," according to that Church, are rules which cannot be obeyed by those who remain in the ordinary life of the world, but only by those who come into holiness by separation from such life. All this is contrary to the New Testament ideal of saintship. Let me put that again in a simple way. If you cannot be a saint in the house of business where you are, you will never be a saint when you enter the Salvation Army. If you cannot be a saint in your own home, you cannot be a saint in this pulpit.

That we are still suffering from these ideas of saintship is evidenced by the converse of saints today concerning saintship. A Christian man says: "I do not profess to be a saint," yet he is a church member, a church officer, sometimes a minister. What does he mean? If not a saint, then not a Christian. If a Christian, then a saint. The fact is that in his mind there still exists a false conception of what saintship really is. Sometimes, moreover, in saying this there is an indication of a contempt for the saint. It is not merely that the speaker does not consider himself a saint; there is a quiet undercurrent of satisfaction in his heart that he is not one. That also is born of this false conception of saintship.

Because the conception is false, the protest is a healthy one. If saintship consists in absolute abstention from the ordinary affairs of everyday life, then it becomes unmanly and anemic, thin, mean, and there is no robust man or woman in the world who ought not to hold it in superlative contempt.

That, however, is not the saintship of the New Testament.

Let me ask you first, then, to remember, gathering up the teaching of the New Testament, that a saint is one who is united with the life of Christ. In the first chapter of this letter, following the words, "To the saints," is a qualifying, illuminative phrase, "the faithful in Christ Jesus." That does not mean such as are faithful, in the sense of fidelity, but those who live upon the principle of faith. These are saints. Every Christian is a saint. The moment in which a man, or woman, or little child hands over the life to Christ is the moment in which saintship begins. I am not denying for a single moment that there may be very great distance between the fact of saintship and the realization of its ultimate perfection of experience; that there may be, as some of our fathers would have put it, a distinction between our standing and our state, between what we are in the economy of God, by the provision of His grace as to resource, and what we are in the actual experience of our lives. This is taught with equal clearness in the New Testament. That is the burden of this letter. It is as though the apostle had said, I am writing to saints, to those men and women in Ephesus, or other churches, who belong to Christ. What have I to say to them? Realize your resources. You are Christians; be Christians. You are saints; live "as becometh saints." That is the burden of the letter.

Let us inquire a little more in detail what this letter teaches concerning the nature of saintship. I am not going to stay to read these three first chapters to you, though that would be a profitable exercise; neither am I going to stay now to turn to them; but I am proposing to remind you that Paul teaches us in the course of these first three chapters three great things concerning our relationship to God. They are illustrations of one great truth, and when we understand them we shall know what saintship really is; and we shall be able to understand the meaning of the Apostle's charge that we live "as becometh saints."

In the first chapter he prays for these Ephesian Christians that they may know what is "God's inheritance in the saints." A little further on, in the second chapter, he declares to them that they are "His workmanship, created in Christ Jesus for good works, which God afore prepared that we should walk in them." Yet a little further on in the same chapter he declares that the saints are being built together for a "habitation of God in the Spirit." Take from these quotations the descriptive phrases and leave all the setting: Inheritance of God, Workmanship of God, Habitation of God.

In these three phrases we have the revelation of the Apostle's conception of the position of every Christian man and woman.

First, the saint is the inheritance of God, His property. Second, the saint is the workmanship of God, one upon whom He is working toward an end. Finally, the saint is the habitation of God, His home. This is not a low ideal of saintship; that would be impossible in the light of New Testament teaching.

It would be well for us if, instead of listening to another voice, we would utter to ourselves in quietness these truths, making them our own, declaring them, affirming them. If I do that, I do it that you may follow and do it for yourselves. Forgive me, therefore, if I use the first person. I am God's property. I am God's workmanship. I am God's home.

I am God's property, absolutely His. I am that by creation. I had lost the sense of that relationship, but now I am His by redemption, by all His infinite work in me, whereby sin is put away as to its guilt, is being dealt with as to its power, and ultimately will be put away as to its presence.

Whatever that personal pronoun stands for, all that is indicated by that simple yet terrible formula, "I," belongs to Him. I am not my own, I am His. Speak, if you will, of spirit, of soul, of body; of the essential spirit, of the body through which the spirit acts, of the mind which is consciousness, either spiritual or fleshly, according to the yielding of my will —I am His. I belong to Him. Speak, if you will, in the terms of that analysis of personality, emotion, intellect, will, all belongs to Him. For the moment I am not discussing the question whether God has possession or not. I am discussing the question of His absolute proprietorship. As a saint I belong to Him. I may be using these hands contrary to His will; I may be using these feet to take me some journey which is out of the way of His appointment; I may be robbing Him, but I belong to Him. The sin of the prodigal son in the far country was that he wasted his *father's* substance in riotous living. I belong to God. That is the first fact of saintship. I would to God I might almost cease speaking, and that that first fact might take possession of the heart of every professing Christian. I am His, not my own, but His.

I take a step further. I am His workmanship. If I simply speak of the fact that the saint is the property of God I recognize the imperfection of God's property. The saint is not an absolutely perfect being who can make no advance. The saint as the property of God may be most imperfect, but, being His, I am His workmanship, and that means that He will take the imperfect thing and make it perfect. Not in a moment, not by some mechanical readjustment of things, so that the imperfect is immediately made perfect, but by processes; by teaching, pain, discipline, affliction, baptisms, fire; by crushing, breaking, making, God will perfect. The first thing is that I am His. The second thing is that I am His workmanship. I never can read that word "workmanship" myself, and

I daresay it is so with many of you, without the Greek word of which it is a translation singing itself into my heart, *poema,* which does not mean rhyming merely, but a thing of beauty, the thought of God revealed in concrete form that others may see it. I never can read the word "workmanship" without the familiar figure of the Old and New Testaments coming to mind, that of the potter and the clay. There is no finer figure to teach the meaning of this truth than that. We are always in danger of spoiling the figure by looking too long at the clay, and at the wheel, and not sufficiently at the potter; yet we must see the clay and the wheel. The clay is the potter's property, that is our first point. It is that when it is still an inert mass, without fashion, or form of beauty; nothing in it attractive. That is the first fact of saintship: without form or comeliness, without beauty, I am His.

Now watch the potter. He takes the clay and puts it on the wheel. The process is very old, but watch it. What is the potter doing? His own foot is turning the wheel. His own hands are upon the clay. What is happening? In the mind of the potter there is a vision of a vessel for use and for beauty. I cannot see what is in the mind of the potter. I do not know the thing he is thinking. I am not familiar with it. Watch, his hands are upon the clay. It is plastic to his touch, and as the wheel revolves the thought that is in the mind of the potter is being revealed in the clay. He is translating his thought of beauty into an appearance of loveliness. "We are His workmanship." As clay in the hands of the Potter, so am I. Unlovely and useless is the clay until the Potter lay His hands upon it, yet what marvelous material it is for the Potter to use. God's hand is upon the saint, molding, making, perfecting something of beauty for all the coming ages. I am His workmanship as well as His property.

I go one step further, to this last thing the apostle says.

The saint is the habitation of God. The figure changes, yet becomes more full of beauty, more full of life. The habitation of God, the home of God. There is a great difference between home and any other dwelling-place. Someone says, the heart has many a dwelling-place, but only once a home. I think there is truth in it. Most of you have a home. Some of you are not at home just now. You are in hotels. No one will ever hear you speak of the hotel as home. What is the difference? Who can answer? No man yet has ever spelled "home." No man yet has ever sung "home." Home is a sigh, a sob, laughter and rapture. Home cannot be defined, but I will tell you what it is. It is the place where you are "at home." I do not mind your smile. I can do no better than that. I know what it means and you know what it means. It is the place where you never need to keep up appearances—unless you have visitors. It is the place where you are supremely conscious that you have right of way, not the right of dogmatic authority, but the right of love. Every door swings open to you. Every picture indicates your welcome. The flowers that are placed by your side breathe an atmosphere of love that makes home. You are the home of God, the place into which He comes and rests, the place where there is no chamber locked against Him. You are the home of God.

That is saintship. His property, poor, worthless, lacking in beauty, but His. And the comfort of it, "His workmanship," feeling the pressure of His hand until I am in agony sometimes, yet knowing the Potter. It is not the principle that helps me. It is the Potter Who helps me. If you emphasize only the principle I am afraid. If you tell me only of the sovereignty of God, I am overwhelmed, but when I know the Potter I know that His crushing hand is crushing only to create. I love that one touch in the old prophetic story about the potter. If he break the vessel he will make it again. If the vessel be marred the potter will make it again. I am His workmanship. That is the second fact. Finally, I am His habitation. He has purchased me for a residence.

It seems to me that I might read the second phrase now almost without a word. "As becometh saints." The only interpretation of its meaning that is sufficient is that of going over these facts again in order to make the simplest application of them.

I am His property. How shall I live as becomes that fact? By seeing to it that all this is His, that of what belongs to Him I am not robbing Him. God may be robbed in many ways. I am not going to deal with the more objectionable and flagrant ways of doing so. The awful possibility of prostituting some power of the life which belongs to God to base uses is admitted. There are other and subtler methods. Some trembling soul who wants to live as becomes a saint may, by taking some weakness in the life and endeavoring to make it strong without His strength, rob Him. You say, I am not worthy to offer myself to Him. But you are His already. But there is this weakness, you say, this infirmity! Do not forget that a great many of the hymns we are singing in evangelistic meetings are for the saint as well as for the sinner:—

> Just as I am—though tossed about
> With many a conflict, many a doubt,
> Fightings and fears within, without,
> O Lamb of God, I come.

He wants you as you are. That is the glory of saintship as revealed here. Counsels of perfection, not in order that you may become a saint, but perfect counsels because you are a saint. To walk as becomes a saint is to recognize that every fiber of the physical life, every movement of the mental life, every power of complex personality is His, and to hand over to Him His property. That is the first law of walking as becomes a saint. The application is more personal and pertinent as we get further on.

Let us take the next. "We are His workmanship." We may learn as much by the disparity as by the similarity in the use of all figures. We speak of the potter and the clay, of the fact that the clay has to be plastic in the hand of the potter; but there is the disparity, and it is at the point of the disparity that our difficulty exists. The clay has no will or wish or desire of its own, but we have will and wish and desire. That disparity reveals the very crux of the condition of saintship. The true attitude is that of yielding the will, the wish, the desire, to the mastery and compulsion of God's will, God's wish, God's desire. To me the profoundest thing in life is submission to the will of God. It is the last thing. It is the rock foundation. It will be the final thing, the capstone with glory gleaming on it. To be in His will, willingly in His will, "as becometh saints." A man ought to speak in the presence of that thought with great tenderness and great delicacy. I do not know that I have learned it. I want to learn it, always to recognize the truth so sublimely sung by Tennyson. How glibly we sing it and recite it, yet what an infinitely beautiful unfolding of the Christian philosophy there is in it:

> Our wills are ours, we know not how:
> Our wills are ours, to make them Thine.

That is the highest function of will, to will to do His will, God's will, so that I am to say, "Not that I have already obtained, or am already made perfect: but I press on": so that I am to say, Where He wills, what He wills, how He wills, when He wills; whether London, America, China, India, or Heaven, does not matter; whether to preach or be silent, to do more or to do less, does not matter; what He wills! Oh, soul of mine, see the vision and pray for strength to answer it. There is no man or woman of us here, comrades in the Christian life, who does not know that that is life, the clay willingly answering the pressure of the Potter. Be in His will. At the front? Yes, if He puts you there, with no mock modesty. At the back? Yes, surely, if He puts you there, with no repining. In His will. "As becometh saints."

Finally, the home of God. Have I any chamber in this habitation locked against Him. You and I must answer that alone. I hate confessions in crowds. I am not going to make any. Is there some compartment, some chamber in your life to which you never admit God? You have given Him right of way over three-quarters of the home, but there is a part locked away from Him. You do not want Him there. You are glad to be here this morning, for you are laying open to Him the sides of your nature where He is welcome, but there is half an hour tomorrow when you would rather not have Him with you or in you. That is not walking as becomes saintship. Have you ever noticed how many days it took them to carry out the things that defiled it when they were cleansing the temple in the olden days of Hezekiah? Make application of the spiritual meaning to yourselves. How many things there are in His temples that dishonor Him. How many rooms of these homes we will not have Him in because we are ashamed. Shall we not open all the doors this morning? Hand over the keys to Him? Yes, if He comes in He will change the setting of things in that room! But He will add to the beauty! He will sweep the pictures from the walls. But He will hang finer ones there. He will burn those books upon the shelves. But He will give you other literature and better! Give Him right of way—forgive the familiarity of it. Make God *at home* in your life! This is what He seeks.

"The whole creation groaneth and travaileth in pain together until now." "For the earnest expectation of the creation waiteth for the revealing of the sons of God." It is a great prophetic word. The principle applies to this moment. London is groaning. New York is groaning. Paris is groaning. Centers of light and fashion and beauty, all are groaning, believe me, this morning. All the things we can hear, and the things that defy our hearing but which are there, the sob, and sigh, and wail of oppressed humanity. What are they waiting for? For you to be a saint and to live as becomes a saint. For me to have done with small thinking about saintship. For us, the property of God, to be at the disposal of God, the workmanship of God to be yielded wholly to God, the home of God to allow Him to possess every chamber.

When He so possesses His own there will be the salt that is aseptic, purifying all the life of the city and the nation; there will be light set upon a hill, illuminating vast expanses, and making all the details of domestic life beautiful, as a lampstand in the home. The world is waiting to see the saints of God, and God is waiting for His own. May God help us His saints, to live "as becometh saints."

CHAPTER XXIII

PREPARATION FOR SERVICE

In the year that king Uzziah died I saw the Lord sitting upon a throne, high and lifted up, and His train filled the temple. Above Him stood the seraphim: each one had six wings; with twain he covered his face, and with twain he covered his feet, and with twain he did fly. And one cried unto another, and said, Holy, holy, holy, is the lord of hosts: the whole earth is full of His glory. And the foundations of the thresholds were moved at the voice of him that cried, and the house was filled with smoke. Then said I, Woe is me! for I am undone; because I am a man of unclean lips, and I dwell in the midst of a people of unclean lips; for mine eyes have seen the King, the Lord of hosts. Then flew one of the seraphim unto me, having a live coal in his hand, which he had taken with the tongs from off the altar: and he touched my mouth with it, and said, Lo, this hath touched thy lips; and thine iniquity is taken away, and thy sin purged. And I heard the voice of the Lord, saying, Whom shall I send, and who will go for Us? Then I said, Here am I; send me. And He said, Go.

ISAIAH 6: 1-9a.

STANDING AS WE DO ON THE THRESHOLD OF OUR WINTER'S work, feeling that we are coming to days of harvest and of gracious ingathering, the question of my own heart has been, Lord, what hast Thou to say to me? I feel that if I can but

295

hear what He has to say to me, I may venture to pass the word on to you.

This passage of Scripture is familiar to us all. In the middle of the ninth verse the revelation of perpetual principles ends. After that we have the commission spoken to Isaiah concerning his own time. He was commissioned to utter a message of devastating judgment. We are not commissioned to utter that message. The local, and the incidental, occupy the last half of this chapter. The essential and the eternal occupy the first part.

The opening words of this passage fix in the history of the Hebrew people the event it recounts. "In the year that king Uzziah died." The reign of Uzziah over Judah, which had lasted for fifty-two years, was over, and his son Jotham was about to succeed to the throne. Israel was suffering under the fearful tyranny of a military despotism. Shallum came to the throne by the murder of his predecessor. Menahem came to the throne by the murder of Shallum. Pekahiah succeeded his father, but was murdered by Pekah. And now Pekah was on the throne, reigning over a people who were soon to be scattered.

The reign of Uzziah had been remarkable in many respects. When he ascended the throne fifty-two years before, as a youth of sixteen, he had set himself to seek God, and the issue had been a period of remarkable prosperity. He had conducted a series of victorious campaigns against the enemies of God, by which he restored much lost territory. Following these, he brought about internal development, the building of towers, the making of cisterns, the planting of the land, its cultivation, and the increasing of husbandry. It was a wonderful reign to a certain point. Then his heart became lifted up, and the man who was victorious over the perils of adversity was overcome by the perils of prosperity. He rebelled against God, and was smitten with leprosy, and for the last period of his life lived in a lazar house. At last he died.

It was at this point that there came to Isaiah, the son of Amoz, the vision recounted in this chapter. He had lived in Judah, and had known no occupant of the throne of his own people other than the king who had now passed away. In the economy of God the time had now arrived when he should come forth to his definite and public ministry. In this wonderful passage we have the story of his solemn ordination.

The passage falls into two parts, first, the vision; and second, the voice.

In the first verse these are the outstanding words, "I saw the Lord." In verse five we have the answer to that. "Then said I, Woe is me!" In verse eight we have the outstanding words of the second division. "I heard the voice of the Lord." In the last part of the same verse is the answer, "Then I said, Here am I; send me."

Take the simplest of these sentences that we may have the outline of the study on our minds. "I saw the Lord." . . . "Then said I." "I heard the voice of the Lord." . . . "Then I said." A vision and a voice, and in that order. First the vision with all that it meant of revelation to the soul of this man of truth concerning God, and consequently of truth concerning himself, and all that it led on to of cleansing. And then, and not till then, the voice, "Whom shall I send, and who will go for Us?" First the vision, and then the voice. First the personal relationship to essential Light, and Love; and then the relative commission in obedience to which, the man illuminated and cleansed, went out to do the work of God. If I am to do anything for my Master, today, tomorrow, and the next day, I must have this vision, I must hear this voice. My answer to the vision must be Isaiah's answer, and my answer to the voice must be his also.

Let us, then, first examine the vision. What did Isaiah see? The first thing that is impressed upon the mind in the study of the passage is that the prophet saw an occupied throne. "I saw the Lord sitting upon a throne, high and lifted up, and His train filled the temple." That is the first truth that broke upon the soul of the prophet, with such terrific force and power that he spoke as though he had never seen the vision before. As a matter of fact, this man had long seen the Lord high and lifted up, but the empty throne was the occasion which revealed to him the true significance of the filled Throne.

"In the year that King Uzziah died." The news spread from street to street, from town to town, from village to village, that the king was dead. There came to Isaiah the sense of loss in the passing of the king. Chaos was everywhere. Israel was in such a terrible condition that she could not exist any longer nationally. Judah was following hard and fast in the wake of Israel to the same defeat and disaster. The one throne to which Isaiah had looked for support was empty. Men said to the psalmist, "If the foundations be destroyed, what can the righteous do?"

And that, perchance, was the first feeling that came to the heart of the prophet when the throne of Judah was empty. Who now will succeed? Then, "In the year that king Uzziah died I saw the Lord sitting upon a throne." Behind the empty throne, there is a throne that is never empty. Over the chaos that appals the heart there is the God of order and government.

I think if we had cross-examined Isaiah, he would have been unable to describe the personality upon which his eyes rested, but he saw the Lord. A Person was manifested to him. Through this whole book of Isaiah there is presented a Personality vague and undefined, a Personality that startles us with contradictions, a Personality robed in splendor, girded with strength, with government sitting upon his shoulder; a Personality stripped, wounded, bruised, suffering; a King reigning in righteousness, and prosecuting His propaganda to the end of the ages, and through all the spheres, a bruised and broken Man Who says, "Who hath believed our report? and to whom hath the arm of the Lord been revealed?" Vague shadowy outlines, never quite clear until the New Testament is in your hand, but nevertheless a Person. Isaiah's first vision of this Person was so vague that he could not perfectly describe it, so definite that he said, "I saw the Lord."

He proceeded immediately from the description of the central Person to that of the surrounding facts; seraphim, flaming glory, smoke, reverberating thunder, and the maintenance of a song, but the Person is mentioned and left, "I saw the Lord." The essential truth is that of a Person enthroned.

There is a very beautiful connection between the twelfth chapter of the Gospel of John and the whole prophecy of Isaiah. It is the chapter of Jesus overshadowed by the Cross. The first incident is that of Mary's coming very near to His grief, and breaking the alabaster box of ointment upon His feet. The second incident is that of His entrance to Jerusalem, which we call the triumphal entry, all full of sorrow to Him. The third incident is that of the coming of the Greeks. The Cross is everywhere. It was the shadow of the Cross that drew forth the adoring worship of Mary, that filled His own eyes with tears as He rode into Jerusalem, that made Him reply when Greeks asked to see Him, "Except a grain of wheat fall into the earth and die, it abideth by itself alone."

Now look at verse forty-one in this chapter. "These things said Isaiah, because he saw His glory." What said Isaiah? "Lord, who hath believed our report?" "These things said Isaiah, because he saw His glory." Isaiah's conception in chapter fifty-three of the mystery and the agony of rejection had been made tremendous because he saw His glory. When did he see His glory? When he was commissioned for his work. "I saw the Lord sitting upon a throne, high and lifted up." The first thing the prophet saw ere he went forth to work that was to be hard and perilous and difficult was the vision of the enthroned God. The throne of Judah is empty. There is chaos everywhere. For this man the Throne is filled, and out of the chaos the cosmos is comng.

He next proceeded to speak of the surrounding glory, the seraphim, the flames of fire; the hosts of the Most High God. Six-winged seraphim. In the presence of that Personality, with two wings they veiled their faces, with two they veiled their feet, with two they were perpetually flying. This is of course symbolic, and we can interpret such symbolism only by Eastern thought. The face is the symbol of intellectual apprehension, the feet are the symbols of governmental procedure, the wings are symbolic of activity Divinely inspired. The unveiling of the nature of the enthroned One is seen in the activity of the burning spirits that surround the throne. They veil their faces, unable to come to perfect intellectual apprehension of the mystery of His Being. They veil their feet, for while they are principalities, dominions, rulers, their governmental procedure gains its strength from submission to His Throne. The veiling of the feet is the hiding of personal authority in the presence of supreme Authority. But the wings, the remaining wings, are ever active, inspired by the very Spirit of life; they perpetually serve under the authority of His Throne.

Now listen to the song. It is a twofold song. First, the song of the nature of the enthroned One. "Holy, holy, holy, is the Lord of hosts." Then it is a song about earth. I am always so thankful when I come to this. It is a song about earth in that high presence chamber, with the enthroned Jehovah revealed personally, but so that He cannot be described; surrounded by the flaming spirits that veil their faces of intelligence, and their feet of government, and beat their wings in perpetual service. What is this they sing of the earth? "The whole earth is full of His glory," or notice the marginal reading of the revised version, "the fulness of the whole earth is His glory." These spirits that surround the throne look down to the earth and see God's glory in it. Isaiah has a different vision of it presently, and these spirits saw his vision also, but they are singing in the presence of God of an ultimate triumph of truth, of a final restoration, of a final victory. They are singing by faith and hope, in the presence of God, of the victory that is to be. "The whole earth is full of His glory." The great psalm of the King, which describes His procedure to ultimate victory, ends with the words that the seraphim sang in the presence of God. "The whole earth is full of His glory." So that the psalm of the glory of God, which is part of the inheritance of the saint here and now amid the chaos and the darkness and the strife and the battle, is the perpetual song which angels sing.

Notice for a moment the effect of the song on the earthly temple. The very "thresholds were moved," trembled. "The house was filled with smoke." We shall be perfectly correct if we translate this word "smoke" by "anger." In Psalm 80, verse four, we read;

O Jehovah, God of hosts,
How long wilt Thou be angry against the prayer of Thy people?

The literal translation of this is, "How long wilt Thou smoke against the prayer of Thy people?" The connection shows that smoke is a symbol of anger. In the day of God's activity it is said by the ancient prophet Joel that there shall be "blood, and fire, and pillars of smoke"; and Isaiah, in that high presence chamber, saw the uplifted God upon His throne; saw the burning spirits round the throne veiling their faces and feet, and ceaselessly moving to do His bidding; heard their song, the song of ultimate victory, in the earth itself; and yet there was the trembling of things in the temple of God. There was the filling of the house with smoke, typical of His anger. So this man stood in the midst of the awful vision, conscious of God's holiness, and His enthronement, conscious of the victory that must be final, and yet conscious that anger was abroad, that judgment was out on the highway of the Most High. The house trembled and was filled with smoke.

And now how did he answer the vision? The answer was not a prepared one. The greatest words men speak in the presence of God, either about God, or to God, are words that come surging out of the deepest consciousness, words that must be spoken because no others are fit. And when this man stood in the midst of the glory, when for a moment his eyes were unveiled, what did he say? Oh, the agony of the cry, "Woe is me! for I am undone; because I am a man of unclean lips, and I dwell in the midst of a people of unclean lips." All of which means that when the prophet had a clear vision of God, he had the true vision of man. And when the prophet had the clearer vision of the Divine order, he had a more overwhelming sense of human disaster. Notice that the cry concerning himself proceeds backward, from effect to cause. The effect, "Woe is me!" The reason of the woe, "I am undone." The reason of the being undone, "I am a man of unclean lips."

Why unclean lips only? Why did he not say unclean heart, why did he not say unclean spirit? Again, the language is symbolic, and it is most simple symbolism. Let us turn over to the epistle of James (3:6). "The tongue is a fire: the world of iniquity among our members is the tongue, which defileth the whole body, and setteth on fire the wheel of nature, and is set on fire by hell. For every kind of beasts and birds, of creeping things and things in the sea, is tamed, and hath been tamed by mankind: but the tongue can no man tame; it is a restless evil, it is full of deadly poison." As in the Divine, the Word is the expression of the God; so in the human, the speech of man is the expression of man, and the lips and the tongue are the instruments of speech. This man standing in the presence of the glory confesses that his lips are polluted. Let Jesus speak, "The things which proceed out of the mouth come forth out of the heart; and they defile the man." Within is the fountain head of corruption, but it is poured out and expressed through the tongue and lips, and so Isaiah says, "I am undone; because I am a man of unclean lips." The words are unclean, because the fact that they have to express is an unclean fact. What has this to do with his work? Everything. I do not know how you all feel, my brethren, but the most stupendous evidence to my heart, every day growing, of the grace of God is not that He saves me. That is a great evidence of grace, amazing grace! But the most stupendous evidence of God's grace is that when He saves me He consents to use me. And, my brethren, one of the first qualifications for being ready is to have stood in the presence of His glory, and to have found out how unworthy I am to utter His message. God almighty is my witness that I am not speaking to you idly. Every day I am more astonished that God should use me at all.

And what follows? I do not know that it would not be good to sit still and read the rest almost without comment. It is so simple. "Then"—I wish I knew how to emphasize that "then," because it is the dividing line. We have tried to look at the glory of God, at the enthroned Jehovah, at this man smitten in his inner consciousness with a sense of unworthiness. Then what? "Then flew one of the seraphim." Taking in his hand one of the sacred vessels from the altar, the place of blood and fire, and catching one of the burning coals from the altar, he comes to that man.

Now, whereas I want to speak especially of the fact that for the man called to service there is perfect cleansing and energizing provided, what I want you to see first is that out of the midst of the overwhelming and awful glory of God comes the most overwhelming vision of His grace. The enthroned Jehovah surrounded by the burning spirits that worship. Do you hear the thunder of the seraphim as they sing? Can you hear anything else? I do not think I can. God can! What did He hear? The cry of a guilty man! Oh, soul of mine, take heart. One guilty man cries out in the consciousness of his sin, and the faint cry of that human soul, conscious of pollution, rises in the ear of God above the thunder of the seraphim. And a seraph must leave the place of worship to work when a human soul is in need. These are Divine measurements. These are not the measures we sometimes put upon evangelistic effort. That was evangelistic effort. And he brought the live coal and he touched the lips of the man, he touched that which the man had made the symbol of his own uncleanness. The man said, "I am undone; because I am a man of unclean lips," and the seraph touched the lips, and said, "lo, this hath touched thy lips; and thine iniquity is taken away, and thy sin purged." This is one of the cases where I am almost inclined to translate iniquity very literally as to the actual meaning of the word. "Thy crookedness has been taken away." Fire has straightened out three! But something more. "Thy sin is purged." Sin is offense, guilt, the thing in a man that is the outcome of his iniquity in his relation to

God. What of that? It is purged, and here you may use the old Hebrew word, "thy sin is expiated." It is the word that the Hebrew made use of when he referred to atonement. It is the word to cover over, not in the sense of covering over a polluted thing, but to atone, to blot out. Thy sin, as against this high excellence and glory of heaven is expiated. Thy personal crookedness is straightened out. Your relative guilt is expiated.

And how was it done? By the coal of fire from the altar, and God Almighty cannot deal with Isaiah in his uncleanness except by the coal of fire that comes from the altar.

What follows? Perhaps a pause. I do not know. There is no pause in the letterpress. I think there must have been a pause, a waiting moment, in which this man rose into the great consciousness that he was undone no longer, that his lips were no longer impure but purified; and it is as he waited in that great consciousness that the voice came. He had seen the vision of God. This was the outcome, and now the voice, and how much it says, "Whom shall I send, and who will go for Us?" Who will go? God is asking for volunteers. God needs someone to be sent, someone who will go. What is the question? Who is ready to be sent? "Whom shall I send?" "Who will go for Us?" and the emphasis in that second question is not on the "Go," but on "for Us." Who will be ready when I send them? Who will be in readiness to be sent, ready to represent Us? And then, thank God, notwithstanding that this man but a moment ago had expressed his consciousness of pollution, immediately came the answer, "Here am I; send me." "Here am I," that is abandonment; "send me," that is readiness. He could not have said that until his lips had been touched by the coal from the altar. The vision cursed him, but the fire cleansed him; and now when God wants help, this cleansed man says, I am at Thy disposal.

That is the whole law of service. In order to do successful service I need first a vision of God enthroned. Have you this vision of God? If you are not quite sure whether God's throne is tottering or not, you had better retire. You remember God's method of sifting an army. It was a wonderful method. Thirty-two thousand came out and said, We are all ready. And the first test was, Let the men fearful and afraid go home. And twenty-two thousand men turned right about face and marched home. Are you sure that was not a mistake? No, for in the day of battle the man who has fear in his heart is a peril. When the victory was won they all came back to shout. God bless them! But when we are fighting we do not want them.

Can we see God on His throne? That is the question. We can see the chaos. We are very blind if we cannot. National corruption, municipal rottenness, dilettante fooling with the problems of poverty that ought to be the problem of every statesman. But high over all earthly thrones is the Throne that never trembles. If you can see God on His Throne, then that Throne is commissioning you to take the evangel of the crucified Christ to cure all the ills of humanity. That is our message. We must have a vision of His enthronement, of His holiness, and we must have this also, the vision of His ultimate glory in the earth. And then we need the vision of self. If I may have a vision of His glory I need the true vision of self. We need also the cleansing that He provides. We are not fit for all this. But to stay there is to dishonor God. Remember the altar is there, and the fire is there. God help us to get to the altar. He will cleanse us and purge us, and with a baptism of fire make us all He wants us to be, if only we will let Him. Let us look up into His face, solemnly and earnestly saying, By the vision of Thine enthronement, by the matchless mercy of the altar and the fire, here am I; send me.

CHAPTER XXIV

POWER FOR SERVICE

But ye shall receive power, when the Holy Ghost is come upon you: and ye shall be My witnesses both in Jerusalem, and in all Judæa, and in Samaria, and unto the uttermost part of the earth.

ACTS 1:8.

IF WE KNOW OUR LORD ONLY AT THE CROSS WE KNOW VERY much, but not all. And if we know Him only in the place of His resurrection, from external observation, we know very much, but not all. After both the Cross and the resurrection He said to the men with whom He had tabernacled for three years, "Tarry ye in the city, until ye be clothed with power from on high." His first command to them after resurrection —first in the order of their obedience, last in the order of His actual utterance—was not to go, but to wait; not to hasten, but to tarry. And in that fact lies great significance.

How shall we describe these men? Let us first remember that they were lovers of the Lord, and loyal to Him. I do not think their question was so ignorant as we sometimes imagine it to be. They were not ignorant of God's ultimate intention. They were ignorant of God's present method. They did not understand the meaning of the Cross. They had never understood it. They had shunned it from its first mention. Attempting to escape it, they had been scattered like chaff before the wind. But they had been gathered again by that inexplicable mystery of His resurrection, and they were perforce compelled to new loyalty to the One Who stood amongst them. That explains their inquiry whether He was now about to fulfil the prophecy of the ancient Scriptures. And "He said unto them, It is not for you to know times of seasons, which the Father hath set within His own authority." That answer was not a rebuke for their conception of the ultimate. He did not say that the Kingdom was never to be restored to Israel. It is as though Christ had said to these men, I am not authorized of My Father to give you any program, or calendar. The Father hath set the times and seasons within His own authority. Israel will be restored, the Kingdom will be set up, the whole earth must yet be brought into submission to the Kingship of God, and all the beneficent results must come, but it is not for you to know the times of these things.

What, then, was necessary? "But ye shall receive power, when the Holy Ghost is come upon you: and ye shall be My witnesses both in Jerusalem, and in all Judæa and Samaria, and unto the uttermost part of the earth." From the viewpoint of the disciples at that moment this was a very unsatisfactory thing to say. Let us endeavor to understand what this meant to these men. How strange their experiences had been. He had disappointed them in His plan and method. They had been brought to despair by His Cross. Strange new hopes and expectations had arisen in their hearts in the light of His resurrection. These were all again extinguished when He said that it was not for them to know times or seasons. All He told them was that they were to be His witnesses, and in order that they might be, they should receive power. A program without a program! No details, no arrangements, none of the things we love so much, but only an attitude and an atmosphere, a duty and a dynamic, a responsibility and a resource! Witnesses in the power of the Spirit. Therefore, He said to them, Wait, tarry. He halted them upon the verge of their going, arrested them at the very moment when they would have been away to tell the mystic story of His resurrection. Just as He had demonstrated His Kingship by resurrection so that there could be no doubt to any honest mind, and they were anxious to tell the story, He said, No, not yet, you are not ready, you must wait.

For what were they to wait? The answer is in one word of the text, and that word I desire to emphasize, and deal with some of its suggestions: "power." "Ye shall receive power, when the Holy Ghost is come upon you." Now in order that we may understand the meaning of the power let us look at these men, for we shall understand the provision by a study of the lack. What did they lack? First of all, they needed a new intellectual power. The use of the word power in that connection is a perfectly accurate one, for we speak of a man of strong mind, and of the strengthening of the mind. These men at the moment lacked the ability to apprehend truth which it was necessary for them to understand if they were indeed to be witnesses of Jesus. This inability they had demonstrated by their attitude toward Him during His public ministry, and by the question they asked as they stood around Him in the light of His resurrection, power and glory. They were ignorant of the very things that they must appreciate intellectually if they were to accomplish the purpose of their Lord. They did not understand the meaning of the halt in the apparent progress of the King to the Kingdom. They did not understand the nature of the Kingdom. They had a correct idea of what its external manifestation would be; but they did not understand all that was necessary to the production thereof. They did not see that the King Who would set up the Kingdom toward which prophets looked, and of which seers sang, must begin, not at the circumference, but at the center. They did not understand that the first movement must be that of spiritual regeneration. They did not understand Him, they did not understand His Cross, they did not understand His resurrection. They did not understand what He was about to do. They needed a new intellectual power. Not long ere He had left them, in those wonderful discourses which are precious to us still, He had said that most remarkable thing, "I have yet many things to say unto you, but ye cannot bear them now," which did not mean merely that He had to tell them of coming suffering, of which they would be afraid, but that the things which He had to tell their minds could not grasp. All through the ministry of Jesus He said things they never understood until the Spirit brought them to their remembrance, and they flamed in new light and meaning.

When I am told it is necessary for me to go back to the Gospels and confine my attention to them, I say I cannot do it. They are not complete, final, and perfect. These men in the olden days did not understand the meaning of the Cross. And we never find the Christ in all His fulness until we have passed through the preliminary and necessary study of the Gospels into the spacious and far-reaching splendor of the Acts of the Apostles, and the Epistles. They needed intellectual power, the quickening of the mind which should enable them to see to the heart of the spiritual mystery.

Then they needed also spiritual power, in the first and simplest sense of the word. Spiritual power as against the power of the carnal life and nature. In the Corinthian letter Paul carefully distinguished between these two things. "I, brethren, could not speak unto you as unto spiritual, but as unto carnal, as unto babes in Christ." These men were still in the grip of their own carnal nature, and in order to be witnesses they had to live before the world the life of spiritual victory. They had to manifest to men the fact that a life can be lived, which never answers the call of the flesh; that it is possible for man, and indeed, it is God's first Divine intention for man, that he should see the upper things, and not the lower; that he should—to use the Apostle's great word—keep the body under, which does not for a moment mean that he is to bruise and chastise and mutilate the body, but that it is to be kept in its proper place, that of subservience. These men had to live that life, and they were unequal to it. The desires of the flesh and of the mind were triumphing within them, and fleshly ideals had undoubtedly crept into their estimate of the work of the Christ. But there came a moment, to quote the great apostle, when he said, "Wherefore we henceforth know no man after the flesh: even though we have known Christ after the flesh, yet now we know Him so no more." But these men had not yet come to that place of spiritual ascendancy and power. They were still living the carnal life, and they needed a power that should set them above the pull of the base and the low, and make them kings over the territory of their own being by spiritual appreciation and spiritual power.

These men needed a new power of the affection and of the will. They were going out to strange days, and He knew it right well. He had told them in some of His earliest discourses of what they would pass through after His crucifixion. He had told them that He would send them forth as sheep in the midst of wolves, that men would hunt and persecute them from city to city, and imagine they did God service; and they needed a new power of the affection and of the will, for the world would be against them. See how they had evidenced that need in recent days. No one can deny—

and I always try to be careful here—that they loved their Lord. They loved Him with all the affection of their nature before the Cross, and yet when the storm burst about His sacred head, and all the malice of hell, expressing itself through men, was let loose upon Him, where were they? "All the disciples left Him, and fled." I am not inclined to blame them. I say it reverently that I am afraid I would have been one of the first to flee. Oh, it was a tragic hour! But they have to face the storm again. The world desiring to crucify Him will desire to crucify them, and if they incarnate His life of truth and perfection the spirit of evil will be against them. They are not going to an easy softness of life, but to heroism, and conflict, and danger; and if the old life was not strong enough to keep them loyal when He was the Center of the storm, how are they to be kept loyal when they themselves become the center of the storm? They need a new power of the affection and the will.

And, finally, they needed a new power which would be with them, and enable them to do the peculiar and remarkable work committed to them, because He had forbidden them to use the things which men usually consider powerful. They were to go and proclaim the Kingdom of God. They were sent forth to proclaim the fact that God's Kingdom centers around God's King, and that God had vindicated the Kingship of Jesus by raising Him from the dead. These men were not sent to preach a theory of God's Kingship. They were sent to bring men into the Kingdom. He did not send these men forth to preach a new philosophy, or a new theory. He sent them to compel wills, and bring men into subjection. And yet—He had already said in the tragic moment of His own rejection, "Put up again thy sword into its place: for all they that take the sword shall perish with the sword"—they were not to win His victories by the unsheathing of the sword. And no victory for Christ has ever been won in that way. To use the sword in order to establish His Kingdom is a blunder and mistake. And, moreover, they were not to establish His Kingdom by policy. They were not to seek the help of other forces, or enter into alliances with them. What, then, were they to do? Tell a story? That was all. The story of the risen, crucified, exalted, coming Christ. There is no government on earth that would not hold you in contempt if you suggested that they should extend their territory by telling a story. Here I do not desire to be misunderstood. They had a great deal more to do when the people, hearing the story, became obedient to it and submitted to the King. Then there was to be organization; then there was to be the realization of the Kingship of God. But the victories were to be won by the telling of the story. When Paul passed through those Greek cities, they said of him in Athens, "This babbler" cometh hither also. The word "babbler" indicates a teller of stories, and they so called him because he told them of Jesus and the resurrection. That is all these men had to do. They were to establish a Kingdom by telling a tale.

Tell me the old, old story of Jesus and His love.

That is the Church's work. It is her initial work. Without banners, or flags, or trumpets, or policies, or sword, she is to go out and tell the story; to herald the evangel.

Now look at these men. Lacking intellectual power, they could not appreciate the meaning; lacking spiritual power, they were not free from the pull of the carnal; weak in their affectional nature, they were not strong enough to stand against the enmity of the world; and devoid of any power upon which they set any value, they were unable to accomplish His work. To them He said, Wait, tarry! It is not for you to have the calendar and the almanac and the program. These things are hidden in the authority of the Father. But you are to be My witnesses, and you will need intellectual power to witness as you should; you will need spiritual power, behind the witness of the lip there must be that of the life; you will need an affectional power if you are to be true to Me amid the storm and stress; you will need a new volitional power in the work committed to you.

We turn for a moment or two, then, to notice the nature of the power promised. We have been attempting to understand it by considering the lack. Now see how this promise of power meets all the need. The power in which these men were to do their work is in no sense of men, and yet it is to be closely united to men. The power in which the Christ triumphed through the testimony of the disciples, and the power in which He still triumphs through their testimony, is entirely apart from the men as to source, but it is closely united to man as to act. And here is the whole philosophy of Christian life, and of service especially. The Spirit of God can do the work of Christ in the world only through human instrumentality. Man can do the work of Christ in the world only through the power of the Spirit. He united forever the souls that trusted Him with the infinite Spirit of power. In them He found a medium for the Spirit to carry on His enterprises and accomplish His victory. In the Spirit He found for them the full and great and gracious equipment which would enable them to do all He was sending them to do. The Holy Spirit, said He, shall come upon you. That promise, so simple, and yet so sublime, stands over against the need of which we have spoken. They lacked intellectual power, but the Spirit knoweth the deep things of God, and discerneth all things. When He came to these men, at once the horizon was flung far back, and the opaque became transparent, and the bloody and brutal Cross flamed into the purple glory of imperial dignity and redemptive power. And no man filled with the Holy Spirit of God ever dares to speak of the Cross in the terms of the human only. These men saw the meaning, and all life was changed in its appearance when God by the Holy Spirit came into intimate and abiding relationship with them. God Himself was new. Christ was new, men were changed, the matters of the moment took on a different appearance. Wherever they looked, they saw the old things, but never again were they the same. Yea, verily.

> Earth's crammed with heaven,
> And every common bush afire with God;
> But only he who sees, takes off his shoes—
> The rest sit round it, and pluck blackberries.

These men had been plucking blackberries! But when the Spirit came they saw the flaming bush! It was the same bush, and other men passed it by and saw it only as the scrub bush of the dreary desert, but they saw it flaming with meaning.

And the coming of the Spirit meant, not merely intellectual power, but also spiritual power. It was when their lives became suffused with that spiritual energy which is of God that they reached the plane of holiness of life and character. Holiness is never merely it, it is Him; never merely something into which a man forces Himself by self-will, but something into which a man forces Himself by self-will, but something into which a man comes by the unveiling of God by the Holy Ghost. And these men went out to show other men what human life might be, a triumph every day, not because they had won by struggling, but by yielding to the Spirit. They found a power mastering the carnal when the spiritual took possession of them.

And did they need a new power of the affection and the will? The coming of the Spirit meant this, that the love of

God was shed abroad in their heart. Is not that another of the phrases that we have done despite to because we have treated it in a temporary and superficial and small way? The love of God was shed abroad in their heart, and when the Spirit came and dwelt in them, He brought God's love for Christ, and made it their love for Christ. And, oh, the change. I need not stay to illustrate it. The Acts of the Apostles is full of revelation. Peter had said, in the presence of the Cross—Spare Thyself! Not that, anything but the Cross. In this new book I turn to the fifth chapter, and I read that he counted it all joy that he was counted worthy to suffer for the Name. I do not read any more of men running from danger. I read of men telling indeed of their troubles, telling how they have been in peril from false brethren, and robbers, on land, and sea, receiving stripes forty save one again and again, being left mauled and half dead by brutal hands; but instead of hearing them speak of suffering in terms of complaint, I hear them say, I glory in my affliction. What is the reason? The Spirit has taken hold of their own weak though loyal affection, and has merged it into the affection of Deity, and the tides of God's love, flowing through them, make them stronger than all the forces that could be against them.

And finally mark this. They have no sword save the sword of the Spirit. They have no program save the orderliness of the Spirit. But when presently I watch these men begin that missionary progress, which has never been completed, and which we are so slow about, I see a group of men who do not impress their age by what they are in themselves. Brethren, remmeber this, the one thing that puzzled, supremely puzzled priests and Pharisees and rulers was how *these* men did these things. How do you account for it? was the question asked, and I hear their own answers, "We are witnesses of these things; and so is the Holy Ghost." That is the answer. One almost trembles as one reads the words. We have wandered so far from the apostolic conception that we dare hardly use them. I wonder if we dare open our next month's church meeting with the words, "It seemed good to the Holy Ghost, and to us." I am here for contemplation rather than application. But this is the ancient picture, and I look at the beginning of things, and I see Peter, rough, magnificent, impetuous Peter—I love him with all my heart—as he begins to talk, and I watch the curious multitude of Hebrews gathered from all the district around, listening to him, with their prejudices and pride, and I watch until I see them swept by the wind of God, and the cry goes up, and men and women are being gathered into the Kingdom.

> See how great a flame aspires:
> Kindled by a spark of grace,
> Jesu's love the nations fires,
> Sets the kingdoms on a blaze.
>
> To bring fire on earth He came;
> Kindled in some hearts it is . . .
> Oh, that all might catch the flame,
> All partake the glorious bliss."

How was it done? "We are witnesses, and so is the Holy Ghost." The saints in fellowship with the Spirit need neither sword, nor policy, nor patronage of earthly power. Their victory is an assured victory.

Did I say a moment ago I was not here for purposes of application? Suffer me one or two words by way of application. Christ's word to us here gathered, whether of this particular fellowship or of another, is exactly the same as to these first disciples. I cannot apply it in all its details. I need not. But He is saying to us, "It is not for you to know times or seasons." There are some who are always trying to arrange times and seasons. I have had a letter from San Francisco which tells me the Lord is coming in seven years, and I am to be ready for Him. I do not like to think He is seven years away. He is at the door. He may disturb me at my preaching. Whether He disturbs me at work or play, oh that I may be able to shout, "Amen, come, Lord Jesus." Burn your almanacs, and give up trying to deal with God's arrangements. What is your work? You are My witnesses, so says the King. Yes, but He is also saying this, You shall be endued with power when the Holy Spirit is come upon you. There is a difference between these men and us. They had to wait, for the Spirit was not yet given. You and I have not to wait. The Spirit is given. Yes, we must wait, unless we have the fulness of the Spirit. Unless we have put out of our life the things He forbids, I had better quit my preaching, and you your Sabbath-school Class, and every form of service. Unless we know the power, we had better tarry, but we need not tarry. The upper room at Pentecost was not more full of the Spirit than is this chapel this morning. O'er all the assembly He broods, close to every life is He. Oh, soul of mine, admit Him. And I can admit Him only as in absolute loyalty I crown the Christ, and give Him right of way o'er all the territory of my being. And if I do that, this Spirit, without sound of mighty rushing wind, without sign of fire, will fill and equip, and I, even I, oh, matchless grace of God, may be His witness too.

CHAPTER XXV

CHRIST'S KNOWLEDGE OF MEN

Now when He was in Jerusalem at the passover, during the feast, many believed on His name, beholding His signs which He did. But Jesus did not trust Himself unto them, for that He knew all men, and because He needed not that anyone should bear witness concerning man; for He Himself knew what was in man.
JOHN 2:23-25.

THE CLOSING STATEMENT OF THESE VERSES EXPLAINS WHY Jesus did not trust certain men who trusted Him. The outward commitment of the life to Him, and the belief which was merely a persuasion toward Him on account of signs seen, were nothing when the heart was not wholly and absolutely abandoned to Him, when in the deepest of the life there was still reserve. The trust was not complete and Christ can never commit Himself to any man who does not commit himself to Christ. I remember once hearing Dwight Lyman Moody says, "Christ is as great a Saviour as your faith makes Him." The perpetual law of Christ's dealing with souls may be expressed in this very simple formula, "All for all." If I have reposed in Him some imperfect and partial trust, He cannot trust me with all His confidence. He cannot commit to me all that He is unless I have committed to Him all that I am. Had we been in Jerusalem at that time, and had we seen the people crowding to Him, and trusting Him, in all probability we should have been eager to count them, to number them; the fever for statistics would have been upon us as it is until this hour. We should have been inclined to say to Him, "Lord, everything is going well! See how these people are trusting Thee!" Then we would have been surprised to notice that He did not commit Himself to them. Why not? Because "He knew all men." He did not require any testimony borne to Him concerning them, "for He Himself knew what was in man."

This statement concerning Christ must be interpreted, not in the light of this immediate paragraph merely, but also in the light of the whole Gospel of John, and particularly in that of the prologue. "He knew all men." Who? To Whom does the personal pronoun refer. For answer we turn back to the opening words of the Gospel. "In the beginning was the Word, and the Word was with God, and the Word was God. . . . And *the Word* became flesh, and tabernacled among us." "He—*the Word*—knew all men. . . . He—*the Word*—needed not that anyone should bear witness concerning man; for He—*the Word*—Himself knew what was in man."

The theme, then, of my message is the knowledge which Christ has of man, and the result of that knowledge in His dealings with men. In the coming weeks—as God shall help me—I propose to consider some illustrations which this Gospel affords of these great truths.

I begin with the general terms: Christ's knowledge of man and His consequent method with men. That will be a message of comfort or of fire according to what we are. There was a time when it was a very common thing to see on the walls of nurseries and schoolrooms a motto which read: "Thou, God, seest me." That statement is perfectly true,

God does see us, but I have often thought that the tone in which it was recited was utterly false. If it was so recited to a child as to make the child think merely of God as present as a moral policeman, watching, it was wholly bad. Do not be surprised that your child has run away from God if you have not interpreted Him. It is a great truth. We need still to put it in the nursery where the child can see it; only God help us so to interpret God that when we put that truth before the child he may know what God is. You say, Would you take away the sternness of the truth of God's knowledge of men? By no means, but neither would I take away the infinite compassion, the love and beauty of the truth. That old truth printed for us to look at as children is fire or comfort according to what we are. Is there some sin gripping your life, mastering you, to which you are yielding yourself. A solemn hush fell on all the congregation tonight as I read, "Thou knowest my downsitting and mine uprising, Thou understandest my thought afar off." How did the reading of the psalm affect you? If you came with sin cherished, you trembled! Are you a broken-hearted sinner, knowing your sin and desiring to break with it tonight? Then, oh, the comfort of the words, "Thou knowest my thought afar off. Thou searchest out my path and my lying down, and art acquainted with all my ways. For there is not a word in my tongue, but, lo, O Lord, Thou knowest it altogether." Oh, there is such relief for the sinner when he is found out. Man, you are found out. He knows. "He knew all men."

This passage is more particular in its assertion than appears at first. To read it carefully is to see that the writer was indeed most careful in his choice of words. He declares that this knowledge which Christ had of men was immediate, was profound, was universal.

It was immediate knowledge. Notice the word Himself.

"Jesus did not trust *Himself* unto them . . . for He *Himself* knew what was in man." He knew man in Himself and of Himself. He needed not that anyone should bear witness concerning man. We are brought into the presence of a knowledge of man that is peculiar to Christ, to that Christ Who is God incarnate. Here is knowledge of man that no other possessed. I cannot know any man apart from testimony. He needs no testimony to give Him knowledge of man. This is brought out in one of the ancient prophecies concerning the coming Messiah, the perfect Judge of men. "He shall not judge after the sight of His eyes, neither reprove after the hearing of His ears: but with righteous judgments shall He judge." How? He knows all men, and, mark this, He knows what is in man. This is the truth of the Bible from cover to cover. It is a fundamental truth of Christianity, a great and startling truth, and yet we do not remember it, or live in the power of it. The meaning of the incarnation is in part that this truth was wrought out into human consciousness. I take up the Gospel of John and in the light of this text I read it through again, and am impressed by the fact that Christ moved amongst men, and had perfect knowledge of them.

There was no hesitation in His dealing with them. They passed before Him, man after man, woman after woman, and in a moment He spoke the word that needed to be said, dealt with them in the one way that met their need. He knew them. He asked them no questions in order to discover the truth concerning them. He perpetually questioned them in the light of truth possessed. He knew men. The Gospel of John works out into visibility this tremendous truth, which, if men can but grasp it, will alter all their lives, mold their character, and drive them in the way in which they should go. His knowledge was immediate, apart from testimony.

Then His knowledge was profound. I have already

touched upon it. Let me emphasize it again. You notice the Apostle says two things. "He knew all men," individualities, units. "He knew what was in man," the generic term, human nature, the human heart, and all the deep truth concerning it. He knew all men, the varied manifestations of the one common humanity. He knew what was in man, the essential being. We fail of knowing men because we do not know man. Here in the presence of the men of His own age stood One Who to their seeing was a man, and yet standing there in their presence as they passed before Him He knew them all. Simon, thy name is Simon, it shall be Peter. He knew the whole make-up of the man. Nathanael, I saw thee under the fig tree. Thou art a worshiper in whom there is no guile. So on and on, with perfect ease flashing the truth of each man's life into the open word so that others knew the man, and the man knew himself as never before. It was profound knowledge. He did not form His estimate of human life and character from external manifestations, but He set the external in the light of the inward fact. He knew what was in man.

This knowledge was not merely immediate and profound, it was universal, as we see from the Gospel instances. Christ's knowledge of men was not the intuition of kinship. By that I mean that a man of one race understand the men of his own race, but this Man understood all races. If He was dealing with a Hebrew, He knew exactly how to speak to a Hebrew in the language of Hebrew thinking. If Greeks came, saying, "We would see Jesus," He used language in reference to them which revealed His intimate acquaintance with the Greek mysteries which were unknown to Hebrews of His own time. "Except a grain of wheat fall into the earth and die, it abideth by itself alone." To the men who stood about Him on that day it was a strange thing to say, but the Greeks understood it. Only recently we have come to know something of these Greek mysteries, and we have discovered that at the heart of one lay the representation of the cutting off of the ear of wheat in order to gain more abundant life. The two Greeks came up to Him. He was a Hebrew prophet, and they found Him a master of their own mysteries. Standing in their presence He knew them, He knew all that was in them.

He knew men of different temperaments: whether it were the retiring, shrinking Philip, having to be called before he followed, and forevermore livng, as my friend Mr. Elvet Lewis has beautifully put it, on the edge of the crowd, or whether it was fiery, impetuous Peter, He knew them and dealt with them according to their temperaments. He so spoke in metropolitan Jerusalem as to arrest the attention of the leaders of the day, men of light and leading, and as to make them say, "How hath this Man letters, having never learned?" He so spoke to the great crowd of poor people that they heard Him and trusted Him. He won them. He knew men of all ages, men of years, young men, little children, men of all habits. He knew man, and because He knew man He knew men. If you and I try to study humanity by studying men we shall never understand humanity. If we come to know man in the light of God's revelation we shall know how to deal with men. Here standing in the midst was one who knew them.

What knowledge had He of man? I take the whole of the Gospels, and I find, if I study them, Christ's conception of humanity. He looked upon man as spiritual in being, as sinning in experience, as salvable by grace.

He dealt with man as spiritual in being. They crucified Him because of that. "Seek ye first the Kingdom of God" was a great spiritual word, startling the valleys and mountain heights of Judea. "Repent ye, for the Kingdom of heaven is at hand," was a clarion call from dust to Deity, from materialism to spirituality. "Be not afraid of them which kill the body, but are not able to kill the soul," evinced a fine scorn for the life that did not count eternities or deal with God. Whether He looked into the face of the impotent man at the pool, a pauper seeking charity, or into the face of the mitred high priest, He dealt with the spirit behind. His conception of humanity was that it was spiritual.

His conception of humanity, moreover, was that it is sinning in experience. Sin was that with which He had come to deal in tears and passion and blood. When He spoke to men upon their highest level and recognized the best in them, He flashed into the midst of His recognition the revelation of man's evil as well as his good. "Ye know how to give good gifts to your children." That is the finest thing you can say about man, it recognizes his tenderness, his compassion, his fatherhood, the most beautiful thing in man. What else? "If ye, then, *being evil*." He knew that man in experience was sinning, and always dealt with him as a sinner.

But this knowledge did not produce hopelessness in Him, for He dealt with men everywhere as being salvable by grace. Sometimes one finds oneself limited, straitened to find words to tell some great truth! So am I now! How shall I tell it? How shall I say what I mean? Thus—He treated men as worth dying for. He looked upon man as possible of being remade through His passion and His death! How a man would like to stay here were he preaching to Christian people rather than to an assembly in which there are those who are seeking Christ. These are the views of humanity which create the evangelistic fervor. Every human face is the outward manifestation of spiritual being. Every human being is in the grip of sin in some form. Every human being can be saved. In the power of these things we dare preach and work. He knew what was in man.

If you look at the truth and ask the question. What did Christ know of man? you are simply overwhelmed by the variety. You find as you go through the Gospel of John that no two men appeared alike before Him, and that He did not deal with any two men alike. We are saying to men perpetually, to every man who crosses our pathway, You must be born again. There is a sense in which it is true, but Christ said it to only one man. It was true of every man, but He did not approach every man from that standpoint. Of the personalities that came into contact with Christ, this Master Winner of souls, He did not deal with two in the same way. He knew the personal peculiarity, the individual idiosyncrasy, and He dealt with it. He was always leading men to recognition of their spiritual being, to abandonment of their sin, to the river of grace which would heal them, but He acted in a thousand different ways. Every man who came to Him was dealt with by the method demanded by his immediate need. Christ knew what was in man.

That leads me to the second thought, some of the general results of this great knowledge. I begin with the broader facts. What did His knowledge of men produce in the Christ? My first answer is the answer of the whole book. His incarnation is the first result. He expressed God to man through man's own nature. "No man hath seen God at any time; the only begotten Son, which is in the bosom of the Father, He hath declared Him." How? By being made flesh. That was the first thing He came to do. That is the burden of my message. If I can see how Christ looked at man I shall know God's attitude. If I can discover the diversity of His method and learn therefrom, that though I am a lonely man, there being no other like me in the world, having peculiar sins and temptations, so that I cannot be classified, Christ can yet deal with me, I shall know that God can deal with me. The incarnation was not the beginning of a new fact, it was the initiation of a new revelation. When the Word became flesh and eternal nearness of God blossomed into visibility, but the psalmist of the olden day had sung the great truth, Thou knowest me, I cannot escape from thee. God was ever present, but the fact became patent when the Man of Nazareth took form and substance and shape, so that these very eyes could see, and this very hand could feel, and this life of mine could come to understand. He did that because of His knowledge of man. His knowledge of man compelled Him to express God for humanity that humanity mght have knowledge of God.

Incarnation is not all. It is the way into the mightier, and the next word I use is salvation. He knew man, and what did He? He came, let me not use any words of my own. We fall back upon His own words, they are so familiar to us, and they are music to us tonight, "The Son of Man came to seek and to save that which was lost."

> Plunged in a gulf of dark despair,
> We wretched sinners lay.
> He saw, and, oh, amazing love,
> He flew to our relief.

Then mark, I pray you, what follows. This is the thing of all things that I want to say in the closing words of my message tonight. Being in human life, visible by incarnation, being there for the saving of men, watch Him carefully, see how He treats every case alone: one issue, but many ways. I take up this Gospel and run through it and see Him in contact first with John the Baptist, and what does He do? He so deals with the prophet who has seen the flaming vision as to make the prophet content to say, "He must increase, but I must decrease." Andrew approaches Him. The adventurous seeker who turns from John with all sincerity to follow and see what some new teacher has to say. Christ turns and sees him. Andrew asks, "Rabbi, where abidest Thou?" How will Christ deal with him? "Come, and ye shall see." You are curious about Me, come along and I will show you where I live. If you had been a worker in some inquiry rooms you would perhaps have put Him outside because His method was not right! Peter, the man of possibility, what will Christ do with him? Tell him his possibility and then through processes realize it. Philip, the reserved man, Christ sees him, calls him. He would never come unless called, so He will call him and Philip comes. Nathanael, the guileless worshiper, brought by another to the Christ. Christ fulfils all that there was in this worship and brings him into such fellowship with Himself that he becomes Bartholomew the apostle. Mary, His own Mother's supreme human affection, He corrects, and at last commits her in human love to John. Nicodemus, the intellectual seeker, the man who thinks that everything is to come by way of knowledge; pure and upright in character so far as he had light, Christ brings him to the wicket gate and says, What you want is not learning, but life, "Ye must be born anew." The woman of Samaria, the flippant sinner who is ready for a theological argument but not for repentance. He searches her, flames upon her His knowledge, and then sends her to be the messenger to the city, having saved her. The nobleman, the sorrowing father with his boy ill, persistent in his appeal, what will Christ do? Heal his son and so win the father, for the whole house believed. There in the porches of Bethesda is an impotent man, utterly unable to lift himself. He will approach him, renew his hope, set him upon his feet, pronounce him whole and bid him sin no more. A woman taken in adultery, condemned. What will He do. Deliver her and lay upon her delivered spirit the great charge not to sin. A man born blind in the great and mysterious economy of God in order that God's works may be manifested in him. He gave him sight and made him the first worshiper outside the Jewish economy. Martha, honest, restless, He will patiently teach. Mary, the lowly disciple, He will fill her soul with His great grace. To Lazarus dead He will give life. Judas Iscariot, the thief, He will expose and exclude. Thomas, the skeptic, He will give him patient and gentle instruction. Annas and Caiaphas, mean and false, He will rebuke and then be silent in their presence. Pilate, the time-server, He will strive to save and then abandon. Joseph of Arimathea, the secret disciple, He will at last bring into such circumstances that his discipleship flames into light. Mary of Magdala, devil possessed, He will cast out the devil and make her the great messenger of His love and of His resurrection. John the rare dreamer, the man seeing visions and attempting to listen to the mystic music of the spheres, He will give him the apocalypse, the unveiling, signs and wonders in the heavens above and the earth beneath. He deals with every man according to his need.

Now hear me, I bring you tonight, in conclusion, the word of the herald in the first chapter of the Gospel, "In the midst of you standeth One Whom ye know not, even He that cometh after me, the latchet of Whose shoe I am not worthy to unloose." He knows you absolutely, perfectly, profoundly, finally. Not only better than your neighbor knows you, better than you know yourself! That is the final comfort to me. As God is my witness, during the last few months if only I had known myself I would have abandoned hope in more than one dark hour, but the memory of the fact that He knows me better than I know myself, that He looked into the face of Peter and said to him, "The cock shall not crow, till thou hast denied me thrice. Let not your heart be troubled," trust Me, is my comfort. Man, where are you? Would God that I could lay hands, violent hands of love, upon you. He knows you. All things are naked and open to His eyes, and He loves you notwithstanding, and is able to save you to the uttermost, and He will deal with you along the line that is necessary to your making. I pray you turn to Him for perfect understanding, for His perfect understanding of you. I said it was a comfort to be found out. Many a man has hidden a sin, a felony, for years, attempting not to be found out, but the morning in which the hand of the law arrested him was a morning of comfort, it was a relief to be found out. Man, you are found out. He knows, God help you, He knows. What does it matter that mother, or wife, or brother or sister, or neighbor or friend does not know, He knows. Oh, but you say, it is not merely sin, it is weakness, difficulty, I cannot get anyone to appreciate the peculiar difficulty of my life. He knows. There is nothing in the wide world so precious as someone who knows. That is friendship. The measure in which you know and understand me is the measure of your friendship. It may make you rebuke me, but it is friendship. He knows. It is the basis of friendship. Oh, if I could get you to Him! I do not care anything about your getting to me. I care nothing about your getting into the church, you will do that after; you cannot help it. Get to Him for perfect understanding and know as you come to Him that there is no necessity for subterfuge, and no use therein; He knows you.

Know also that when you come to Him you will have not merely perfect understanding, you will have faithful dealing. He will not put His hand upon you in false pity and say these things do not matter. If your right hand offends you, cut it off. If your right eye is making you stumble into lust, gouge it out, fling it away. That is what He will say to you. No man here wants a medical man who faces a disease and tells you it does not matter. You want a man who will take hold of it and with knife and strength cut it out. The Physician of souls is such. He will be faithful with you.

Blessed be God, there is another word. You come not merely for perfect understanding, faithful dealing, but for certain salvation. Demonstrate to me that He cannot save you and I quit preaching. Prove to me that your case is beyond the power of Christ and the evangel breaks down. But you cannot prove it. Oh that there may come to us sooner or later a great baptism of passionate honesty. Witnesses are everywhere here, men and women who know His power; who could not, but can; who were fast bound in sin and nature's night, but who awoke as a ray of light came into the dungeon from His presence, whose chains fell off and who went forth to live, serve, and follow Him. If you will but come to Him because He knows you and let Him deal with you in all His faithfulness, you will find Him able to save you. May God in His grace bring you to this Christ Who knows you, that He may save you.

CHAPTER XXVI

CENTER AND CIRCUMFERENCE

Look unto Me, and be ye saved, all the ends of the earth: for I am God, and there is none else.
Face unto Me, and be ye set free, all the ends of the earth: for I am God, and there is none else.
                                            ISAIAH 45:22.

THIS IS THE GREAT DIVINE WORD TO MAN, THE PERPETUAL call of love; it is therefore the Church's all-inclusive message. All the prophets, seers and psalmists of the past in varied tones and with differing emphases have uttered the same message. Upon man's answer to the message—when he has heard it— has depended his condition, his character, his destiny. "Face unto Me, and be ye set free, all the ends of the earth: for I am God." God gave the highest revelation of Himself to humanity in the incarnation, therefore these words of the ancient prophecy are supremely the words of Christ. The context of my text is quoted by the writers of the New Testament in direct application to Him. We are warranted, therefore, in dealing with this passage as finding its most powerful delivery in the Person and ministry of Jesus. It is through the fact of that ministry, not merely the ministry of nineteen centuries ago, which was straitened and limited, but the perpetual ministry of the Christ from Pentecost until now, that the Church is able to deliver this message. I think you will see what is on my own heart and mind this morning. We are facing, so far as our union as ministers and people is concerned, a new year of work. I am very much inclined to forget the things that are behind in order that we may press toward those that are before. As we face the future we are far more conscious this morning than we were three years ago of the problems, perplexities, and difficulties of our work. As we come to know the neighborhood in which we are called to serve we are sometimes almost overwhelmed. We are, morover, conscious that there are currents of thought which three years ago were undercurrents, but now are more evident and on the surface. It is well for us, therefore, quietly to get back for a morning's meditation to first principles, to remind our hearts, together as ministers and church, of what indeed is the Church's business. I gather up my whole message as we start our new year together and express it thus. We exist for one simple and all-inclusive purpose, to say in this neighborhood, and so far as we may be able to make our voice heard and our influence felt, one thing only, and that, "Look unto Me, and be ye saved, all the ends of the earth." We cannot at Westminster say that as it ought to be said. By that I mean to say the message is too full, too varied, too infinite for one church to deliver it. The Word of God is symbolically referred to in that great book of dreams and visions, signs and symbols: thus, "His voice as the voice of many waters." If here we can express the music of one of the streams which mingle into the many waters, we shall thank God. Yet it is well for us to understand the full music to which our contribution is to be made. We go back, then, to this old text that we all know so well, that everyone here who has ever preached has preached about, not to discover in it something new, but to find in it the old without which the new is always useless, but in the power of which there is perpetually springtime following winter, new beauties blossoming out of the essential root. So I bring you back to first principles this morning as we face another year's work.

Because the One Who here speaks has revealed Himself to us in Christ finally and perfectly I shall ask you to think with me first of the center, "Look unto Me," God as revealed in Christ; then of the circumference as here indicated, "All the ends of the earth"; then of the great claim as here made, "Look unto Me, and be ye saved." If one were seeking for a title for this morning's meditation, it might be described as, Center and Circumference, the Story of a Circle.

First, then, let us turn our thought to the Center. "Look unto *Me*, and be ye saved, all the ends of the earth: for *I am God*, and there is none else." The ultimate revelation of God to man was made in the Christ. As I read the story of Christ in the New Testament I discover that the Man of Nazareth was but the revelation of One Who has been—and now the tenses are all at fault and there is no help for it—and must always be the Center, the age-abiding Center of the universe of God. I am not going to tarry there. The ultimate, final words were written long ago by the Apostle-Seer to whom was given to see things for all who should follow him. In those opening verses of the Gospel which bears his name, he has revealed to us the fact that the One Who came into time as Jesus was, in the deepest fact of His actual personality, "the Word." In the beginning with God, Himself God, present at and presiding over creation, sustaining all things by the word of His power, so that nothing has been made save by Him: Himself the Light that lighteth every man that cometh into the world, and so present in some sense to every human consciousness. All these things are mysteries of which there can be no final explanation. I mention them only that our hearts may be reminded of them as we proceed a little further. This Christ Whom we are called to preach is the age-abiding Center of the creation of God, the Word of God Himself.

Leaving that, I ask you to remember that Christ is the center of human history. All that preceded Him led to Him and culminated in Him. Everything since the time of His manifestation in the world has been affected by His presence here. All the highways of the past led to Him. All the highways from His coming unto this moment have proceeded from Him. He was the consummation of the old hopes and aspirations. We may think of the world on Hebrew or Gentile side, taking those old and convenient divisions with which we were familiar in our childhood, and we shall discover that everything led toward Himself. The Hebrew nation lived by hope in the coming of One: they were looking for Him; they were unable to produce Him; when He came they did not know Him as a nation. Yet as the centuries have passed since His coming we see how in His own Person He perfectly fulfilled all their expectations, and was the incarnate music which had expressed itself in their singing. All that was high and noble and ideal in their aspirations found fulfilment in the Man of Nazareth Who was at once the King with government resting upon His shoulder, and the suffering Servant bruised and broken and battered Who had been described in their ancient writings. All the lines of the strange and wonderful Hebrew history led to Him. When He came ritual was fulfilled, aspiration was realized. There came with Him the dawning of that day the gleaming glory of which the men of the past had caught glimpses of from many a mountain peak. There came the clear articulation of that truth, certain parts and emphases of which the teachers of the Hebrew nation had spoken to the people through the centuries. All that perhaps is readily granted. It is equally true that in the historic Christ there was found the consummation of all that was excellent in the Gentile world, and there had been much. We are greatly mistaken, and upon the basis of that mistake shall misinterpret history, if we imagine that God had abandoned the world outside Hebraism. There had been mighty figures in the Gentile world. Take the testimony of the greatest of them preceding Christ; they themselves claim that they had been able to do no other than to teach men to ask questions. Socrates and Plato both practically declare in so many words that their mission was a mission of instructing men how to inquire. What were the questions they had asked? Questions concerning the immortality of man, concerning the destiny of the soul, concerning the character of the Creator. When one reads some of the writings of those Gentile thinkers one is inclined to think that God was leading them as distinctly and clearly as He was leading the Hebrew prophets in their doings and declarations, leading them to inquire. Yet remember this, they had been unable to give any answer to their questions. In some senses the world reached its greatest intellectual height before Christ came: Greek eloquence, sculpture, philosophy, poetry, we still go back to them for the standards. Yet the Greeks had not been able to answer these supreme questions. He came, a Man of Nazareth, and the very questions they had been asking were all answered. He "brought life and incorruption to light through the gospel." He, not in any long and set discourse, but by the familiar manifestation of His everyday speech, tore away the veil and revealed to men the destiny of the soul, and the nature and character of God, this last supremely. So that the idea of God which is embodied in the best thinking of the century in which we live has come absolutely as the result of His presence in the world and His teaching. He was thus not merely the One Who consummated and completed all that was excellent in the centuries before He came. He became the starting point of a new history. The old history had commenced with the creation of man. The new history commenced with the incarnation of God. By His coming new forces were introduced into human life, new aspirations were felt in the human heart. Men began to see, dimly, and yet as they had never seen before. That theme is a fascinating one. I remit it to your own thinking. I beg you often to think of it in these days. Every look of man outside the Church, I am not speaking merely of men in the Church, every look of man toward better conditions and the realization of brotherhood is the result of the light that flashed by Galilee and over the Judean valleys. Every high and noble conception of human life which we cherish, and which some men cherish who are telling us that the churches have done their work, was born with Jesus. I am not proposing to enumerate any of the things of which I am thinking. You know and are thinking of them. Every conception that is high and noble that is in the mind of man today was born with the Man of Nazareth. So I say that He stands at the center of human history. All before Him leading toward Him: all after Him coming forth from Him.

Again He stands at the center of life today. He still retains His absolute pre-eminence as the ideal man. It is to this Man of Nazareth that men turn even after they have denied some things that we of the evangelical faith teach concerning Him, and they point to Him at least as the ideal man, as the One Who has revealed in human history a type of humanity that had never been dreamed of. If I say that all men recognize that He is the ideal man, I do not mean to say that they are willing to conform to the pattern. They are not. While men stand in the presence of the sublime dignity of the manhood of Jesus they never answer or obey it save as they are brought by the power of the Spirit into the place of submission to Him first as Saviour. There He stands amid the men of His own age, a peasant, garbed in simplicity, girt as a slave, always serving. Hear me when I tell you this, that there is no thinking man in the East or West, whether East or West refer to London or the world, who does not recognize the dignity and beauty of that ideal, even though he do not obey it and is not prepared to follow it. Christ stands at the center of individual life revealing the ideal.

There is another word which is a supreme word and may be dismissed in a sentence. He stands at the center not merely revealing an ideal but communicating the dynamic. That is the burden of the preaching here perpetually, and I need not detain you to argue it this morning. That is the supreme and lonely splendor of this Christ, not that He flashes upon human life that is paralyzed an ideal—that He does; but that He touches the paralyzed life with power until it also becomes the ideal life. That is the loneliness of the Christ. The other is His loneliness also, for we refuse to put into comparison with Him any teacher the world has ever had in revelation of the possibility of human life. Yet this is the final loneliness today, that He stands amid men, with all their advancement and all their progress and all their new philosophies, and wherever a man comes to Him, from the East or West, North or South, paralyzed, helpless, beaten, broken, damned so far as a man can be in this world, this same Imperial One touches him with power to purpose, and he stands upon his feet and lives. That is why I continue to preach Him.

Then He stands at the center today of society, teaching men that there can be no regeneration of society save upon the basis of the regeneration of individuals. We are told that socialism is Christianity. That depends. So far as the men who are uttering their convictions concerning the social ideal have seen the realization of life upon the plane where war of every kind shall cease, that is Christianity: but so far as they are attempting to realize their dream while men are still in themselves evil and sinning, that is not Christianity. Jesus Christ confronts the individual man and says with passion and tenderness, "Ye must be born anew." I will give you life.

He stands at the center of the nations. They are not looking at Him, but He stands there. He has given to the world all truth concerning government. He has revealed to the world the fact that humanity can finally live out its perfect life only under an absolute monarch. He has also revealed to the world that there is only one absolute monarch, and that is God. He is calling men everywhere—mark the emphasis of the familiar word—to "seek—first the Kingdom of God." God is the absolute monarch He came to preach. In one brief sentence He flashed upon the world the whole conception of the true constitution of a nation, "One is your teacher, and all ye are brethren. . . . One is your Master, even the Christ." I do not know how you feel, but I am startled anew by the comprehensiveness of that word of Christ, by its profound philosophy. I am startled by the fact of how far the world is from understanding it.

What is He saying? "Look unto Me." I quoted the text in other words, attempting to convey the real force of the Hebrew, for this word, "Look," is not the word that is most commonly translated so; it is a word that literally means "face," "Face unto Me," that is the call. Mark if you will in the simplest way what this word is, and what it is in regard to the Christ. If only we were simple enough and I dare have a blackboard in this pulpit! Imagine it for a moment, and that upon it you have a diagram of a circle. You take a point which is the center, mark the sweep of your circle. At the center write the word "Me"; around it write "the ends of the earth." Look for a moment or two at that circle, and let me say some of the simplest things that you have nearly forgotten, though you learned them once. Look at the circle for a moment. You cannot draw a straight line from the center but it touches the circumference. There is no point in any circumference from which you cannot draw a straight line to the center. If you attempt to draw a straight line from the circumference which does not touch the center it touches the circumference again, getting back to its own dead level, and continues on into the distance never touching the center. That you may see it more clearly, with your eye fixed on the diagram, look at the center; we have drawn a circumference. You cannot put your pencil or chalk anywhere outside the center but that you touch a circumference. You can sweep a circumference anywhere outside the superficial area exposed to your view. I like Isaiah's "the ends of the earth." At the center God revealed in Christ, for we may add to Isaiah's vision the revelation of the New Testament. What then? All the straight lines from that center touch the circumference, the myriad circumferences that sweep around the center. I do not think that the psalmist was thinking of circles and circumferences, yet he was in the midst of the same philosophy when he exclaimed, "How precious also are Thy thoughts unto me, O God! How great is the sum of them." All the lines and forces of God are out toward His humanity. You are in a circumference which is related to that center, nor can you escape therefrom. Round the center there sweep myriad circumferences, and there is not one who can escape. We are all in His purpose. We are all in the provision of His infinite grace, in some sense related to Him by purpose. It is possible that I am not experimentally related to Him, that

I am not receiving the light He came to give, or the life He came to bestow, that I am not responsive to the love that is in His heart: but I cannot escape Him. If you will let me put that for one minute in another way, not for the sake of the multitude of Christian people, but for the sake of the one man who has drifted in here and does not know Christ as Saviour, there is a straight line from where you are to the heart of God; you have no journey to take, you are in relation to Him already in His economy and purpose: "Look unto Me, and be ye saved, all the ends of the earth: for I am God, and there is none else."

Follow me now as we come to that last great word, the claim: "Face unto Me." What is the thought conveyed in that call? That what is the matter with man, whether you use the term individually or generically, is that his face is not toward God. That is the trouble with human life individually. That is the trouble with human life socially. That is at the root of the agony of international dispute and war and armament. It is but a dream we are allowed to dream, we cannot hurry the processes of God; the consummation is not yet, but it will be. How will it come? All the nations of the earth are to face to God. That is the end. I am at the circumference of which He is the center. Sweeping lines round about that central personality in the universe include me, pass through my life. The cry that comes from the center, transcendent, immanent—I do not care for these words—the cry that comes from the center, from the center of this life and light, is this, "Face unto Me." God has never turned His back upon humanity. With that statement perfectly agrees the language of the apostolic writers. They never asked or suggested that God should become reconciled to man. It is always that man should be reconciled to God. It is the same great figure as Isaiah's. We speak of reconciliation as though

God had turned His back on man and that man had turned his back on God. It is not so. Man has turned His back upon God. God has never turned His back upon man. Because He has never turned His back upon men—oh, I know the humanness of it and the incompleteness, and the difficulty of the figure, yet hear it—the face of the Father is still looking toward the far country where the prodigal has gone; the cry of the Father, "Face unto Me, and be ye saved," indicates the only way of salvation for a man, for society, for a nation.

For a man, "Face unto Me."

There is life for a look at the Crucified One.

We do not all like that hymn. Some speak of it as being unworthy of the singing of a great congregation, but that is because their understanding of it has been so feeble. There is the profoundest philosophy in it for me.

> There is life for a look at the Crucified One,
> There is life at this moment for thee,
> Then look, sinner, look unto Him and be saved,
> Unto Him Who was nailed to the Tree.

You say it was borrowed from the old story of the brazen serpent. Certainly, but what is the story of the brazen serpent? It is the story of people who had broken God's law and turned their backs upon Him, beaten, suffering, turning back to the brazen serpent because that was the symbol of His authority. The great truth is that they turned back to God. That is human salvation. "Look unto Me." Oh, the comfort of it this morning. It is the voice of thunder that comes to us out of the infinite space. It is the voice of Galilee. I hear the voice of Jesus saying, "Come unto Me, all ye that labour and are heavy laden, and I will give you rest." That voice was so simple and winsome that His mother loved it in babyhood and loved the music of it in manhood. It was so gentle that the men and women who came into contact with Him never trembled at the thunder. Yet behind it there was the infinite majesty and mystery of the calling of God to man, "Face unto Me." Man, you can do it where you are. You can do it without an inquiry room. You can do it without any sacramentarian interference on the part of priest or preacher. "Face to Me." That is His call.

That is His call to society. That is His call in the presence of all the problems that vex us. I am not expressing any opinion now as to the question at issue, but this Christian congregation this morning believes with all its heart that if directors and men would face to Him there would be no railway strike. "Face to Me" is the great cry. Remember that in this same great chapter of Isaiah a little way before our text these words occur, "Declare ye, and bring it forth; yea, let them take counsel together: who hath shewed this from ancient time? Who hath declared it of old? Have not I the Lord? And there is no God beside Me; a just God *and a Saviour.*" If you are going to take away from Christ the fact that He is a Saviour, then you are going to take away that in which when men look they find life. If you take that away you cannot reconstruct society. "Look unto Me." Not merely the ideal, the social reformer, but a Saviour and a just God.

That is His word to the nations. We are looking in other directions. We are still looking to armaments and to policies. Oh that we might be delivered from them and look unto Him. What then?

"Be ye saved." I do not want us to drop that word saved but to understand it. "Be set free." The facing of man, the turning of man to God is the liberation of man from all the things that bind him. It is not license. Man is not let loose upon the universe uncontrolled. That would be but to work ruin and havoc everywhere. He is brought back into true relation to the center of the universe. His life then indeed becomes in tune with the infinite in the deep and true sense of that word. He has found His way back to the path from which he had wandered. He is set free from all the things that spoil by being bound to the central throne of righteousness and judgment. "Be ye set free." Yes, saved, set free. This is what we need in our sociology. You may hold your meetings and discuss plans and pass resolutions, divide up and get angry and quarrel, but it is only as you can set men there that you can bind them together. It is only as men are bound to the throne of God that they are bound to each other. It is only as men are set free from lust and passion and selfishness that they can be bound together in a great society, a great brotherhood. "Saved"! It is not a narrow word. It is not the peculiar property of the Salvation Army. Let no one go away imagining I am saying a critical thing of the Salvation Army. I wish I could have had you all with me at the Albert Hall recently as I sat and rested my soul and thanked God for the Salvation Army. It is not, however, their peculiar word. It is their word, blessed be God that it is. But it is our word also to this district of the West so far as we can touch it, and to the East so far as we are responsible for it. Being saved means being set free from all the things that spoil the soul. There is only one way: "Face unto Me," says God. Let me use my geometrical figure once more and I have done. If my memory serves me right it was in the third book of Euclid that we learned that concentric circles are such as have a common center. If that be true, then the ends of the earth—and what does that mean? The Hebrew word means cessation, the point where it leaves off. What is beyond it? I know not. I am at the ends of the earth. The circles are still sweeping round and round, what? The same throne, the same center, concentric circles having the same center, the same throne, the same God, the same Saviour. I leave you to make your application. Take the lines which in imagination I drew upon that first circle a little while ago. You remember that a line that proceeded from the center to the circumference of your first circle can be carried out and it touches all the rest. The line that commences at the circumference but was not drawn toward the center goes into ever increasing distance from the center. From all these simple things learn this at least, that if I am in right relation to the center here, so am I, so shall I be, through all the ages of which I do not know the mystery. It is when a man finds himself in right relation to the center there that he laughs at death with the laughter of holy victory, and recognizes that passing is but transition from limitation to larger life. Do not let us be at all anxious to prepare for dying, but very anxious to prepare for living. Am I ready for heaven? Yes, if I am ready for London. Am I ready for eternity? Yes, if I am fit for time. If my face is toward the center here,

> Then let the unknown morrow bring with it what it may,
> It can bring with it nothing but He will bear me through.

That applies not merely to changing seasons and years of quickly passing life, but to the up-heaped ages that baffle my thinking and yet rejoice my heart, the "for ever" more of which I am a part.